Adventures in Phonics

Florence M. Lindstrom

Level B

Christian Liberty Press

Copyright © 1996 by Christian Liberty Press

2002 Printing

All Rights Reserved. No part of this workbook may be reproduced or transmitted in any form or by any means, electronic or mechanical, without written permission from the publisher. Brief quotations embodied in critical articles or reviews are permitted.

A publication of

Christian Liberty Press

502 West Euclid Avenue

Arlington Heights, Illinois 60004

Written by Florence M. Lindstrom

Edited by Edward J. Shewan

Copyediting by Belit M. Shewan

Designed by Eric D. Bristley

ISBN 1-930092-77-6

Printed in the United States of America

This book is dedicated
to my precious children's children
who are such a joy and blessing from the Lord.

May those students who complete these lessons
seek to glorify God in their preparation
to be our country's future leaders.

The fear of the Lord is
the beginning of knowledge: but
fools despise wisdom and instruction.
My Son, hear the instruction of thy father,
and forsake not the law of thy mother:
for they shall be an ornament of
grace unto thy head, and
chains about thy neck.
Proverbs 1:7–9

Introduction

The importance of being able to read cannot be overstated. It gives our minds access to important knowledge—the greatest being God's Holy Word. Surely it is such a blessing to gain understanding through listening and speaking. But how wonderful it is to know how to read and write as thoughts and friendships are shared.

Each loving and caring teacher knows the joy of seeing a student, after many diligent hours of study, suddenly realize that he understands how to read. It is as if a light turned on. The student knows he can do something that is most valuable to him. To this end, *The Adventures in Phonics* program seeks to open a new world of understanding to the student.

The phonics lessons contained in this workbook have been successfully used in the Christian Liberty Academy day school for over fifteen years. In addition, *The Adventures in Phonics* program has been field tested over a period of several years with numerous home school families who have found the pages to be very helpful. Much of the material has been developed with the help of many ideas obtained over the past thirty years from teachers and other resources.

The general plan of this workbook includes the introduction of phonetic principles in a logical sequence, along with a consistent dose of drill and repetition to insure comprehension. Students are often directed to demonstrate their comprehension of lesson material by way of written exercises. Ideally, students should be encouraged to complete most of these exercises by themselves. However, some students may become unnecessarily frustrated with the quantity of written work which appears throughout the workbook. Therefore, instructors should feel free to allow their students to complete some of the workbook lessons orally. Instructors are encouraged to be sensitive to the individual capabilities of each of their students, especially in the area of handwriting development.

This book is only possible because of God's gracious goodness in direction and strength. His faithfulness has granted perseverance and guidance. From the beginning to the end of our life of learning, line upon line and precept upon precept, may we always be conscious of the fact and thankful that it is God who has fearfully and wonderfully made us. May each of us show our love and gratitude to Him as we constantly seek to be lovingly obedient. He alone deserves the praise.

Florence M. Lindstrom
Arlington Heights, Illinois

Table of Contents

Short Vowel Sound ✎ A a

The short sound of **A a** is found in many words that you say and hear each day.
Notice that the short vowel sound is usually heard at the beginning or middle of the words.

✔ Say the sound of **A a** (as in **ant**) as you circle and print the vowel.

✔ Many of these words begin with the short sound of **a**. If a word begins with an **a**, underline the **a** and circle that word. Listen as your teacher reads them to you.

ant	antler	sand	and	am	Andy	men
Andrew	tent	apple	map	add	sit	act
ax	Ann	fill	at	him	ash	big

✔ Carefully print the missing **a** in these words, and say the words. Do you hear the sound of **a**?

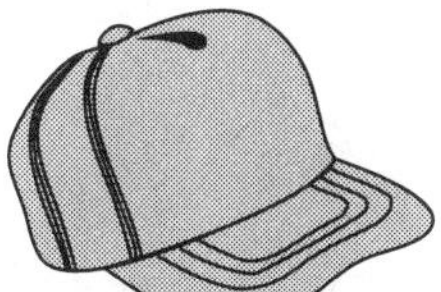

c p	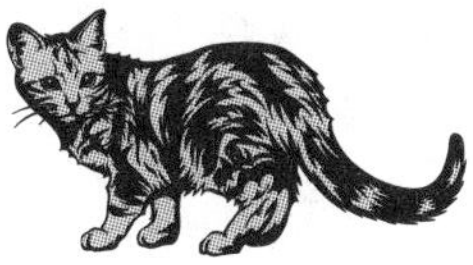 c t	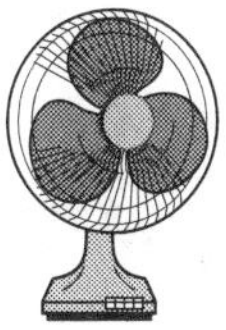 f n	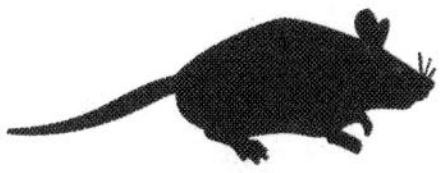 r t	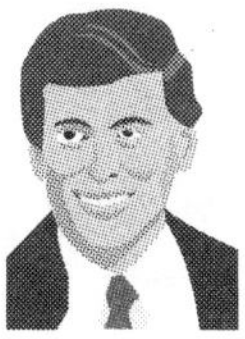 m n
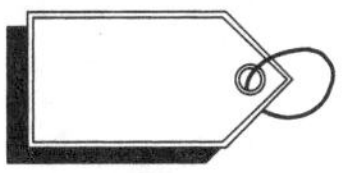 t g	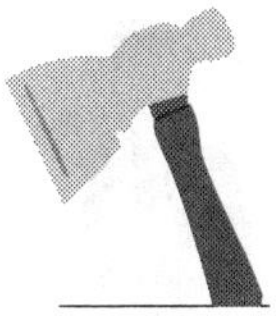 x	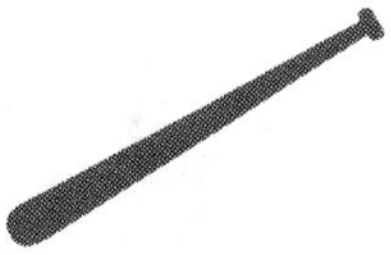 b t	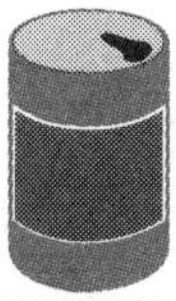 c n	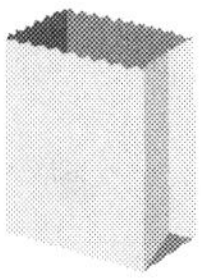 b g
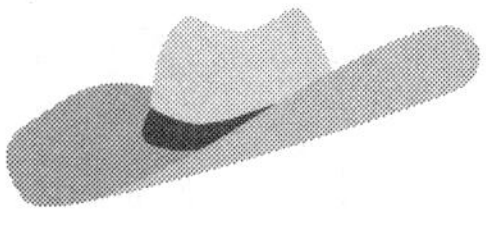 h t	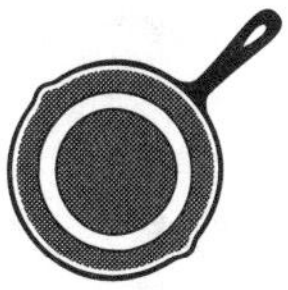 p n	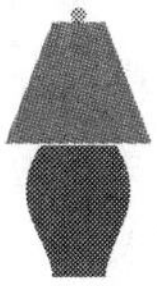 l mp	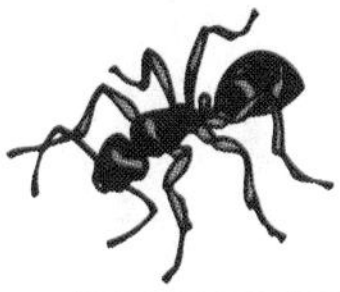 nt	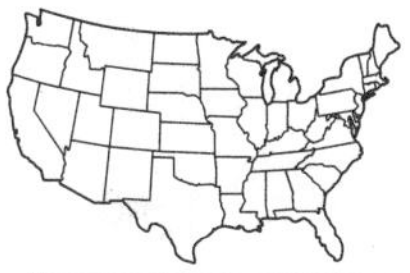 m p

Short Vowel Sound ✎ E e

The short sound of **E e** is found in many words that you say and hear each day.
Notice that this short vowel sound is usually heard at the beginning or middle of the words.

E e

✔ Say the short sound of **E e** (as in **egg)** as you circle and print the vowel.

E t r e E w e b E e

e E e E e s E s e E

E E ee

✔ Many of these words begin with the short sound of **e**. If a word begins with an **e**, underline the **e** and circle that word. Listen as your teacher reads them to you.

egg	ant	engine	edge	Ted	Ethel	elder
enter	ten	end	map	ever	Elmer	jam
Ed	Emily	dog	elbow	fast	exit	empty

✔ Carefully print the missing **e** in these words, and say the words. Do you hear the sound of **e**?

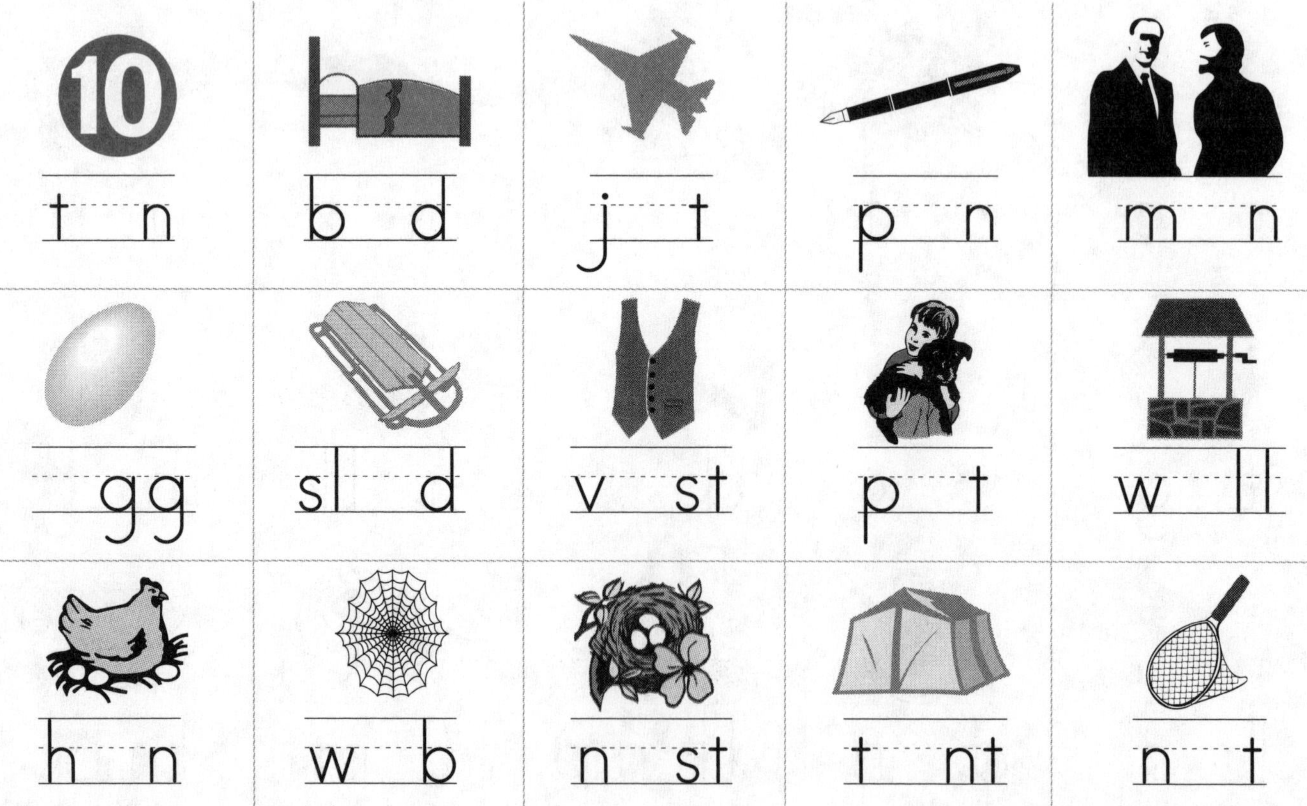

Short Vowel Sound ✎ I i

The short sound of **I i** is found in many words that you say and hear each day.
Notice that this short vowel sound is usually heard at the beginning or middle of the words.

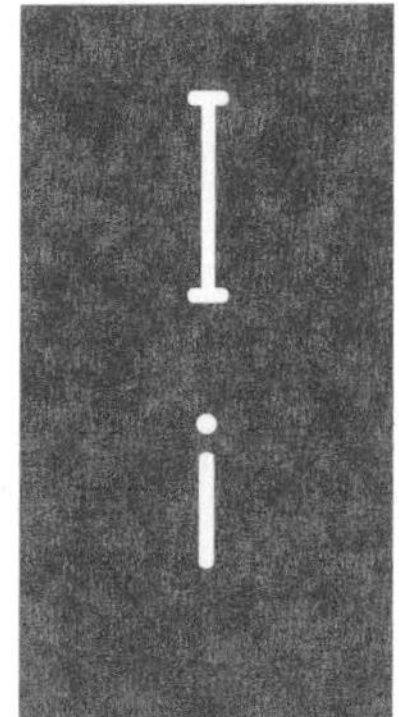

✔ Say the short sound of **I i** (as in **insects**) as you circle and print the vowel.

i g i t i I e i i a

i i s I i a i I s i

I I i i

✔ Many of these words begin with the short sound of **i**. If a word begins with an **i**, underline the **i** and circle that word. Listen as your teacher reads them to you.

into	under	image	did	include	add	cat
inside	apple	inland	ant	itch	Italy	in
if	inner	infect	enter	invite	is	igloo

✔ Carefully print the missing **i** in these words, and say the words. Do you hear the sound of **i**?

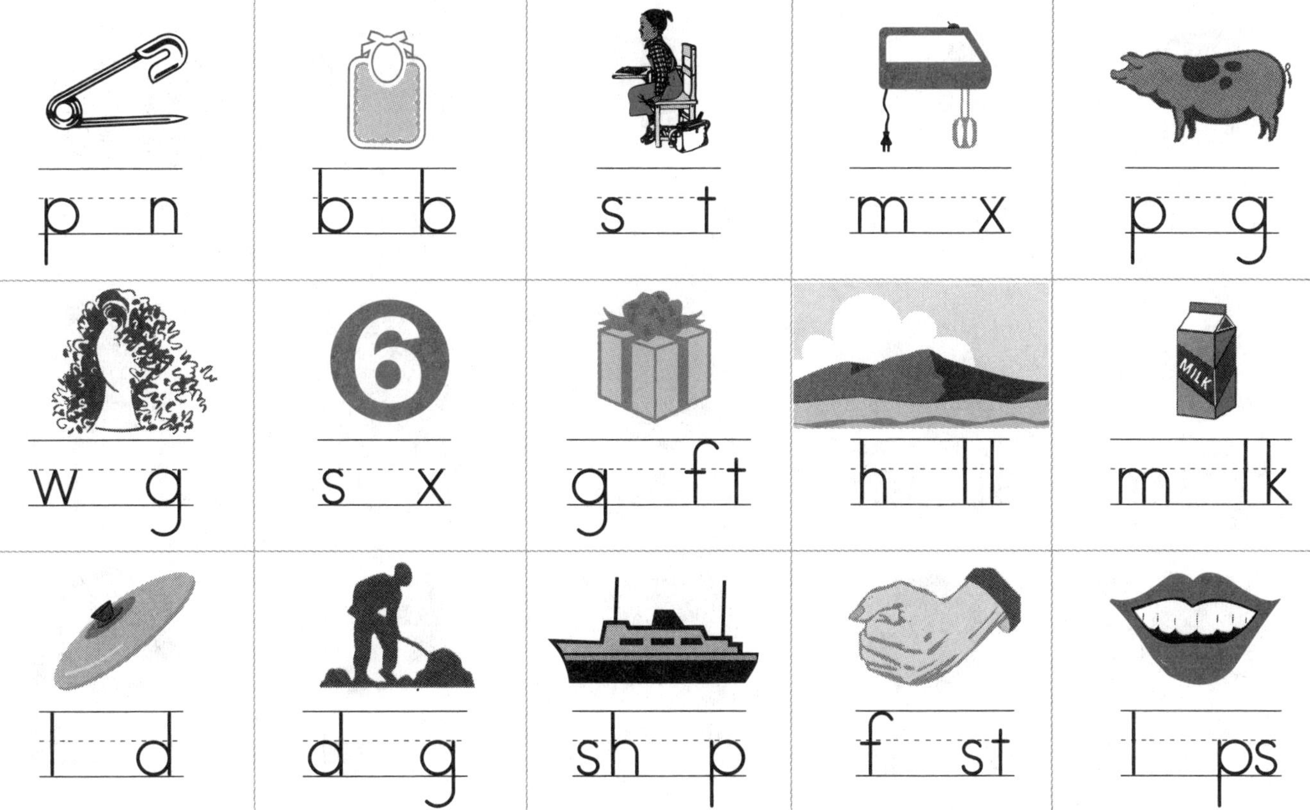

Short Vowel Sound ✎ O o

The short sound of **O o** is found in many words that you say and hear each day. Notice that this short vowel sound is usually heard at the beginning or middle of the words.

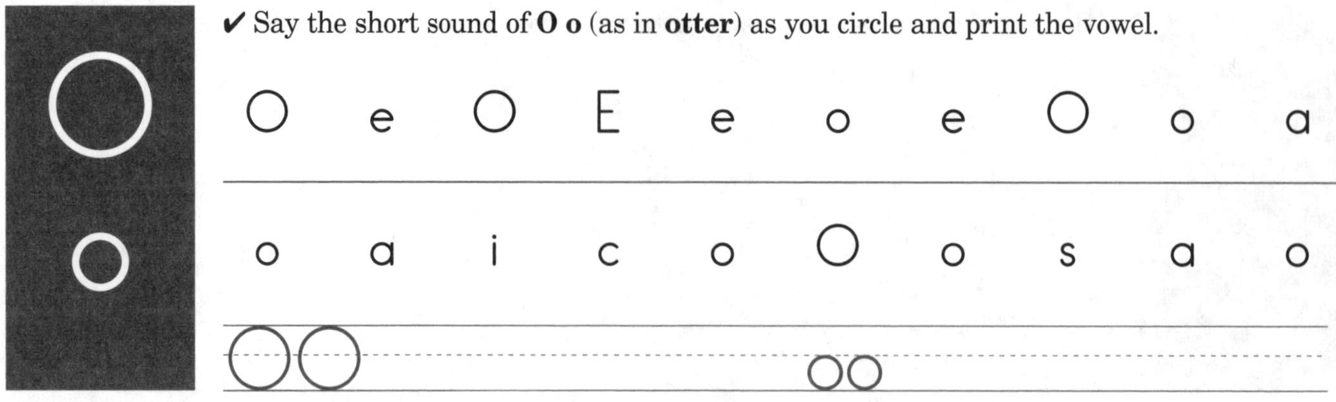

✔ Many of these words begin with the short sound of **o**. If a word begins with an **o**, underline the **o** and circle that word. Listen as your teacher reads them to you.

ox	on	hop	apple	oxen	pot	end
odd	object	enter	onto	even	ask	sock
add	olive	into	act	box	clock	cot

✔ Carefully print the missing **o** in these words, and say the words. Do you hear the sound of **o**?

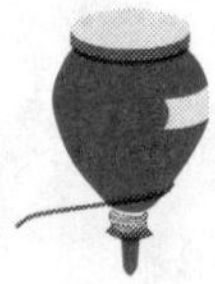

t_p	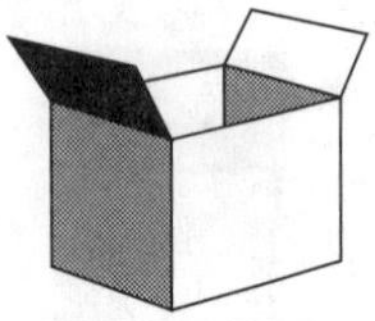 b_x	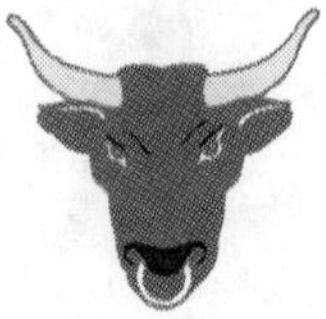 _x	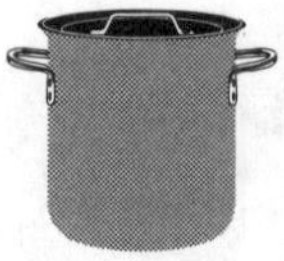 p_t	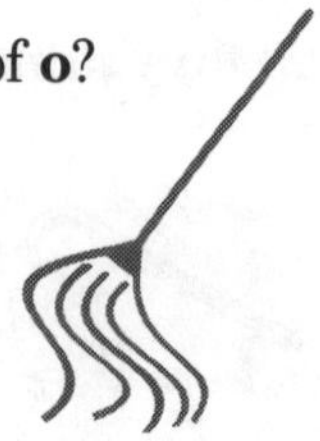 m_p
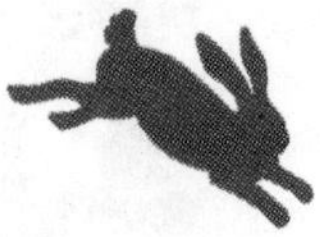 h_p	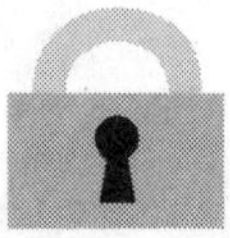 l_ck	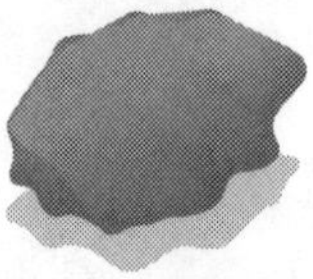 r_ck	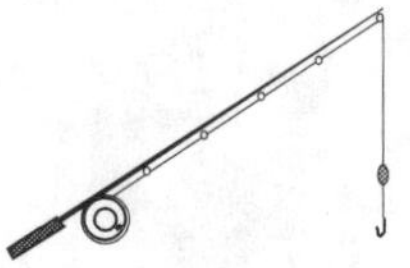 r_d	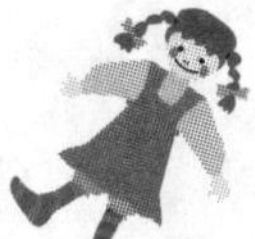 d_ll
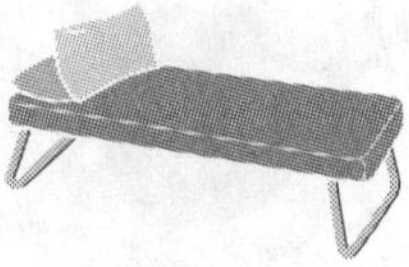 c_t	st_p	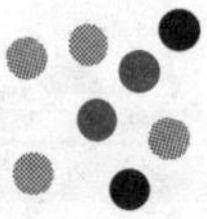 d_ts	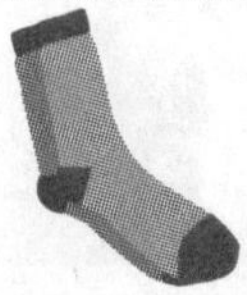 s_ck	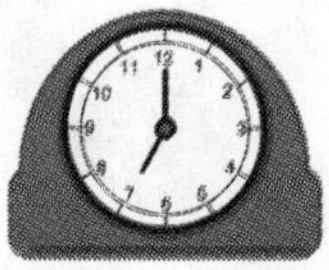 cl_ck

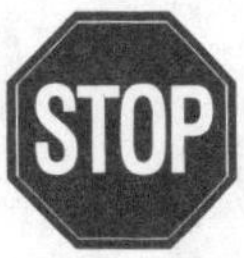

Short Vowel Sound ✎ U u

The short sound of **U u** is found in many words that you say and hear each day. Notice that this short vowel sound is usually heard at the beginning or middle of the words.

✔ Say the short sound of **U u** (as in **under**) as you circle and print the vowel.

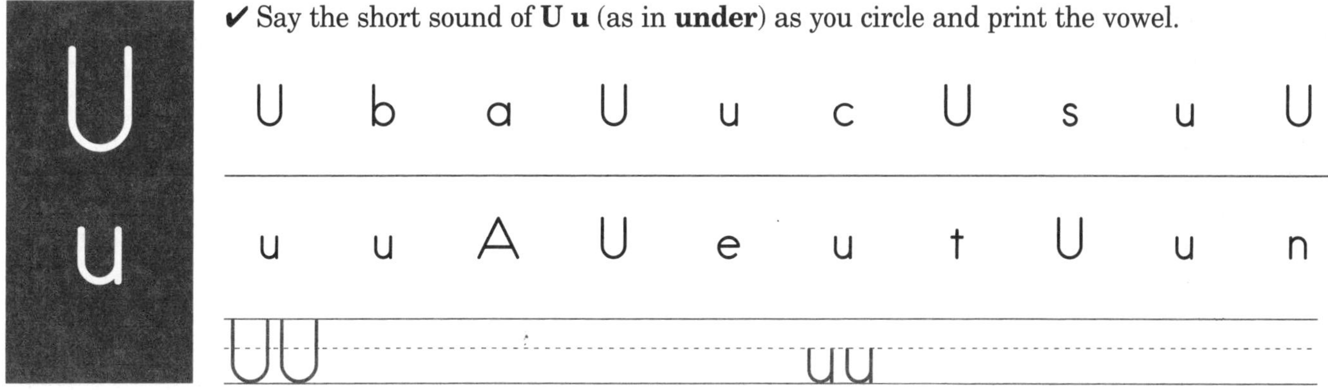

✔ Many of these words begin with the short sound of **u**. If a word begins with an **u**, underline the **u** and circle that word. Listen as your teacher reads them to you.

until	upset	cattle	ant	exit	umpire	ugly
under	egg	us	upon	ever	unfair	am
uncle	up	inch	umbrella	gum	unhook	apple

✔ Carefully print the missing **u** in these words, and say the words. Do you hear the sound of u?

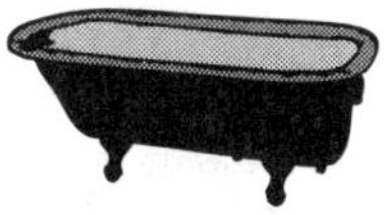

t b	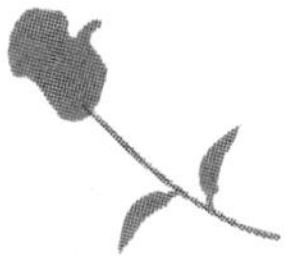 b d	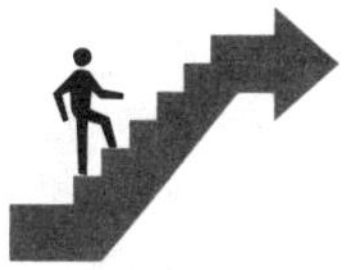 p	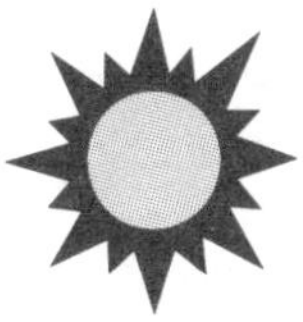 s n	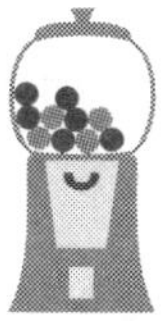 g m
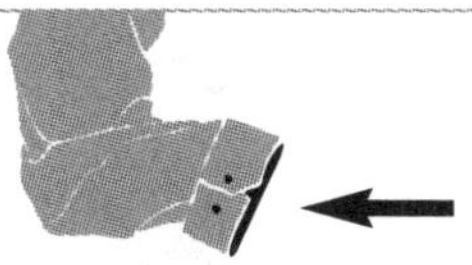 c ff	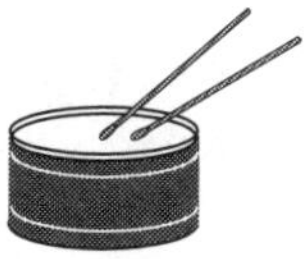 dr m	b s	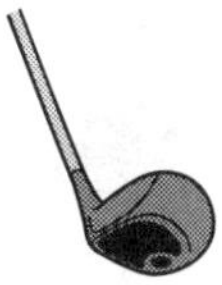 cl b	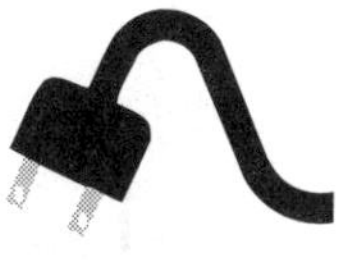 pl g
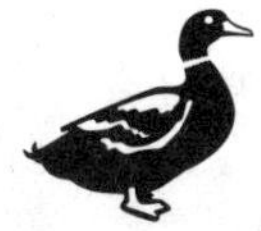 d ck	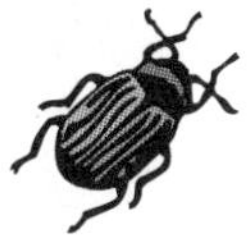 b g	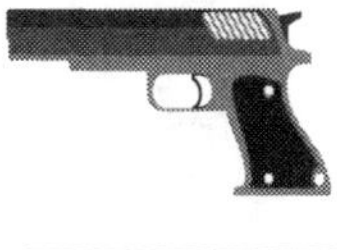 g n	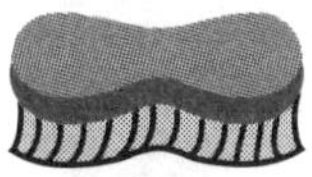 scr b	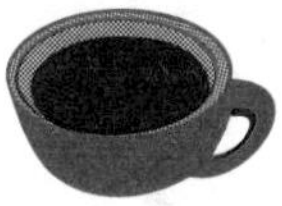 c p

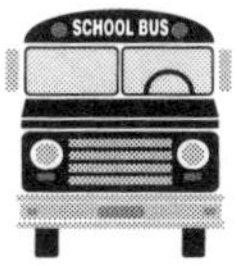

Consonant ✎ S s

The consonant **S s** can be found at the beginning, middle, or ending of words. It is an easy and fun sound to learn.

S
s

✔ Say the sound of **S s** (as in **squirrel**) as you circle and print the consonant.

S h s E e s E s e S

s E e S w s b S s m

Ss ss

✔ Many of these words begin with the sound of **s**. If a word begins with an **s**, underline the **s** and circle that word. Listen as your teacher reads them to you.

sun	ant	Sally	simple	sad	Sam	and
sell	sand	end	supper	scroll	snail	stamp
Seth	soap	log	until	smell	sick	sin

✔ Practice saying **s** with each of the short vowel sounds. Print the correct sounds in the blanks.

sa
se
si
so
su

___n	___x	___ck	___nd
___t	___b	___nk	___ven
___ck	___d	___ck	___ng

Consonant ✎ T t

The consonant **T t** can be found at the beginning, middle, or ending of words.
It is an easy and fun sound to learn.

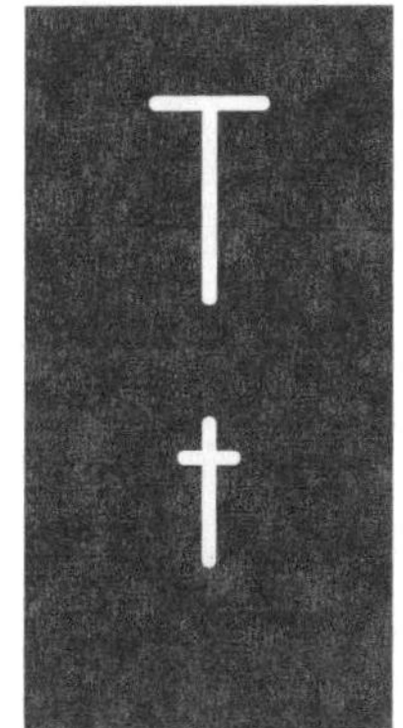

✔ Say the sound of **T t** (as in **turtle**) as you circle and print the consonant.

T n t T t u T a t T

t s a T s t b T t u

T T t t

✔ Many of these words begin with the sound of **t**. If a word begins with **t**, underline the **t** and circle that word. Listen as your teacher reads them to you.

ten	top	Tom	talk	sit	Sam	tent
tell	band	tag	tower	told	nail	camp
Terry	toad	tip	uncle	smell	tickle	tin

✔ Practice saying **t** with each of the short vowel sounds. Print the correct sounds in the blanks.

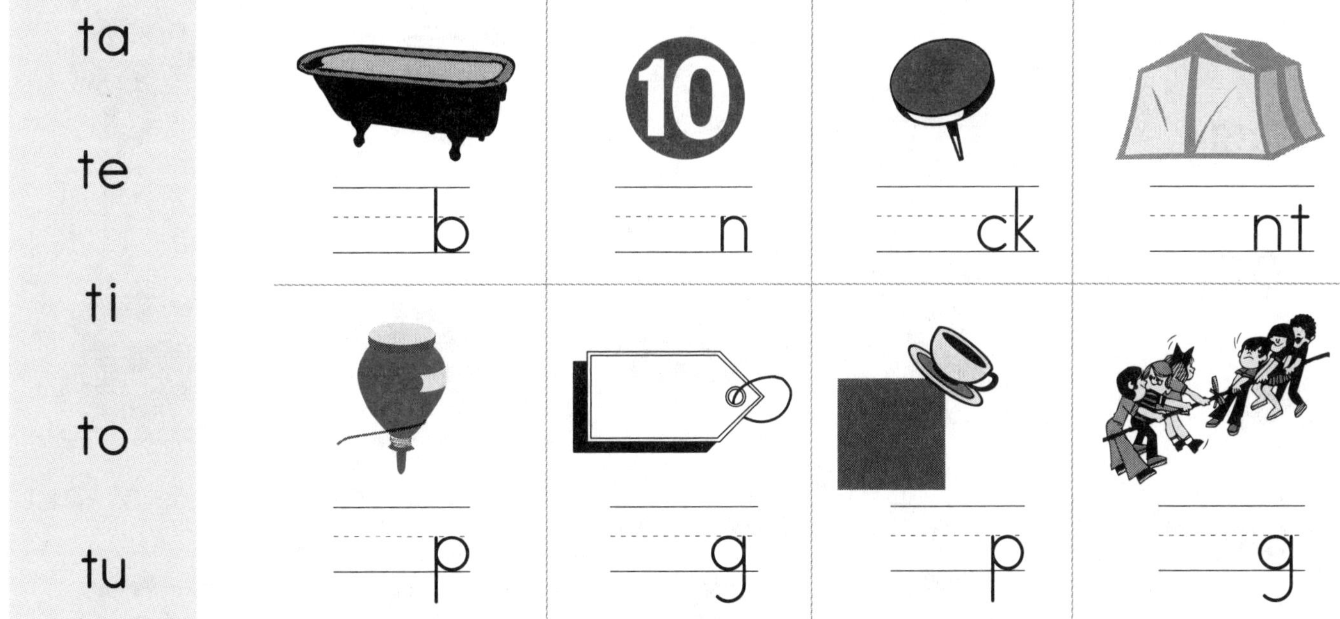

✔ Sound out these words and see how quickly you can read them.

as is at it sit sat set test

Consonant ✎ B b

The consonant **B b** can be found at the beginning, middle, or ending of words. See how quickly you can learn this important sound.

✔ Say the sound of **B b** (as in **Bible**) as you circle and print the consonant.

t B a B b b B t b T

b f b B e i o B b s

BB bb

✔ Many of these words begin with the sound of **b**. If a word begins with **b**, underline the **b** and circle that word. Listen as your teacher reads them to you.

bat	bent	Ben	tag	bad	Bill	band
bell	bass	bend	under	box	bait	bag
Beth	boat	and	oxen	tell	brick	belt

✔ Practice saying **b** with each of the short vowel sounds. Print the correct sounds in the blanks.

ba
be
bi
bo
bu

___d	___ll	___nk	___lt
___t	___g	___x	___s
___b	___d	___ck	___g

SCHOOL BUS

Consonant ✎ H h

The consonant **H h** is usually found at the beginning of words. See how quickly you can learn this important sound. It is made by giving a short breath from your mouth.

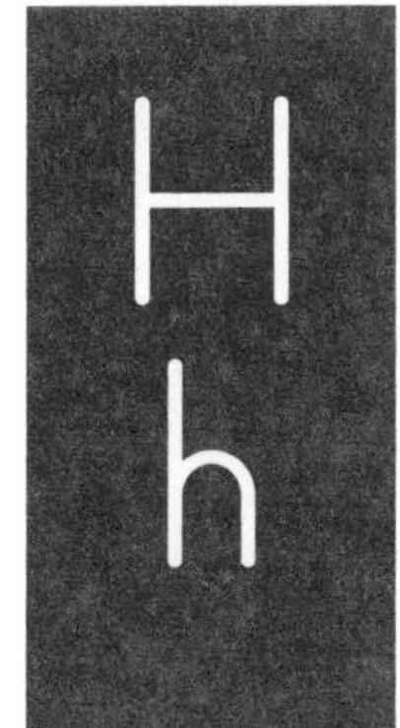

✔ Say the sound of **H h** (as in **horse**) as you circle and print the consonant.

h a H b H e h o H h

b H s H h t H s h H

H H h h

✔ Many of these words begin with the sound of **h**. If a word begins with **h**, underline the **h** and circle that word. Listen as your teacher reads them to you.

hat	hot	hen	tan	had	hill	hand
bell	has	help	hard	sat	hello	hum
harp	sand	holy	tent	home	hike	hem

✔ Practice saying **h** with each of the short vowel sounds. Print the correct sounds in the blanks.

✔ Sound out these words and see how quickly you can read them.

has his hat hit hot he hut hub

Consonant ✎ F f

The consonant **F f** can be found at the beginning, middle, or ending of words. See how quickly you can learn this important sound.

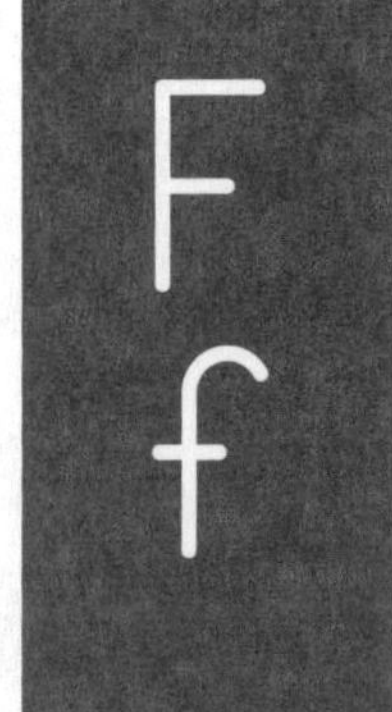

✔ Say the sound of **F f** (as in **fox**) as you circle and print the consonant.

t F a F f f F t b F

f f b F e h o F f H

FF ff

✔ Many of these words begin with the sound of **f**. If a word begins with an **f**, underline the **f** and circle that word. Listen as your teacher reads them to you.

fact	fin	fan	fox	food	fill	band
tell	fast	fire	first	belt	fence	fun
fish	fist	hen	sock	fell	front	felt

✔ Practice saying **f** with each of the short vowel sounds. Print the correct sounds in the blanks.

✔ Sound out these words and see how quickly you can read them.

fast fit fell fist fuss if huff fib

Consonant ✎ M m

The consonant **M m** can be found at the beginning, middle, or ending of words.
See how quickly you can learn this important sound.

✔ Say the sound of **M m** (as in **mother**) as you circle and print the consonant.

h M a M m m M t m H

m f m M a s e M m s

M M m m

✔ Many of these words begin with the sound of **m**. If a word begins with **m**, underline the **m** and circle that word. Listen as your teacher reads them to you.

mat	men	met	man	oxen	tell	brick
mill	mask	mend	work	mad	bill	mouse
map	goat	milk	mix	hill	made	mop

✔ Practice saying **m** with each of the short vowel sounds. Print the correct sounds in the blanks.

ma

me

mi

mo

mu

___n ___lk ___n ___p

___p ___lt ___x ___g

✔ Sound out these words and see how quickly you can read them.

mat man mad men must mess Sam am

Consonant ✎ K k

Both of the consonants **C c** and **K k** can make the **k** sound.
The **k** usually comes before vowels ***e*** and ***i*** as in **key** and **king**.

✔ Say the sound of **K k** (as in **king**) as you circle and print the consonant.

t K u K k k w A a k

K b k K a k r f K h

KK kk

✔ Circle the words that begin with **k**. Say the sound of **k** as you underline it. Listen as your teacher reads them to you.

kitten	kind	key	kick	kill	tune	kept
snake	king	keep	kettle	help	cap	bake
happy	kite	book	can	kid	stick	kit

✔ Print **ke** or **ki** where they belong in these words.

✔ Sound out these words and see how quickly you can read them.

kit cub kid cat book kiss cup cap

Consonant ✎ C c

The consonant **C c** makes the **k** sound when it comes before vowels ***a, o***, and ***u*** as in **cat**, **cot**, and **cut**. The **C c** usually makes the sound of the **s** when it is followed by ***e*** or ***i***, but this will be reviewed later.

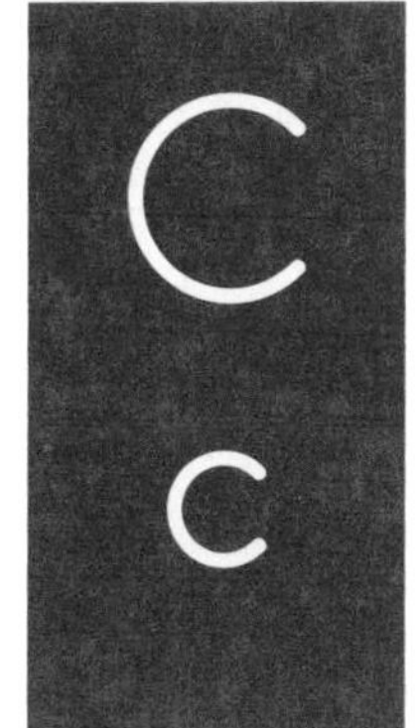

✔ Say the sound of **C c** (as in **king**) as you circle and print the consonant.

c b c m c C w A a C

f C s C h c r f c e

CC cc

✔ Circle the words that begin with **c**. Say the sound of **k** as you underline it. Listen as your teacher reads them to you.

cow	calf	bark	color	can	cup	kick
coat	cape	cane	stork	camel	keep	come
jerk	corn	cub	cone	cut	call	take

✔ Print **ca**, **co**, or **cu** where they belong in these words.

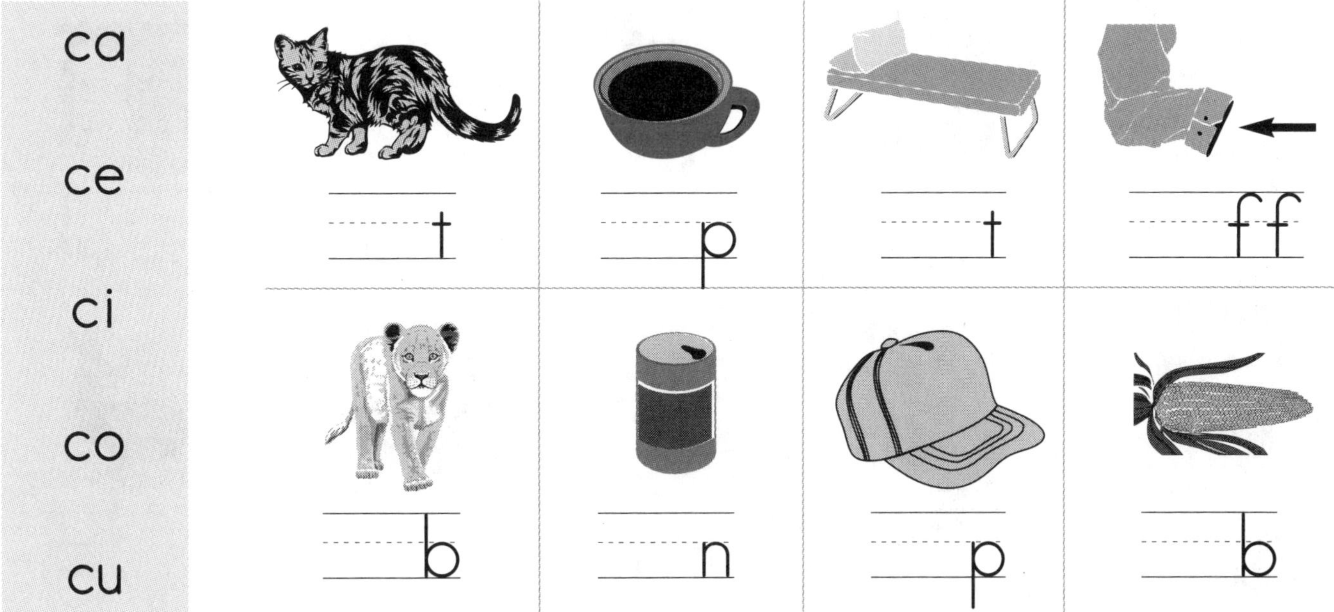

✔ Sound out these words and see how quickly you can read them.

cab kit cub cuff cat back cut cap

Consonant ✎ D d

The consonant **D d** can be found at the beginning, middle, or end of words. See how quickly you can learn this important sound.

✔ Say the sound of **D d** (as in **duck**) as you circle and print the consonant.

d D a B d d D h d S

b d b D e o u D b d

DD dd

✔ Many of these words begin with the sound of **d**. If a word begins with **d**, underline the **d** and circle that word. Listen as your teacher reads them to you.

dot	desk	Ben	Dan	dab	dill	dam
doll	bass	dent	dump	door	date	deer
bell	dime	dog	dug	dell	Dick	belt

✔ Practice saying **d** with each of the short vowel sounds. Print the correct sounds in the blanks.

✔ Sound out these words and see how quickly you can read them.

dab sad bad had mad dot dad add

Consonant ✎ J j

The consonant **J j** can be found in many words.
See how quickly you can learn this important sound.

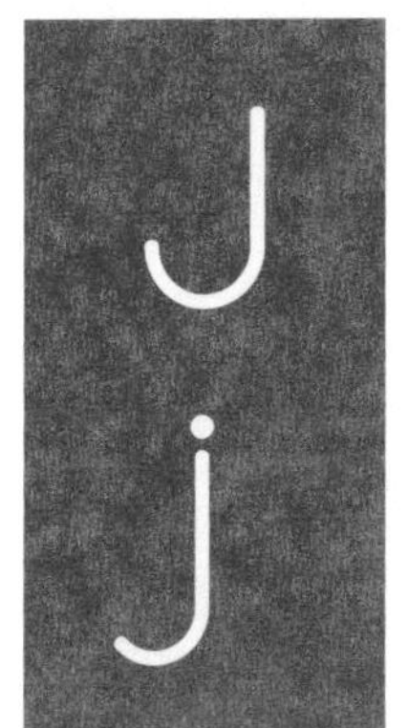

✔ Say the sound of **J j** (as in **jam**) as you circle and print the consonant.

t J a J j j B h j S

j f j J m e u J B j

J J j j

✔ Many of these words begin with the sound of **j**. If a word begins with **j**, underline the **j** and circle that word. Listen as your teacher reads them to you.

jam jet Jean and jab Jill Jan

jell just jungle junk cold job jump

✔ Practice saying **j** with each of the short vowel sounds. Print the correct sounds in the blanks.

ja je ji jo ju Ja Je Ji Jo Ju

__m __cks __mp __t __g

✔ Draw lines to the correct pictures.

Jim has a fat cat.
Dad has a hat.
A bus is fast.

✔ How quickly can you read these words?

jam	dim	Jim	job	jet	Jeff	jab
cab	ham	hot	cob	set	jiff	jot

Consonant ✎ R r

The consonant **R r** can be found in many words.
See how quickly you can learn this important sound.

✔ Say the sound of **R r** (as in **rabbit**) as you circle and print the consonant.

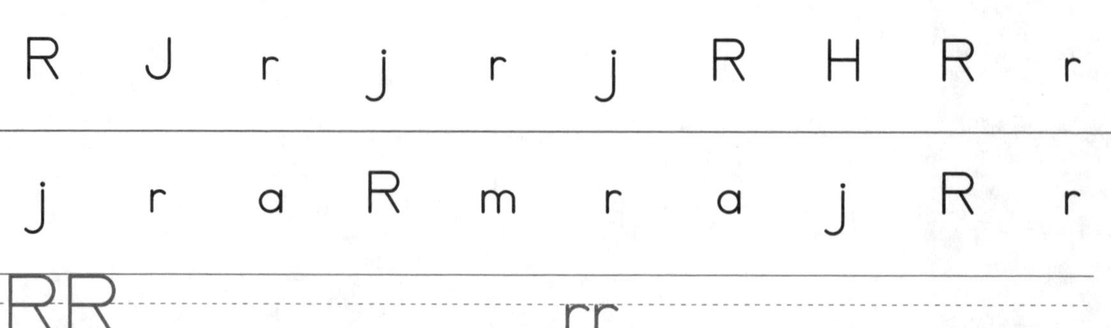

✔ Many of these words begin with the sound of **r**. If a word begins with **r**, underline the **r** and circle that word. Listen as your teacher reads them to you.

ran	red	read	sand	rug	Ruth	rock
roll	rest	thank	rim	rat	real	Rick

✔ Practice saying **r** with each of the short vowel sounds. Print the correct sounds in the blanks.

ra re ri ro ru Ra Re Ri Ro Ru

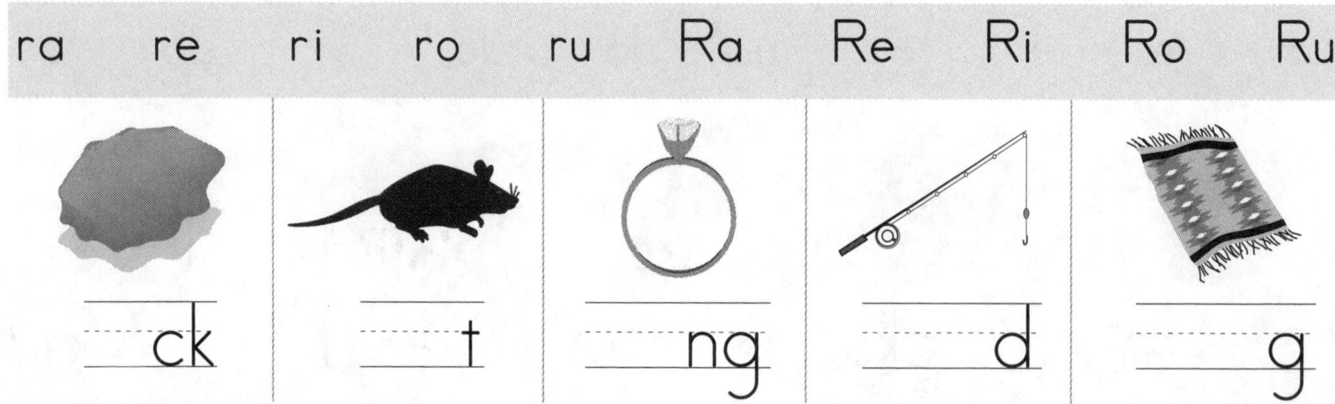

✔ Draw lines to the correct pictures.

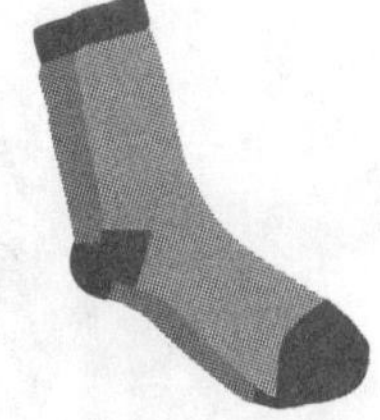

Rick has a red sock.
A rock hit Sam's fist.
A cat has a fat rat.

✔ How quickly can you read these words?

ran	rob	red	rat	rut	rid	rest
tan	sob	bed	sat	cut	hid	best

Consonant ✎ G g

The consonant **G g** can be found in many words. The typewriter can print it this way – **g**, and students print it this way – g. See how quickly you can learn this important sound.

✔ Say the sound of **G g** (as in **goose**) as you circle and print the consonant

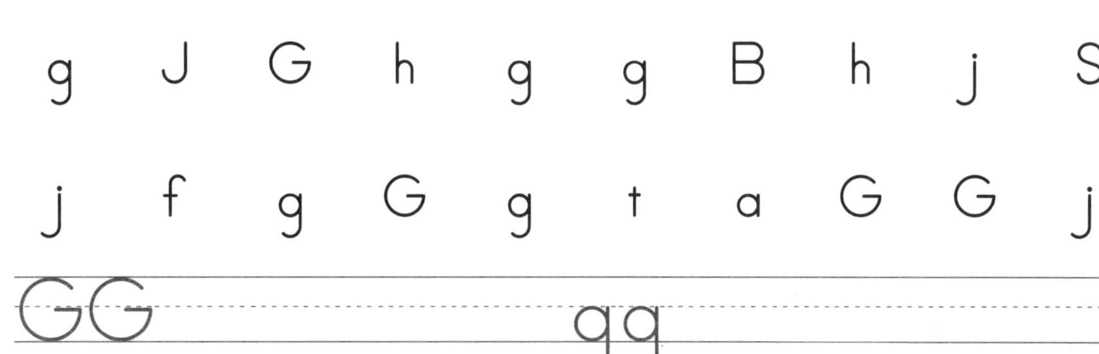

✔ Many of these words begin with the sound of **g**. If a word begins with **g**, underline the **g** and circle that word. Listen as your teacher reads them to you.

game gate dad got ant gull goat

get just girl gold goose gab Jan

✔ Practice saying **g** with each of the short vowel sounds. Print the correct sounds in the blanks.

ga ge gi go gu Ga Ge Gi Go Gu

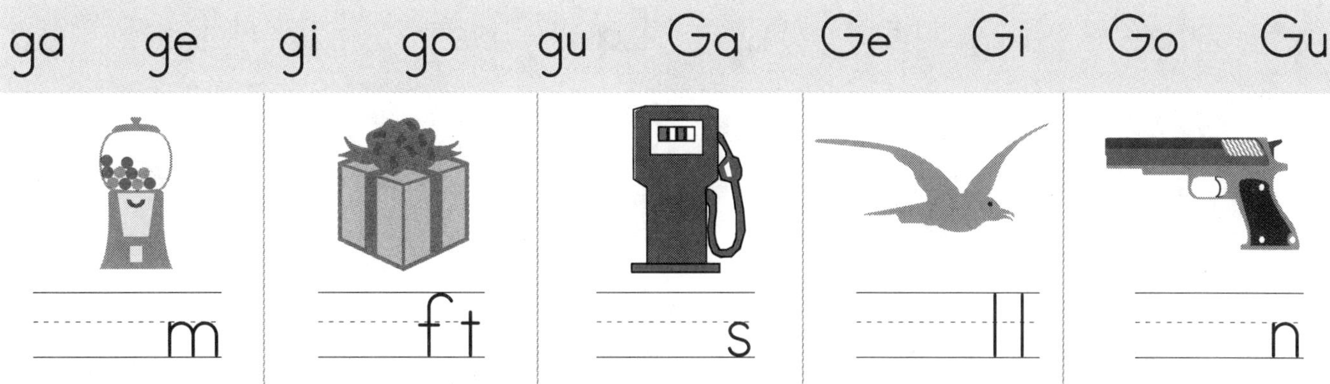

✔ Draw lines from the sentences to the correct pictures.

Dad got a gift.
It is a big mug.
Dan hugs Dad.

✔ How quickly can you read these words?

bag bug big rag tug hum get
tag hug dig gag rug gum set

Consonant ✎ L l

The consonant **L l** can be found in many words.
See how quickly you can learn this important sound.

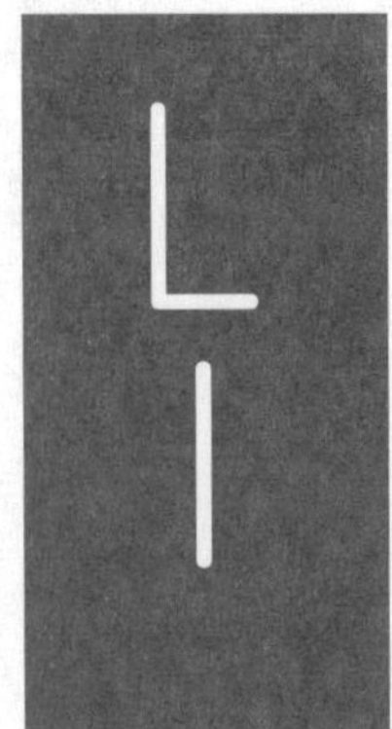

✔ Say the sound of **L l** (as in **lion**) as you circle and print the consonant.

l L i J L f F l j S

L t l J l L i L T l

L l

✔ Many of these words begin with the sound of **l**. If a word begins with **l**, underline the **l** and circle that word. Listen as your teacher reads them to you.

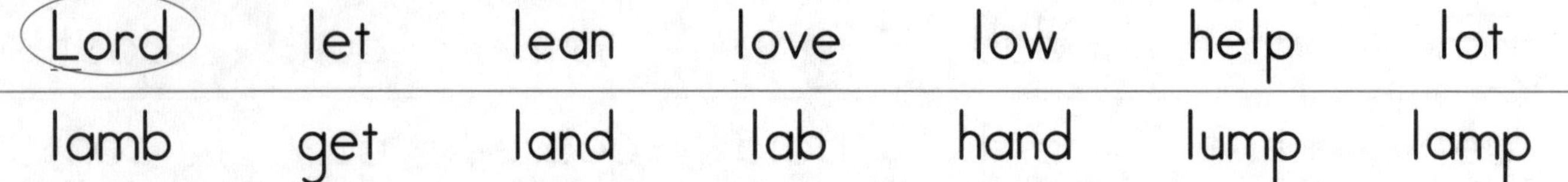

Lord	let	lean	love	low	help	lot
lamb	get	land	lab	hand	lump	lamp

✔ Practice saying **l** with each of the short vowel sounds. Print the correct sounds in the blanks.

la le li lo lu La Le Li Lo Lu

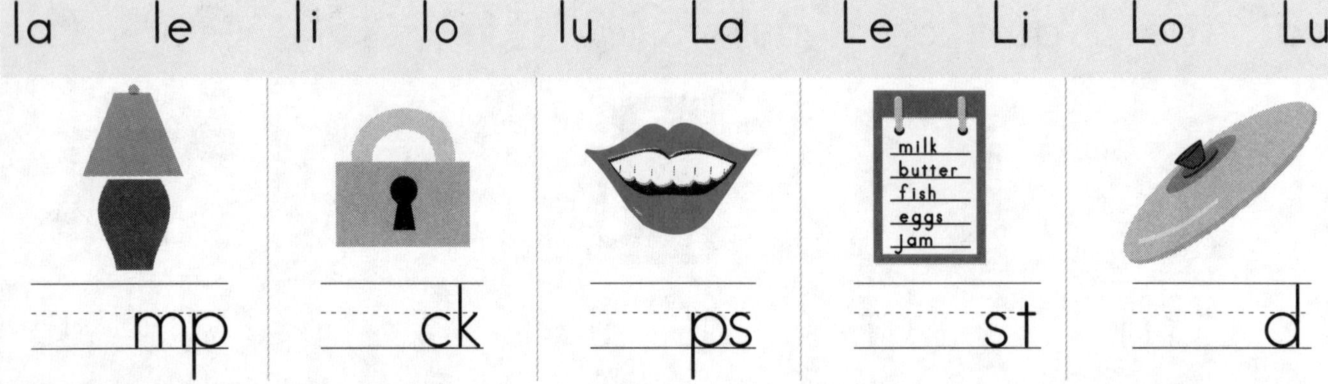

__mp __ck __ps __st __d

✔ Draw lines to the correct pictures.

A ball hit Bill's leg.
Jan hugs a doll.
Jack ran up a hill.

✔ How quickly can you read these words?

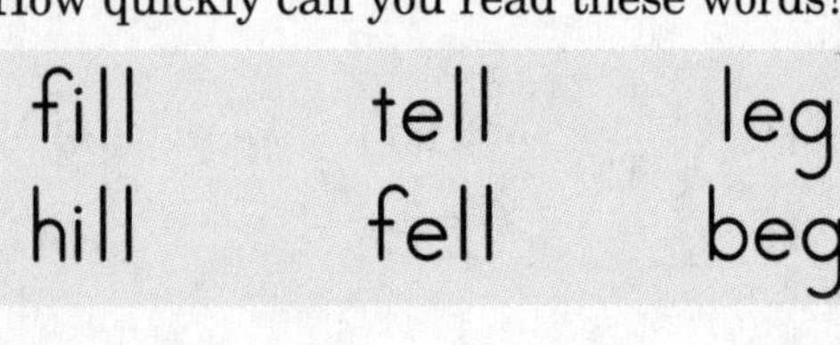

fill	tell	leg	lad	mad	led	bed
hill	fell	beg	sad	bad	red	fed

Consonant ✎ N n

The consonant **N n** can be found at the beginning, middle or end of words.
See how quickly you can learn this important sound.

✔ Say the sound of **N n** (as in **nose**) as you circle and print the consonant.

t N n J n j N u n m

j n u N m s u N N r

NN nn

✔ Many of these words begin with the sound of **n**. If a word begins with **n**, underline the **n** and circle that word. Listen as your teacher reads them to you.

nap faith nice nurse need nail not

net never nose egg nut girl tent

✔ Practice saying **n** with each of the short vowel sounds. Print the correct sounds in the blanks.

na ne ni no nu Na Ne Ni No Nu

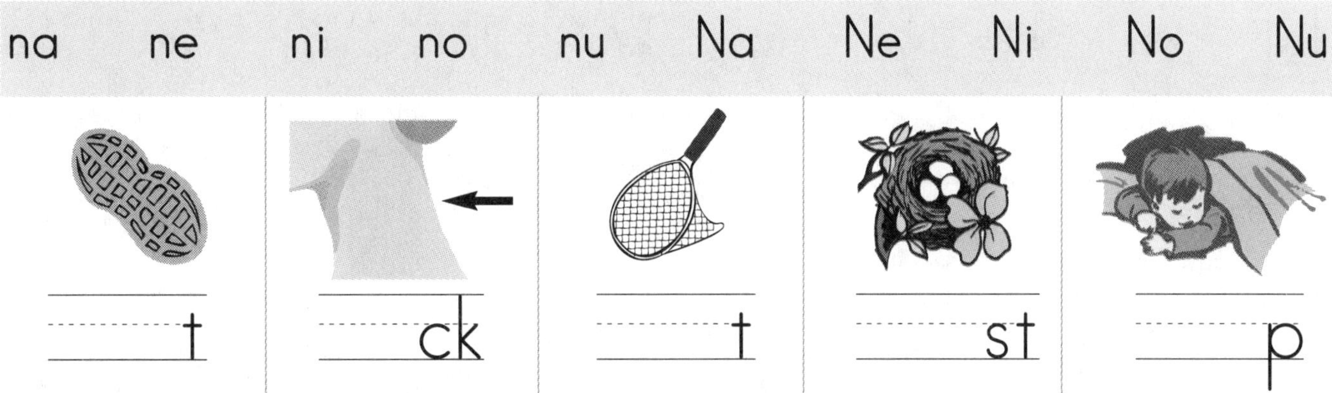

__t __ck __t __st __p

✔ Draw lines to the correct pictures.

Ned has a red hen.
It sits on eggs on a nest.
Jan went in a big tent.

✔ How quickly can you read these words?

nap	net	set	bed	hen	ten	run
tap	let	met	Ned	den	men	fun

Consonant ✎ W w

The consonant **W w** can be found in many words.
See how quickly you can learn this important sound.

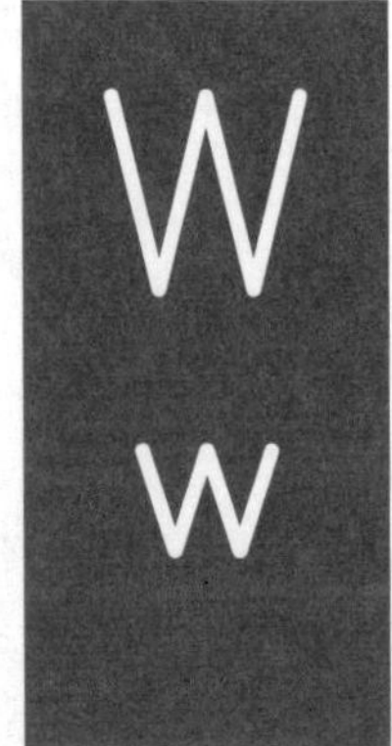

✔ Say the sound of **W w** (as in **walrus**) as you circle and print the consonant.

t W a w j W B w j W

w m w W n a w W w T

W W w w

✔ Many of these words begin with the sound of **w**. If a word begins with **w**, underline the **w** and circle that word. Listen as your teacher reads them to you.

went	wet	weed	will	wade	hit	web
sad	west	seed	water	wit	win	well

✔ Practice saying **w** with each of the short vowel sounds. Print the correct sounds in the blanks.

wa we wi wo wu Wa We Wi Wo Wu

b ll n x g

✔ Draw lines to the correct pictures.

Bill and Al went in a tent.
A web fell as Mom hit it.
Wag is sad as Jill is ill.

✔ How quickly can you read these words?

win	wet	will	fill	till	mill	well
fin	get	bill	sill	hill	dill	bell

Consonant ✎ P p

The consonant **P p** can be found in many words.
See how quickly you can learn this important sound.

✔ Say the sound of **P p** (as in **pear**) as you circle and print the consonant.

p b d P p p P h d M

p k j P m p a P B p

PP pp

✔ Many of these words begin with the sound of **p**. If a word begins with **p**, underline the **p** and circle that word. Listen as your teacher reads them to you.

pan pet map pen pat hill sand

pill pond puzzle bunk pin pit pump

✔ Practice saying **p** with each of the short vowel sounds. Print the correct sounds in the blanks.

pa pe pi po pu Pa Pe Pi Po Pu

✔ Draw lines to the correct pictures.

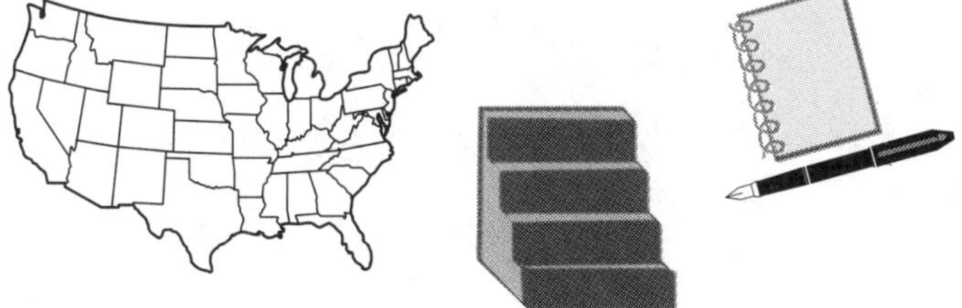

Pat has a big map.
Will has a pen and a pad.
Pam fell on the steps.

✔ How quickly can you read these words?

pan	sand	hand	pill	hot	cap	tip
can	band	land	will	pot	nap	tap

Consonant ✎ V v

The consonant **V v** can be found in many words.
See how quickly you can learn this important sound.

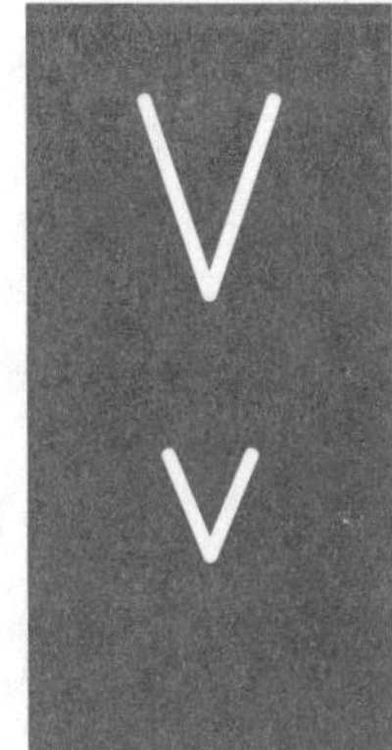

✔ Say the sound of **V v** (as in **vine**) as you circle and print the consonant.

v V s v v B h v W V

v t W v V s w V v u

V V v v

✔ Many of these words begin with the sound of **v**. If a word begins with **v**, underline the **v** and circle that word. Listen as your teacher reads them to you.

van	run	win	vent	visit	vote	wig
vine	vase	vest	vast	hen	verse	very

✔ Practice saying **v** with each of the short vowel sounds. Print the correct sounds in the blanks.

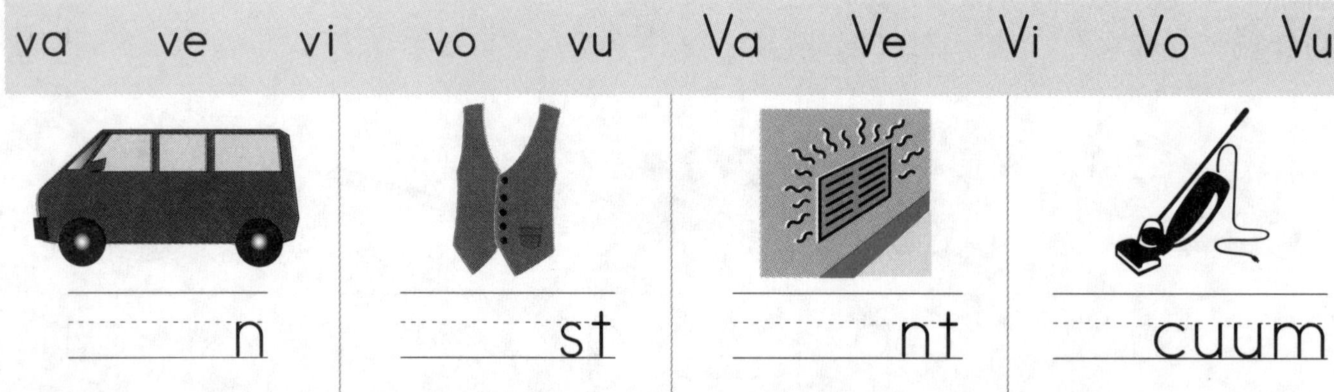

✔ Draw lines to the correct pictures.

Pam will get in a van.
Bob has a red vest.
Can a hen run fast?

✔ How quickly can you read these words?

vet	vest	test	vent	vast	last	wit
set	west	best	tent	past	fast	pit

Consonant ✎ Qu qu

The consonant **Q q** can be found in many words. In English, it always has the **u** next to it. **Qu qu** makes the sound of ***kw***. See how quickly you can learn this unusual sound.

✔ Say the sound of **Qu qu** (as in **queen**) as you circle the consonant and print **Qq** with the vowel **u** on the line below.

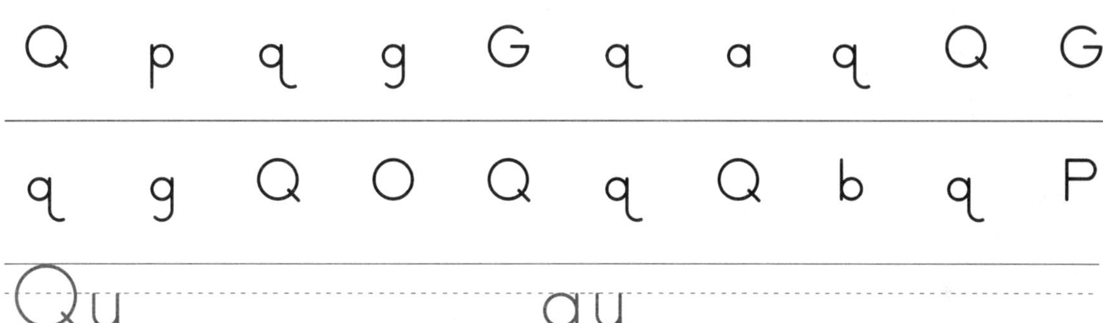

✔ Many of these words begin with the sound of **qu**. If a word begins with **qu**, underline the **qu** and circle that word. Listen as your teacher reads them to you.

quit quill pill queen quest quiz quail pail

quick quote poke quart quack quilt guilt quiet

✔ Practice saying **qu** with each of the short vowel sounds. Print the correct sounds in the blanks.

qua que qui quo Qua Que Qui Quo

___lt ___ck ___ll ___z

✔ Draw lines to the correct pictures.

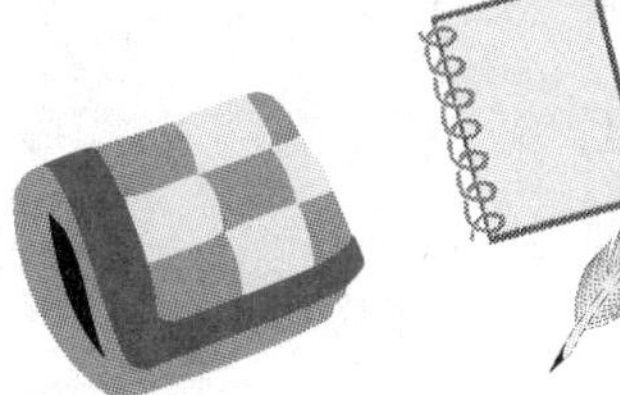

Ben has a quill and a pad.
Pam had a quiz.
A quilt is on a bed.

✔ How quickly can you read these words?

quit	quill	pot	quick	pack	sick	quilt
pit	pill	gill	quest	quack	best	got

Consonant ✎ Y y

The consonant **Y y** can be found at the beginning of many words.
See how quickly you can learn this important sound.

✔ Say the sound of **Y y** (as in **yard**) as you circle and print the consonant.

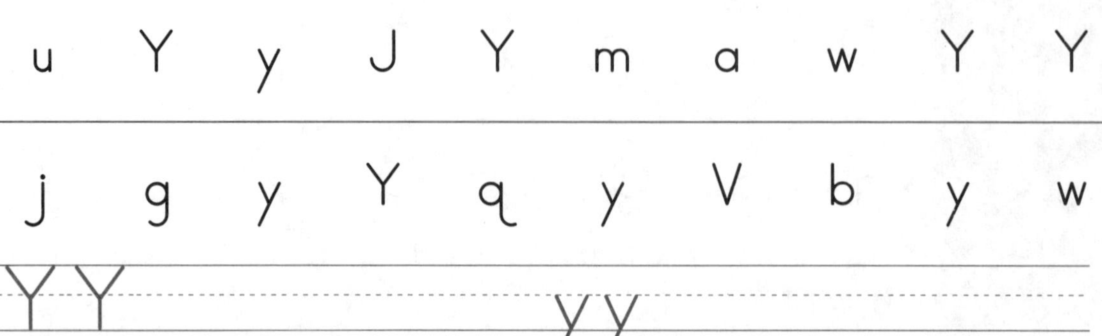

✔ Many of these words begin with the sound of **y**. If a word begins with **y**, underline the **y** and circle that word. Listen as your teacher reads them to you.

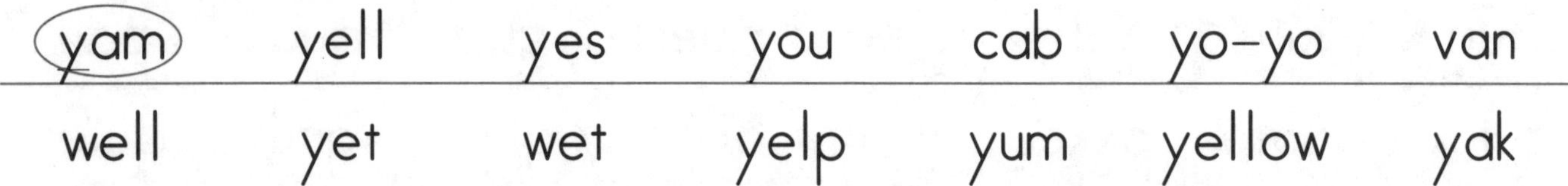

✔ Practice saying **y** with each of the short vowel sounds. Print the correct sounds in the blanks.

ya ye yi yo yu Ya Ye Yi Yo Yu

✔ Draw lines to the correct pictures.

The sun is big and yellow.
A pan has a yam in it.
Jill will not yell at Wag.

✔ Draw lines to the correct words.

1. Bob has a	big.	4. Ann has a	yet?
2. A pup can	hat.	5. Dad has a	yo–yo.
3. The box is	yelp.	6. Is Bill six	van.

Consonant ✎ X x

The consonant **X x** is made by saying the sounds of ***k*** and ***s***.
The **x** is usually at the end of words.

✔ Say the sound of **X x** (as in **ax**) as you circle and print the consonant.

t X a x X x B h x k

X f j x x e u X B j

✔ Many of these words end with the consonant **x**. If a word ends with **x**, underline the **x** and circle that word. How many words can you read? Listen as your teacher reads them to you.

wax	fax	box	boy	ox	joy	ax
tax	will	six	fix	mix	sat	fox

✔ What letters must be printed to complete these words?

___x

___x

___x

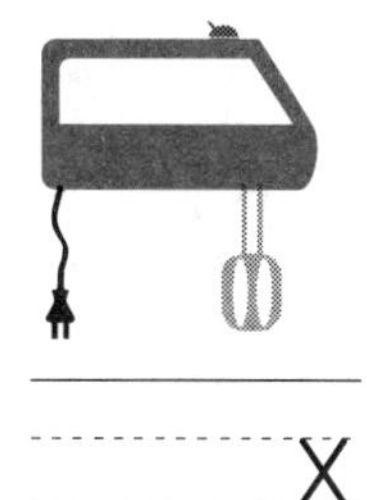
___x

___x

✔ Draw lines to the correct pictures.

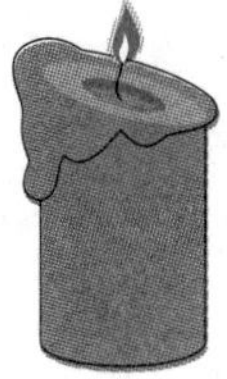

A hen sits on six eggs.
The hot wax will drip.
A big ox can help a man.

✔ Can you draw these pictures?

ax	fox	ox	box	wax	six

Consonant ✎ Z z

The consonant **Z z** can be found in many words.
See how quickly you can learn this important sound.

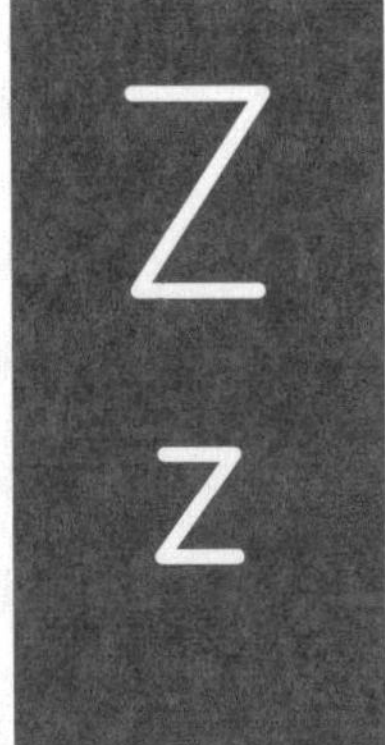

✔ Say the sound of **Z z** (as in **zebra**) as you circle and print the consonant.

t Z s Z z s K c z Z

z s x Z z m n S Z s

Z Z z z

✔ Many of these words begin with the sound of **z**. If a word begins with **z**, underline the **z** and circle that word. Listen as your teacher reads them to you.

zero	zip	zigzag	sip	top	zoo	sand
jell	zone	zoom	zipper	zing	sob	hump

✔ Circle the words that name the pictures.

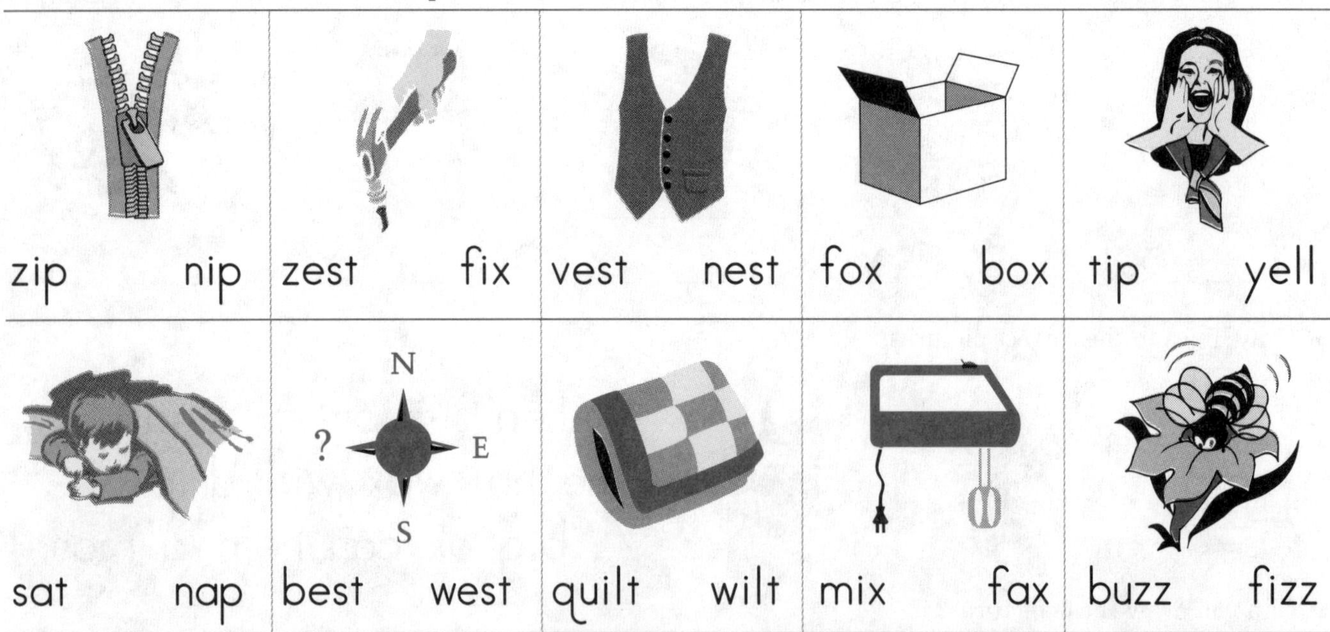

✔ Draw lines to the correct pictures.

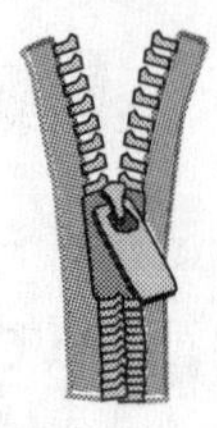

Can Jan zip a zipper?
The quilt has a zigzag.
Tom's pup has zest.

Review of Short Vowels a e i o u

When a word or syllable has only one vowel and it comes at the beginning of the word or syllable, or between two consonants, that vowel usually has a short sound.

✔ Read both words, circle the word for the picture, and carefully print it on the line.

map lap	pan hand	ant van	cap bag	sand man
leg net	ten pen	sled well	men tell	desk west
pig fig	sit bit	fill quill	fix six	lid bib
hop top	box fox	stop drop	hot cot	pot doll
rub tub	run sun	mug tug	bus bug	pup cup

✔ Read the sentences carefully. Choose the correct word from the box, and print it on the line.

1. Tim had a nap on his big ________.
2. A man will fix his tan and black ________.

van
bed

Short Vowel ✎ a Words

When a word or syllable has only one vowel and it comes at the beginning of that word or syllable, or in between two consonants, then that vowel usually has the short sound.
The short vowel sound for *a* may be marked like this: căt.

✔ Listen closely to the short vowel sound of **a** in this lesson. Mark the short vowels as you read the lists. Circle the correct word that names the picture next to each list, and write it on the line below.

păn (măn) răn	wax tax → fax	bad mad pad ←	lag wag tag	hat cap gap
tan van fan	bag sag rag	pat mat fat	Sam Pam yam	had sad Dad
hand band sand	cab map tap	ant plant flag	as has gas	am ham jam
sat cat rat	tab can gab	lad bat lap	jam can ax	and tap nap

✔ You can read many words now that you know the short vowel sound **a**. Choose the correct words from the box on the right to complete the sentences. Print the words in the blanks.

1. A fast cab will pass a tan ________.
2. Dan sat on Dad's lap as Sam sat on a ________.
3. Pam will run as fast as a cat and ________ Jan.

mat
tag
van

Short Vowel ✎ e Words

When a word or syllable has only one vowel and it comes at the beginning of that word or syllable, or in between two consonants, then that vowel usually has the short sound.
The short vowel sound for ***e*** may be marked like this: pĕn.

✔ Listen closely to the short vowel sound of **e** in this lesson. Mark the short vowels as you read the lists. Circle the correct word that names the picture next to each list, and write it on the line below.

pĕn mĕn hĕn	get wet pet	jest vest best	well bell tell	let ten den
bed Ted fed	get set jet	leg peg egg	led red sled	best rest nest
Jed web pep	pet net met	hem bend stem	tent sent test	dent west steps

✔ You can read many words now that you know the short vowel sound **e**. Choose the correct words from the box on the right to complete the sentences. Print the words in the blanks.

1. Jed went and fed his pet ________.

2. Ted will get his dad a red ________.

3. Jan and Ben did best on a ________.

4. Nell will help Jill mend a ________.

5. An ant bit Jim on his ________.

test
hen
hem
vest
leg

Short Vowel ✎ i Words

When a word or syllable has only one vowel and it comes at the beginning of that word or syllable, or in between two consonants, then that vowel usually has the short sound.
The short vowel sound for ***i*** may be marked like this: sĭt.

✔ Listen closely to the short vowel sound of **i** in this lesson. Mark the short vowels as you read the lists. Circle the correct word that names the picture next to each list, and write it on the line below.

bĭt kĭt hĭt	sit kit big	fit gift pit	fig spin pig	did lid hid
dim rim mix	him bin pin	bib win sin	tin crib spin	fib rib milk
silk fist mist	list his is	till miss quilt	bill hill fix	wig fin lips

✔ You can read many words now that you know the short vowel sound **i**. Choose the correct words from the box on the right to complete the sentences. Print the words in the blanks.

1. Bill is sick and has a __________ on his lap.

2. Jill will sit still and fix him a get-well __________.

3. Jill will help mom mix eggs and __________.

4. His pan has a lid and it fits on its __________.

5. Did a pig dig a big pit in the __________?

gift
rim
quilt
milk
hill

Short Vowel ✎ o Words

When a word or syllable has only one vowel and it comes at the beginning of that word or syllable, or in between two consonants, then that vowel usually has the short sound.
The short vowel sound for *o* may be marked like this: bŏx.

✔ Listen closely to the short vowel sound of **o** in this lesson. Mark the short vowels as you read the lists. Circle the correct word that names the picture next to each list, and write it on the line below.

hŏt nŏt dŏt	hot tot pot	rock on Tod	Tom cot mom	ox sod lot
pox rot fox	box flop pod	blot tot cob	pond pop stop	nod on hop

✔ Print the two letters on the lines below to make new words. See how quickly you can read them.

ot	od	ob	op	ox
j	G	s	t	b
l	n	m	dr	p
bl	s	r	fl	f

✔ You can read many words now that you know the short vowel sound **o**. Choose the correct words from the box on the right to complete the sentences. Print the words in the blanks.

1. Don will lift the lid on a ________.

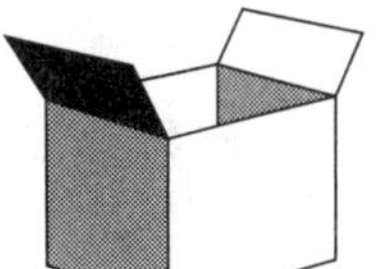

2. The box has ________ in it.

3. Scott will plant a crop in black ________.

4. Tod is a tot and naps on a ________.

sod
cot
pop
box

Short Vowel ✎ u Words

When a word or syllable has only one vowel and it comes at the beginning of that word or syllable, or in between two consonants, then that vowel usually has the short sound.
The short vowel sound for ***u*** may be marked like this: sŭn.

✔ Listen closely to the short vowel sound of **u** in this lesson. Mark the short vowels as you read the lists. Circle the correct word that names the picture next to each list, and write it on the line below.

bŭn rŭn gŭm	sun fun but	mud hut cut	fuss cuff dug	puff stub cup
tub rub bump	dump mum mug	cub hub rut	suds hum bug	lump tug plug
bus dull buzz	us nut yum	gull club jump	hug muff jug	fuzz bud pup

✔ An important word to learn is **the**. The vowel **e** says the short sound of **u**.
In some words the vowel **o** makes the sound of the short vowel **u** as in **other**, **mother**, and **brother**.

come	dove	shove	front	of (uv)	some	none
ton	love	glove	son	from	done	color

✔ Use the underlined words from the list above to complete the following sentences.
Print the correct words in the blanks.

1. Dad got ________ gifts ________ his son.

2. God is glad if a son does ________ his dad.

3. A dove has ________ to our ________ steps.

✎ Consonant Blends

Many words begin or end with two or three consonants. When each of these consonants says its usual sound, we call it a blend. You have seen blends in such words as **steps** and **tent.**

✔ Underline the blends in these short vowel words. Circle the correct word that names the picture next to each list, and write it on the line below.

slant sent next	drift left slept	lift dent scrub	fact 5 crept +4 drift 9	hand stamp melt
west N fast ? E crust S	clamp stamp hump	quilt cast milk	lamp lump limp	husk swift dent
wilt text raft	belt must grasp	risk list stump	act desk stand	gift twist pond

✔ Choose the words with consonant blends from the box on the right to complete these sentences. Print the correct words in the blanks.

1. A tan ________ ran past the pond.

2. The bed has a big ________ on it.

3. Ted ________ on a cot in his tent.

4. Mother will set the ________ on the desk.

5. Jim will fix the ________ of the lamp.

quilt
gift
plug
elk
slept

✎ Double Consonant Endings

When a word has a short vowel sound, usually the consonants **s, l, f,** and **z** will be doubled. Double consonant words, such as **bell**, **gull**, and **cuff** have been used in previous lessons. Some exceptions to the doubling rule are ***bus***, ***gas***, ***yes***, ***as***, ***is***, ***has***, ***was***, and ***his***.

✔ Underline the double consonants in these short vowel words. Circle the correct word that names the picture next to each list, and write it on the line below.

dull doll sell	bell fell tell	mess fuss press	buzz fuzz fizz	sniff kiss miss
class bless glass	staff stuff bass	pass cuff puff	pills pass still	kill ill grill
lass fill grass	cliff bill quill	well swell still	Jill muff hill	fell dell yell

✔ Choose the words with the double consonants from the box on the right to complete these sentences. Print the correct words in the blanks.

1. Bob fell and his left leg is ______________.
2. Will has some milk in a big ______________.
3. The milk will ______________ on him if the glass tips.
4. Nan has on a red silk ______________.
5. Sam will help Dad cut the ______________.

dress
grass
stiff
glass
spill

Consonant Ending ✎ c k

Remember this RULE: Four letters that are usually doubled when they come at the end of a short vowel word are as follows: **ff** as in **cuff**, **ll** as in **bell**, **ss** as in **bless**, and **zz** as in **buzz**.
Remember this RULE: When a short vowel is followed by a **k** sound, it is made by **ck** as in **duck**.

✔ Underline the **ck** at the end of these short vowel words. Circle the correct word that names the picture next to each list, and write it on the line below.

tock sock stock	tuck buck truck	crack deck peck	pick pack puck	jack sack black
click brick quick	stick trick prick	trick lick tick	dock flock clock	duck cluck stuck
rack quack tracks	crock cluck rock	neck click Dick	smack kick stock	snack lack back

✔ Choose the words ending with **ck** from the box on the right to complete these sentences. Print the correct words in the blanks.

1. Dick had a sack of nuts as a ________.
2. A ________ of ducks swam in the pond.
3. Jack has a ________ in his black backpack.
4. A dump ________ got stuck in some mud.
5. Mother will fix dinner in the ________ pot.

truck
jacket
snack
crock
flock

Consonant Endings ✎ **ng** and **nk**

Many words end with the letters **ng** as in **sing** and **nk** as in **sink**.
Think about these sounds as you do this lesson.

✔ Underline the **ng** and **nk** at the end of these short vowel words. Circle the correct word that names the picture next to each list, and write it on the line below.

bring dunk sing	mink ink stink	tank rank sting	blink bank wink	Hank rang swing
drink plink fling	pink ding ring	dunk link sink	bang hang trunk	crank blank rang
sling cling clank	rink ping wing	yank link king	tank string gang	bunk planks junk

✔ Choose the words ending with **ng** or **nk** from the box on the right to complete these sentences. Print the correct words in the blanks.

king
drank
ring
hang
sing
spring

1. A man will ____________ a song.

2. In the ____________ the robin sat on six eggs.

3. An elk ____________ from the pond.

4. The ____________ has a ____________ on his finger.

5. Pam will ____________ up her pink dress.

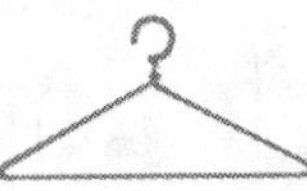

✎ Review Lesson

You have learned many lessons about our language and are able to read hundreds of short vowel words. This lesson uses rhyming words. **Jack's cat slept on a mat.** If any words are to rhyme, they must have the same vowel sound and same ending consonants: **swell–smell**, **pass–class**, **quick–sick**, **buzz–fuzz**.

✔ Circle the correct words that rhyme with the underlined words in the sentences below.

Sentence			
1. Jack is quick as he <u>picks</u> up	stacks	(sticks)	stuck
2. Mother will help Anna <u>press</u> a	grass	muss	dress
3. This bug has <u>wings</u> and it	spring	swings	stings
4. Did Jim spill some <u>stuff</u> on his	cuff	cliff	fluff
5. Can Dick's <u>rocket</u> fit in his	bucket	pocket	racket
6. Dan and Jan <u>swing</u> and	sling	string	sing
7. Men will fix the <u>crack</u> on the	track	stock	slack

✔ Draw pictures of these words.

hill	truck	swing	clock	grass	stump

✔ Draw lines to match the rhyming words below.

quack	sniff	blank	press	fuzz	bang
dull	smack	string	crank	block	stock
stiff	gull	bless	sing	rang	buzz

Consonant Digraphs ✎ sh ch

A consonant digraph has two consonants that make one sound. They may be at the beginning or ending of a word. Two of the digraphs are: **sh** as in **ship** and **ch** as in **chin**

✔ Underline the digraphs **sh** and **ch** as you read these short vowel words. Circle the correct word that names the picture next to each list, and write it on the line below.

branch ranch chip	such shell shop	rush crush brush	chap check chuck	smash ship splash
shed shelf shin	fish wish sash	dash dish blush	ranch bunch chin →	chick chat chop

✔ Add these digraphs to the blanks below to make new words. See how quickly you can read the words.

sh		ch		tch	
___ock	sma___	___ap	ran___	ca___	pi___
___ut	cra___	___unk	pin___	hi___	ba___
___ack	blu___	___ess	pun___	Du___	ma___

✔ Choose the words with digraphs **sh** or **ch** from the box on the right to complete these sentences. Print the correct words in the blanks.

shut	chick	lunch	sash

1. Mitch has a fresh plum in his ________.
2. Ashley ________ the lid on the box of shells.
3. Beth has a pink and tan ________ on her dress.
4. A little ________ sat on a bench in the shed.

Consonant Digraphs ✎ th wh

Remember this RULE: A consonant digraph has ***two*** consonants that make ***one*** sound.
The digraph **th** with two sounds: the hard **th** sound as in **the** or the soft **th** sound as in **think**.
Learn the digraph **wh** as in **whip**.

✔ Underline the digraphs **th** and **wh** as you read these short vowel words. Circle the correct word that names the picture next to each list, and write it on the line below. NOTE: the **b** in thumb is silent.

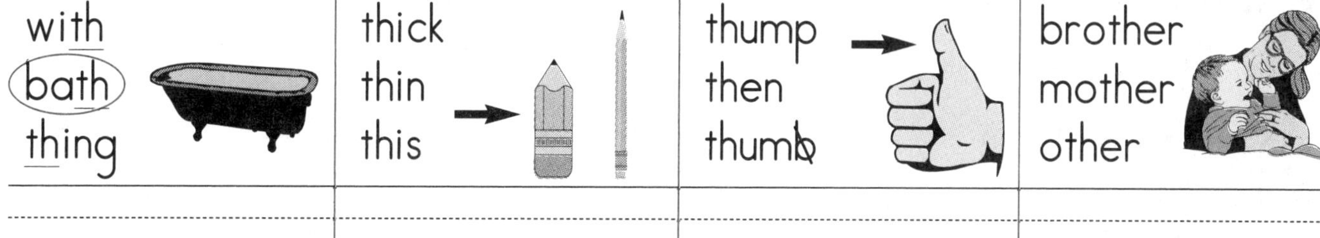

with bath thing	thick thin this	thump then thumb	brother mother other

✔ Add these digraphs to the blanks below to make new words. See how quickly you can read the words. NOTE: **th** refers to the hard ***th*** sound as in **the**, and **th** refers to the soft ***th*** sound as in **think**.

th	th	th	wh
__at	o__er	__in	__iff
__an	mo__er	__ick	__ich
__em	bro__er	__ank	__en
__en	ga__er	__ink	__ip
__is	bo__er	__ing	__isper

✔ Choose the words with digraphs **th** or **wh** from the box on the right to complete these sentences. Print the correct words in the blanks.

mother	thank	gather	which

1. Let us ________ God for blessing us.
2. Tim is glad that his ________ loves him.
3. Is this the path ________ is the best?
4. Josh will ________ flowers for his mother.

Long Vowel ✎ A a

Remember this RULE: When there is only ***one*** vowel at the beginning or in the middle of a word, it usually has a short sound. This lesson begins teaching the **long vowel** rule.
Remember this RULE: When ***two*** vowels are in a word, usually the first vowel says its name, and the second vowel is silent: **ai** as in rāin, **a_e** as in cāke, **ay** as in prāy.

ai
a_e
ay

✔ Practice saying these short vowel words with the long vowel words.
NOTE: the **b** in lamb is silent.

ran	rain	can	cane	hat	hate
pal	pail	cap	cape	mad	made
bat	bait	Sam	same	pad	paid
pan	pain	lamb	lame	man	main

✔ Mark the ***two*** vowels as you read these long vowel **a** words. Circle the correct word that names the picture next to each list, and write it on the line below.

sāil nāil tāil	cake take make	vail hail pail	tape cape ape	came name game
quail trail mail	brain train pain	vane pane mane	fail sail vail	stain rain main

✔ From the box on the right, choose words that rhyme with the underlined words in these sentences. Print the correct words in the blanks.

1. God made the quail and the little ________.
2. Jake will help his mother bake a ________. 
3. Wag is the name of the pet that is ________.
4. He will sit and wait as a fish gets his ________.

snail
tame
cake
bait

Long Vowel ✎ A a

Remember the long vowel RULE: When ***two*** vowels are in a word, usually the first vowel says its name, and the second vowel is silent. The letter **y** is a vowel when it is at the end of a word or syllable. It is silent in the following **ay** words.

✔ Practice saying these **ay** words.

pray	lay	hay	ray	clay
bay	may	stay	way	sway
say	jay	pay	gray	stray

✔ Mark the vowels as you read these long vowel **a** words. Circle the correct word that names the picture next to each list, and write it on the line below.

plāy dāy (prāy)	wake skate bake	saint faint paint	wave save pave	sway tray gay
scale pale trail	fake lake quake	rake sake stake	snail frail fail	Kay hay pay

You have learned that <u>short vowels</u> are marked like this: Bŏb's pĕt hăd a băth in a tŭb.
<u>Long vowel</u> words are marked like this: Jāke tākes a trāin in Māy.

✔ In the box below, mark the long vowel words as shown above. Choose words from this list to complete the following sentences. Print the correct words in the blanks.

dāy faint play fade train name

1. The sun rays may ______ the stain on her dress.

2. Ann may ______ if a snake came on the trail.

3. God made this ______, and Ray is glad.

4. Jay will ______ with his gray ______.

Long Vowel ✎ E e

Remember the long vowel RULE: When ***two*** vowels are in a word, usually the first vowel says its name, and the second vowel is silent. This lesson teaches the long vowel sound of **e** as in **he**, **tea**, **bee**, **key**.

e ea
ee
ey

✔ Practice saying these short vowel words with the long vowel words.

set	seat	hell	heal	fed	feed
fell	feel	met	meet	tell	teal
ten	teen	men	mean	den	dean
step	steep	bet	beat	sell	seal

✔ Mark the ***two*** vowels as you read these long vowel **e** words. Circle the correct word that names the picture next to each list, and write it on the line below.

bēe hē wē	glee flee three	sea ear tea	gear tear dear	sleep deep reach
creek leaf deed	mean steam sheep	seem feed key	bean fear seen	greet wheat feet

✔ From the box on the right, choose words that rhyme with the underlined words in these sentences. Print the correct words in the blanks.

1. It is such a treat to ________ the team.
2. Jean can hear a bee ________ a green tree.
3. The seal was glad to get a fish as a ________.
4. She has seen three sheep ________ and play.

meal
greet
leap
near

Long Vowel ✎ E e

Review the long vowel RULE. This lesson teaches more of the long vowel sound of **e**.

This is how long vowel **e** words may be marked: clēan, frēe, and kēy.
If a word has ***one*** vowel and it comes at the end of the word, that vowel usually has a long sound:

bē hē mē shē wē

✔ Mark the following long vowel words as shown above. See how quickly you can say these words.

creek dear	steep wheat	screen greed	teach zeal	key she

✔ Mark the ***two*** vowels as you read these long vowel **e** words. Circle the correct word that names the picture next to each list, and write it on the line below.

mēal (hēel) zēal	heed need wheat 	flea deal leap 	seam peek peas 	seat peep real
steal creek peel	neat deed bean 	seed weed feed 	beam team seem	beat feet meet 

✔ Choose long vowel **e** words from the box at the right to complete these sentences.
Print the correct words in the blanks.

1. Shhhh! Look at the ________ in the pond.
2. It peels and eats a tree as a ________. 
3. It will ________ its tail if we come ________ it.
4. See its heap of sticks near the ________.
5. God gave it big ________ to help it eat.

stream
beat
treat
near
beaver
teeth

Long Vowel ✎ I i

Remember the long vowel RULE: When ***two*** vowels are in a word, usually the first vowel says its name, and the second vowel is silent. This lesson teaches the long vowel sound of **i**.

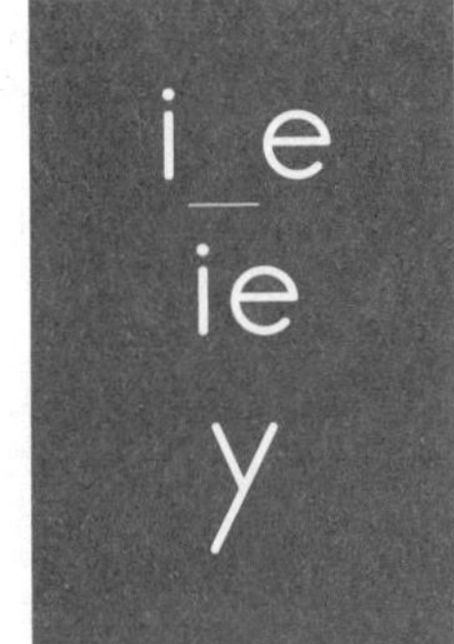

✔ Practice saying these short vowel words with the long vowel words.

pin	pine	hid	hide	dim	dime
Tim	time	bit	bite	rid	ride
slid	slide	kit	kite	pill	pile

✔ Mark the ***two*** vowels as you read these long vowel **i** words. Circle the correct word that names the picture next to each list, and write it on the line below.

white die pie	time dime lime	side chime line	dive five hive	hide tide bride
wire hire tire	fire file wipe	mine vine wide	smile while side	bite kite pipe

✔ From the box on the right, choose words that rhyme with the underlined words in these sentences. Print the correct words in the blanks.

1. The grapes from the vine are ________ to eat.
2. Mike will clean and wipe the ________ grape.
3. Steve has seen five ducks ________ in the lake.
4. A wire got stuck in the ________ of his bike.
5. Mother has a dime to get a ________.

dive
fine
lime
ripe
tire

Long Vowel ✎ I i

Review the long vowel RULE. This lesson teaches more about the long vowel sound of **i**. You have learned that a **y** is a vowel when it is at the end of a word or syllable. If it is the only vowel in the word, it has the long vowel sound of **i** as in **fly**.
This is how long vowel **i** words may be marked: fīve, pīe, and crȳ.

✔ Mark the following long vowel words as shown above. See how quickly you can say these words.

shīne	chime	mine	shy	white
twīne	Nile	why	try	kite

✔ Mark the ***two*** vowels as you read these long vowel **i** words. Circle the correct word that names the picture next to each list, and write it on the line below.

sīze prīze rīse	sly sky spy	by why fry	fly dry sty	bike like hike
five hive drive	shine mine twine	my tie pie	kite bite white	smile file pile

ATTENTION! A few words have two vowels, but the first vowel has the **short** sound as in **have**, **give**, and **live**. A silent **e** is added because words usually do not end with **v**.

✔ Choose long vowel **i** words from the box at the right to complete these sentences.
Print the correct words in the blanks.

1. Did you see that bug ________ by the hive?
2. It is not ________ to lift the lid of that box.
3. A bee will get mad if we look ________.
4. It may sting us and make us ________.
5. Stay away from that ________.

hive
cry
wise
fly
inside

Long Vowel ✎ O o

Remember the long vowel RULE: When ***two*** vowels are in a word, usually the first vowel says its name, and the second vowel is silent. This lesson teaches the long vowel sound of **o**.

o oa
o_e
ow

✔ Practice saying these short vowel words with the long vowel words.

cot	coat	got	goat	cod	code
hop	hope	rod	road	glob	globe
not	note	tot	tote	Tod	toad

✔ Mark the ***two*** vowels as you read these long vowel **o** words. Circle the correct word that names the picture next to each list, and write it on the line below.

vōte bōat quōte	tone zone stone	poke smoke woke	boast roast toast	toad road spoke
note moat pose	hope rose joke	hoe toe stole	bone lone cone	chose nose globe

✔ From the box on the right, choose words that rhyme with the underlined words in these sentences. Print the correct words in the blanks.

1. Jon <u>woke</u> up when his mother ________ to him.
2. He likes to smell the <u>rose</u> with his ________.
3. Dad made a <u>hole</u> for the flag ________.
4. Can a <u>goat</u> have on a ________?
5. The <u>note</u> from Joan had a ________ on it.

pole
spoke
quote
coat
nose

Long Vowel ✎ O o

Review the long vowel RULE. This lesson teaches more about the long vowel sound of **o**.
If a word has ***one*** vowel and it comes at the end of the word, that vowel usually has a long sound as in: gō, nō, and sō.
The letter ***w*** acts as a vowel when it follows another vowel as in: snōw, rōw, and blōw.

Long vowel **o** words may be marked like this: gō, grōw, and tōe.

✔ Mark the following long vowel **o** words as shown above. See how quickly you can say these words.

nō spōke	close boat	stove snow	toast toe	foam joke

✔ Mark the ***two*** vowels as you read these long vowel **o** words. Circle the correct word that names the picture next to each list, and write it on the line below.

slōw (snōw) glōw	bow tow low	hope rope soap	nose rose hose	goat coat boat
toe foe hoe	blow row grow	note vote quote	stove cove drove	soak poke coat

VOTE

✔ Choose long vowel **o** words from the box at the right to complete these sentences.
Print the correct words in the blanks.

1. The black ________ did fly near my home.
2. It went in a ________ in an ________ tree.
3. I can hear it crow as if it did ________.
4. Its black ________ has a shine and a glow.
5. It will ________ its beak in the grass for food.

oak
crow
boast
coat
poke
hole

Long Vowel ✎ U u

Remember the long vowel RULE: When ***two*** vowels are in a word, usually the first vowel says its name, and the second vowel is silent. This lesson teaches the long vowel sound of **u**.

✔ Practice reading these short vowel words with the long vowel words.

us	use	cut	cute	fuss	fuse
cub	cube	tub	tube	mutt	mute

Luke will use his flute and play a tune.

✔ Mark the ***two*** vowels as you read these long vowel **u** words. Circle the correct word that names the picture next to each list, and write it on the line below.

sūit	cure	fruit	use	tube
cūte	pure	rule	fuse	prune
mūte	mule	due	glue	mule
______	______	______	______	______

✔ Mark the following long vowel **u** words. See how quickly you can say these words.

cūbes	suit	cute	flute	blue
frūit	tube	June	use	tune

✔ Choose long vowel **u** words from the box above to complete these sentences.
Print the correct words in the blanks.

1. It is a hot day in the month of ______.

2. Sue needs a big glass of ______ juice.

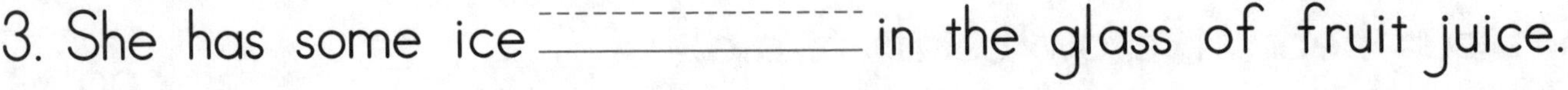

3. She has some ice ______ in the glass of fruit juice.
4. She will ______ a ______ of glue to fix a doll.
5. The doll has on a ______ hat and a white ______.

Long Vowel ✎ U u

Remember the long vowel RULE: When ***two*** vowels are in a word, usually the first vowel says its name, and the second vowel is silent. This lesson teaches more about the long vowel sound of **u**.
The letters **ew** also make the long vowel sound of **u** as in **new** or **yu** as in **few**.

✔ Practice reading these **ew** words.

dew	blew	screw	grew	drew	pew
hew	flew	slew	threw	few	knew
new	chew	stew	crew	Jew	yew

✔ Underline the ew vowels and mark the ū_e vowels as you read these long vowel **u** words. Circle the correct word that names the picture next to each list, and write it on the line below.

drew new few	cube tube rule	blew pew chew	June flute due	threw screw crew

ATTENTION! Two important words have the vowel **o** that makes the long vowel sound of **u**.
They are **do** and **to**. Example sentence: **It is time to do a few tunes on the flute.**

✔ Circle the words in the box at the right which complete the following sentences.
Print the correct words in the blanks.

1. Don got a ________ from the screw. — cute / cut
2. Sue will ________ some glue to fix a box. — use / us
3. God gave us teeth that help us ________. — crew / chew
4. The pup did not like a bath in the ________. — tube / tub
5. A block has the shape of a ________. — cube / cub
6. We sit still in the ________ as we praise God. — flew / pew

✎ Long and Short Vowel Words

Remember the long vowel RULE: When ***two*** vowels are in a word, usually the ***first*** vowel says its name, and the ***second*** vowel is silent.
Remember the short vowel RULE: When a word or syllable has only ***one*** vowel and it comes at the beginning or between two consonants, that vowel usually has the ***short*** sound.

✔ Mark the vowels of the words in the box at the left. Print the correct words under the pictures.

snāil
bōat
sūit
rake
globe
sheep
pray
toast
key
mule
five
tie
lake
kite
tree
glue

✔How do you spell these short vowel **a** words?

✎ Long and Short Vowel Words

Remember the long vowel RULE: When ***two*** vowels are in a word, usually the ***first*** vowel says its name, and the ***second*** vowel is silent.
Remember the short vowel RULE: When a word or syllable has only ***one*** vowel and it comes at the beginning or between two consonants, that vowel usually has the ***short*** sound.

✔ Mark the vowels of the words in the box at the left. Print the correct words under the pictures.

vīne
nōte
fēet
cone
ear
tube
coat
tray
kite
rain
seal
flute
teach
cake
fruit
nine

2+2=4

✔ How do you spell these short vowel **e** words?

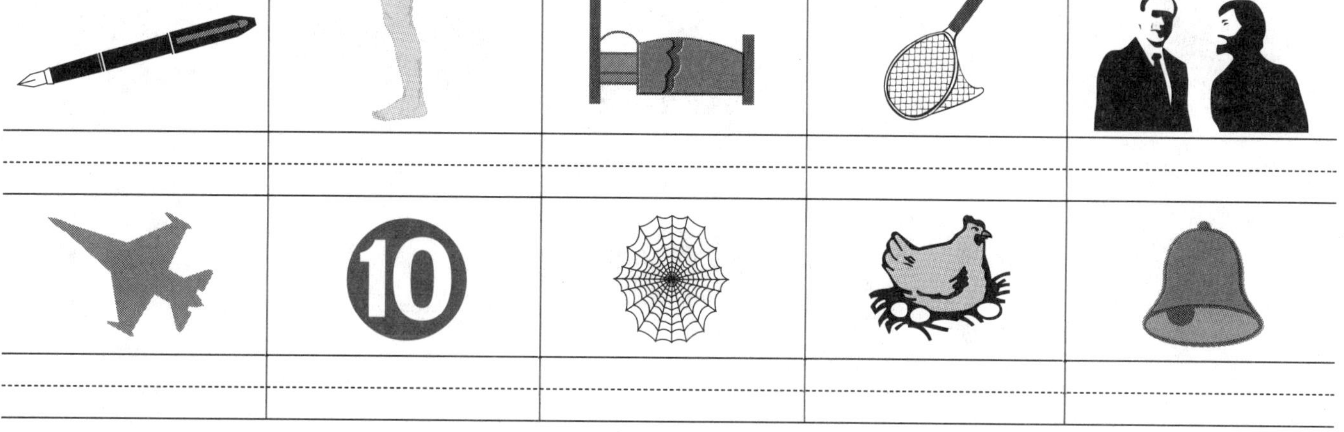

✎ Long and Short Vowel Words

Look back to the two previous pages if you need to review the long and short vowel rules.

✔ Use the vowels in the boxes to spell the long vowel words below.

✔ How do you spell these short vowel **i** words?

✎ Long and Short Vowel Words

Look back to page 50 or 51 if you need to review the long and short vowel rules.

✔ Use the vowels in the boxes to spell the long vowel words below.

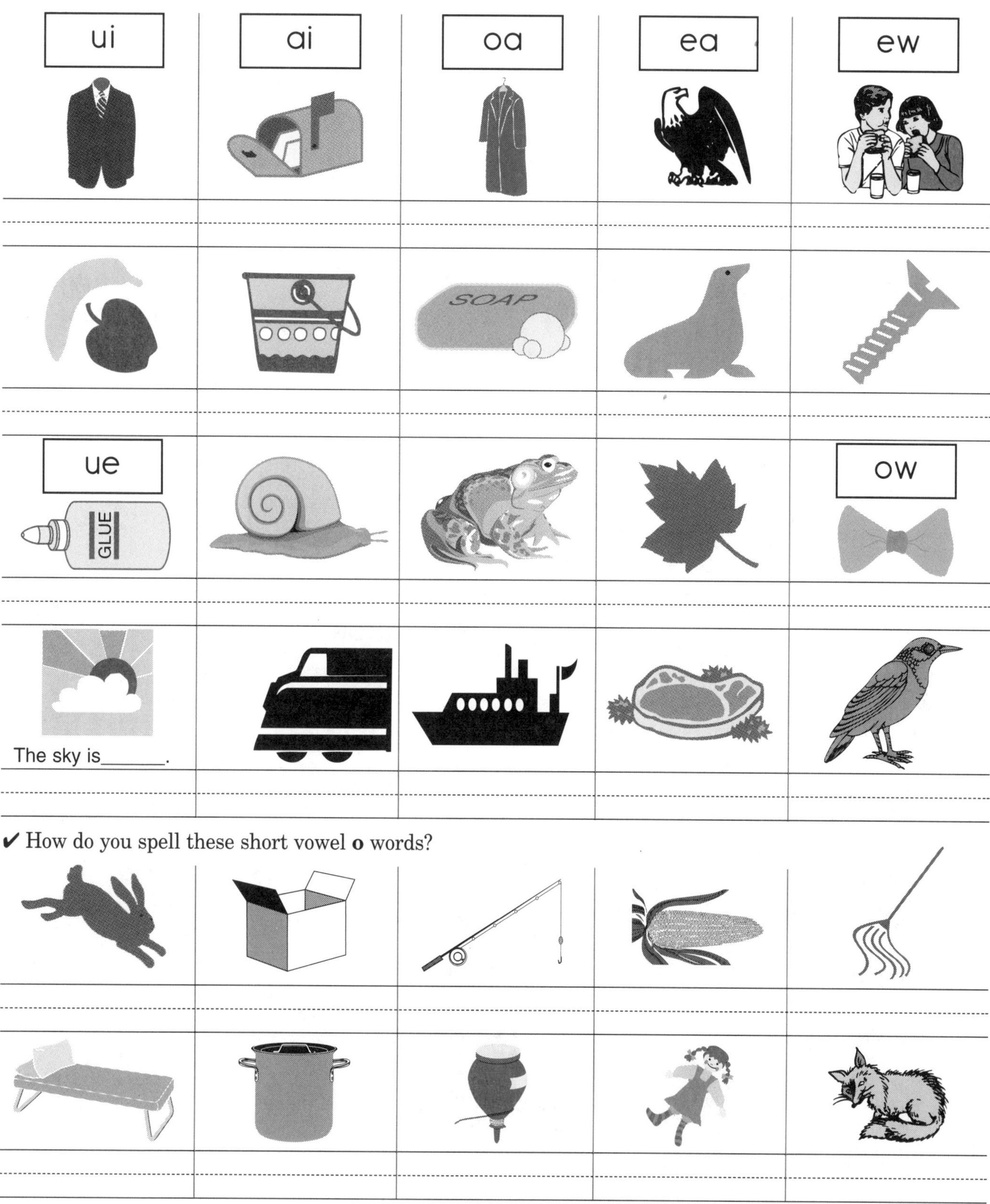

✔ How do you spell these short vowel **o** words?

Long Vowel ✎ i

Usually the vowel **i** is short when it is alone in a word.
This lesson teaches that the **i** is long when it is followed by **ld, nd,** or **gh.** The **gh** is silent.

✔ Mark the vowel ***i*** as you read these long vowel **i** words. Circle the correct word that names the picture next to each list, and write it on the line below.

tīght sīght (līght)	find grind mind	wild child mild	night might tight	nigh sigh fight
bind wind kind	behind hind remind ? legs	right sight fright ? hand	kind blind flight	child find bright

✔ Choose the long vowel **i** words ending in **ld**, **nd**, and **gh**(**t**) from the box at the right to complete these sentences. Print the correct words in the blanks.

behind	night	fight	child	bright

1. God made the sun to give a ______ light.
2. It is not kind to ______ with pals.
3. Tim is first and I am ______ him.
4. I am glad that I can rest at ______.
5. The ______ likes to play hide-and-seek.

✔ How do you spell these short vowel words that end with **ck**?

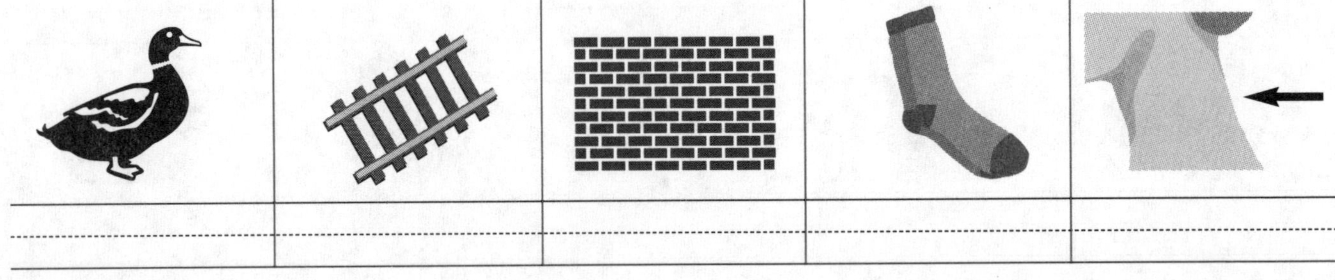

Long Vowel ✎ o

Usually the vowel **o** is short when it is alone in a word.
This lesson teaches that the **o** is long when it is followed by **ld, st, th, ll, or lt**

✔ Mark the vowel ***o*** as you read these long vowel **o** words. Circle the correct word that names the picture next to each list, and write it on the line below.

hōst (pōst) mōst	cold sold told	colt bolt jolt	roll stroll scroll	old fold gold

✔ Choose the long vowel **o** words ending in **ld**, **st**, **ll**, and **lt** from the box at the right to complete these sentences. Print the correct words in the blanks.

1. Men of old had to print on a ________.
2. The ________ wind made Joe go inside his home.
3. It is fun to see a ________ jump and run.
4. Chad has done ________ of his jobs today.
5. James will help Dad get a ________ in a hole.
6. Bill had to ________ the pup when it bit his sock.
7. The bright sun made the chunk of ________ shine.

most
colt
cold
scold
scroll
post
gold

✔ Be careful as you spell these short vowel words that end with double consonants.

Diphthongs ✎ **ou** and **ow**

A diphthong is ***two*** vowel sounds in ***one*** syllable. The diphthong **ou** makes the sound that is heard in **house**. Another diphthong that makes this sound is **ow** which is used at the end of words as in **cow**, or when words with dipthongs end with **l** as in **owl** or **n** as in **crown**.

✔ Underline the vowels that make the **ou** sound as you read these words with diphthongs. Circle the correct word that names the picture next to each list, and write it on the line below.

how now cow	owl wow pow	growl crowd vowels	town down frown	house proud mouse
crown brown gown	tower flower power	bound found round	sound hound pound	count ounce cloud
allow clown plow	out shout snout	mound blouse ground	ouch couch pouch	south scout mouth

a e i o u

N W E ?

✔ Choose the words with diphthongs **ou** or **ow** from the box at the right to complete these sentences. Print the correct words in the blanks.

1. Dry the hound with a brown __________.
2. The trail up the __________ is steep.
3. Jed has about a __________ stamps.
4. A bell has a __________ sound.
5. At night a light shines on a __________.

thousand
loud
towel
fountain
mountain

Diphthongs ✎ ou and ow

A diphthong is ***two*** vowel sounds in ***one*** syllable. The diphthong **ou** makes the sound that is heard in **house**. Another diphthong that makes this sound is **ow** which is used at the end of words as in **cow**, or when words end with **l** as in **owl** or **n** as in **crown**.

✔ Underline the vowels that make the **ou** sound as you read these words with diphthongs. Circle the correct word that names the picture next to each list, and write it on the line below.

sound scout pout	fowl growl tower	hour flour our	crowd amount towel	sprout out doubt

✔ Choose the words with the diphthongs **ou** or **ow** from the box at the right to complete these sentences. Print the correct words in the blanks.

1. The brown hound slept on the ______________.
2. A pig can sniff a sprout with its ______________.
3. An owl can act like a wise ______________.
4. Mother got mad at a mouse in the ______________.

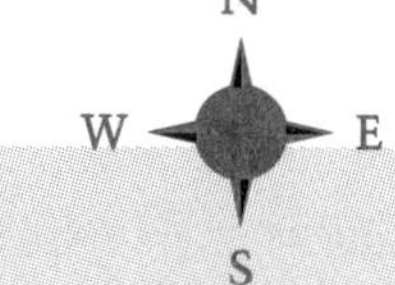

snout
house
fowl
ground

✔ Complete the words by adding the diphthongs. See how quickly you can read the words.

N W E S

ow		ou	
b___	d___n	th___sand	s___th
h___	fl___er	m___ntain	___ch
n___	cr___d	am___nt	c___nt
pl___	ch___der	bl___se	ab___t
c___	t___el	gr___nd	sh___t

Diphthongs ✎ **oi** and **oy**

A diphthong is ***two*** vowel sounds in ***one*** syllable. The diphthong **oi** makes the sound that is heard in **noise.** Another diphthong that makes this sound is **oy** which is used at the end of words or syllables as in **boy** or **royal**.

✔ Underline the vowels **oi** and **oy** as you read these words with diphthongs. Circle the correct word that names the picture next to each list, and write it on the line below.

oil toil spoil	Roy toy joy	join void coin	soil moist hoist	avoid voice joints
coil foil broil	enjoy boy joys	royal foil loyal	Floyd Lloyd boil	boil point joyful

✔ Choose the words with the diphthongs **oi** or **oy** from the box at the right to complete these sentences. Print the correct words in the blanks.

1. Mother will fold ________ around Joy's cupcake.
2. It will help to keep it fresh and ________.
3. Our class ________ it when Roy sings.
4. His ________ sounds loud and clear.
5. Floyd helps his father dig a hole in the ________.
6. He will ________ a flag on a post in the hole.
7. Mother will ________ some meat on the grill.

moist
broil
soil
enjoys
foil
voice
hoist

Diphthongs ✎ **oi** and **oy**

A diphthong is ***two*** vowel sounds in ***one*** syllable. The diphthong **oi** makes the sound that is heard in **noise.** Another diphthong that makes this sound is **oy** which is used at the end of words or syllables as in **boy** or **royal**.

✔ Remember the rule above as you print the correct diphthong in the blanks below.

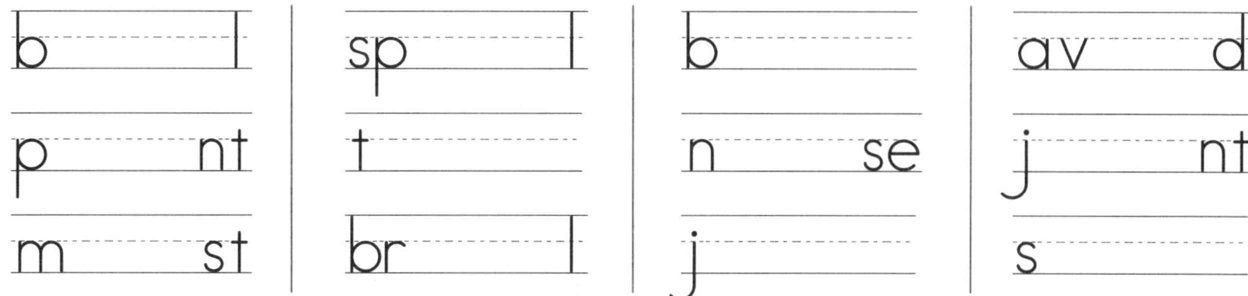

✔ Choose the correct words from the box at the left and print them in the blanks under their pictures.

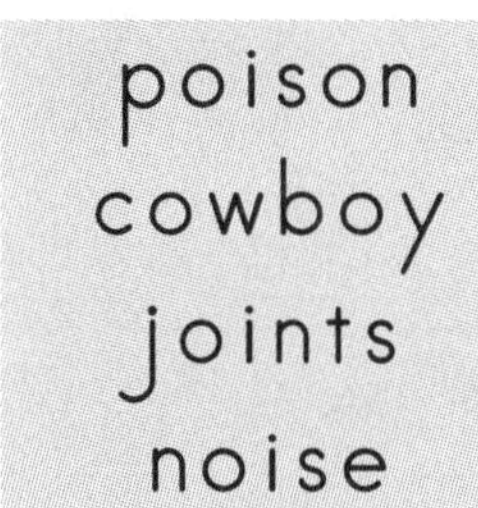

✔ Choose the correct words that complete the following sentences. Print the words in the blanks below.

cowboy	poison	enjoy	noise
join	joints	joyful	broils

1. Joy hears the loud ________ Roy makes with his horn.

2. Both of them will ________ the club.

3. Can you see the ________ lead the cows?

4. He will ________ it after he ________ it on a grill.

5. God made our hands with lots of ________.

6. We feel ________ as we sing about God.

Vowel Digraph ✎ oo

A vowel digraph has ***two*** vowels that make ***one*** sound. The double vowels **oo** make two sounds. This lesson teaches the sound of o͞o as in zo͞o.

✔ Mark the vowel digraph **oo** as you read these words. Circle the correct word that names the picture next to each list, and write it on the line below.

lo͞on (mo͞on) no͞on	spoon soon boost	fool cool tools	spool stool too	boot pool coop
booth tooth proof	goose groom loose	mood food pooch	snoop stoop hoop	shoot broom toot

✔ Choose the words with the vowel digraph **oo** from the box below to complete these sentences. Print the correct words in the blanks.

noodles	poodle	smooth	choose
balloon	rooster	school	moose

1. Don wakes up as he hears the ____________ crow.

2. He will not have ____________ this afternoon.
3. It is his birthday and Jill will give him a ____________.
4. The shape of the balloon is a white ____________.
5. He will choose to eat cheese and ____________.

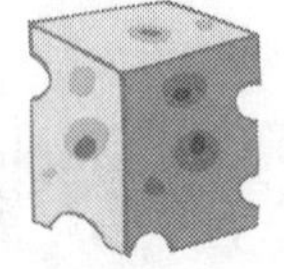

6. He can see a big ____________ outside his home.

Vowel Digraph ✎ oo

A vowel digraph has ***two*** vowels that make ***one*** sound. The double vowels **oo** make two sounds. This lesson teaches the sound of o͝o as in bo͝ok.

✔ Mark the vowel digraph **oo** as you read these words. Circle the correct word that names the picture next to each list, and write it on the line below.

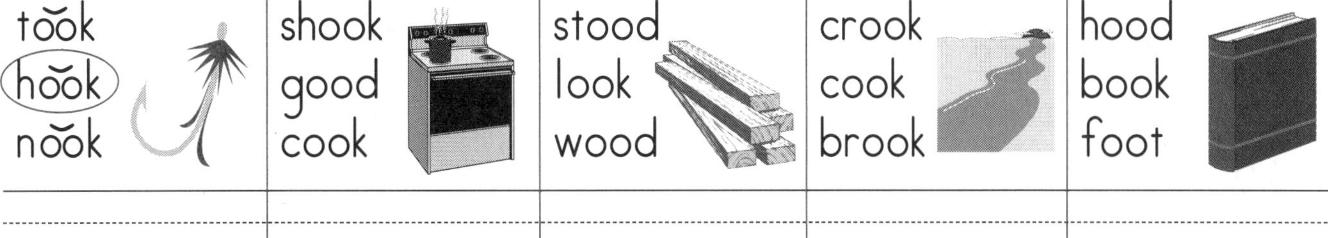

to͝ok ho͝ok no͝ok	shook good cook	stood look wood	crook cook brook	hood book foot

✔ Choose the correct words from the box at the left and print them in the blanks under their pictures.

bush
push
pull
wolf

✔ Choose the words with the **oo** sound as in **book** from the box at the right to complete these sentences. Note that sometimes **o**, **u**, and **ou** can also make the **oo** sound as in **book**. Print the correct words in the blanks.

1. Cal would like to play ball if he ________.
2. June felt ________ after she ate six cookies.
3. It is good if we do as we ________.
4. A ________ ran by a bush in the woods.
5. Dan will give his brother a ________ on a swing.
6. Mother made some good ________.
7. Jim took some cookies down to the ________.

brook
full
should
cookies
push
could
wolf

Modified Vowel ✎ ar

When the consonant **r** comes after the vowel **a**, it changes the sound of the vowel as in **ark**. The **ar** sound may be marked with two dots over the **a** like this: **ärk.**

✔ Mark the vowel **a** like this **ä** as you read these words. Circle the correct word that names the picture next to each list, and write it on the line below.

bärn härm chärm	bark car dark	mar arm part	harp hard carp	far art card
jar tar bar	park star arch	shark mark spark	sharp cart dart	farm tart yarn

✔ Choose the **ar** words from the box at the right to complete these sentences. Print the correct words in the blanks.

1. Mark would like to be a ________.
2. He must keep the pigs in a ________.
3. He could plant a big ________.
4. His job would be ________ each day.
5. Some crops will be sold at a ________.

garden
market
farmer
yard
hard

✔ Draw lines to match the rhyming **ar** words below.

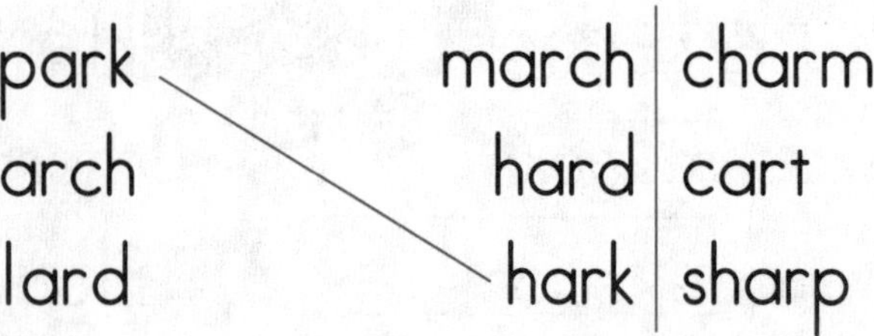

park	march	charm	harp	star	mark
arch	hard	cart	harm	spark	chart
lard	hark	sharp	start	smart	car

Modified Vowel ✎ or

When the consonant **r** comes after the vowel **o**, it changes the sound of the vowel as in **corn**. The **or** sound may be marked with a caret (**^**) over the **o** like this: **côrn.**

✔ Mark the vowel **o** like this **ô** as you read these words. Circle the correct word that names the picture next to each list, and write it on the line below.

Lôrd dôor flôor	cork pork fork	stork short sport	more sore core	horse store wore
born horn torn	snore forth corn	porch torch port	shore organ storm	thorns score corner

✔ Choose the **or** words from the box at the right to complete these sentences. Print the correct words in the blanks.

1. Jordan will start to make a card ________ Carl.
2. His pal is sick with a ________ throat.
3. Jordan has a gift for him from the ________.
4. Soon Jordan will bring it to Carl's ________.
5. He will pray to the ________ for Carl this morning.

store
for
sore
Lord
door

✔ Draw a line to match the rhyming **or** words below.

forth ——	north	storm	fork	door	fort
torch	border	stork	dorm	horn	thorn
order	porch	shore	snore	sport	floor

Modified Vowels ✎ er ir ur

You have learned that **r** modifies **a** as in **ark**, and **o** as in **corn**. The other three vowels are also changed. When **e**, **i**, and **u** are followed by **r**, they usually make the same sound as a rooster makes, like **er** in **verse**, **ir** in **girl**, and **ur** in **church**. This sound is a combination of the ***schwa*** (ə) and ***r*** sounds.

✔ Underline the letters that make the **er** sound as you read these words. Circle the correct word that names the picture next to each list, and write it on the line below.

derby verse serve Blessed is the nation whose God is the LORD. Psalm 33:12	father dirt sister	first fern firm	third whirl bird	burn nurse church
turtle burst curb	turn curls purple	mother cracker hammer	hurry hurt purse	herd disturb girl
injure churn squirrel	person sir shirt	skirt thirsty fir	during stir fur	turkey rocker zipper

✔ Choose the words with the **er** sound from the lists above to complete these sentences. Print the correct words in the blanks.

1. God will bless us as we go to ____________ each Sunday.

2. He is glad as we read a ____________ from our Bible.

3. Bert has a little pet ____________ that lives in a box.

4. He made the wooden box with nails and a ____________.

5. A gray ____________ ate the seeds for the birds.

Modified Vowels ✎ ear wor

You have learned that **e**, **i**, and **u** say the same ***schwa*** sound when followed by an **r**. Two more ways to make the ***schwa*** plus ***r*** sound are with the letters **ear** as in **earth** and **(w)or** as in **world**.

✔ Underline the letters that make the **er** sound as you read these words. Circle the correct word that names the picture next to each list, and write it on the line below.

worth worm worse	earn early earth 	learn heard words 	worship worry working 	worthy world pearls 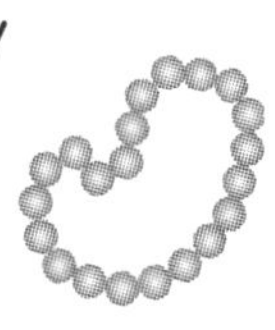

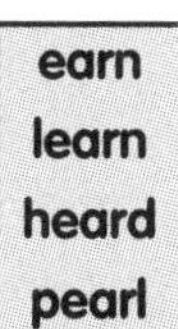

✔ Choose the correct words from the box at the left and print them in the blanks under their pictures.

turkey worship birthday rooster				

✔ Choose the words with the **er** sound from the lists above to complete these sentences. Print the correct words in the blanks.

1. As you read ________ you will learn many new things.
2. Another name for God's earth is God's ________ .
3. A fat, brown ________ went into a hole in the ground.
4. Each day we should love and ________ the Lord.

✔ Draw lines to match these rhyming words. NOTE: The ***schwa*** sounds are spelled differently.

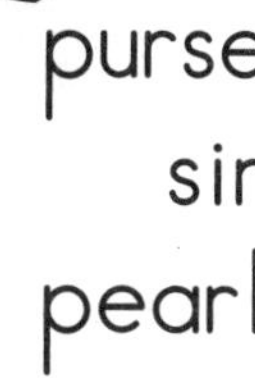

earn	word	burst	whirl	girl	purse
earth	learn	heard	first	stir	sir
herd	birth	curl	bird	nurse	pearl

Modified Vowels ✎ âr

You have learned the sound of **är** as in **arm**. These letters may also make the sound of **are** as in **square**. This **ar** sound is marked with a caret (**^**) over the **a** like this: **squâre**. This sound may also be made as follows: **arr** as in **carrot** , **air** as in **chair**, **err** as in **berry**, **ear** as in **bear**, and **ere** as in **where.**

✔ Underline the **âr** sound as you read these words. Circle the correct word that names the picture next to each list, and write it on the line below.

stare snare square	rare carry carrot	hare fare care	tear wear bear	air hair fair
where dare beware	share spare stairs	error merry errand 3 +5 = 9✓	dairy cherry declare	bare pair air ? of shoes
carry chair there	blare chair berry	pear swear dare	marry scary parrot	ferry barrel berry

✔ Choose the **âr** words from the lists above to complete these sentences.
Print the correct words in the blanks.

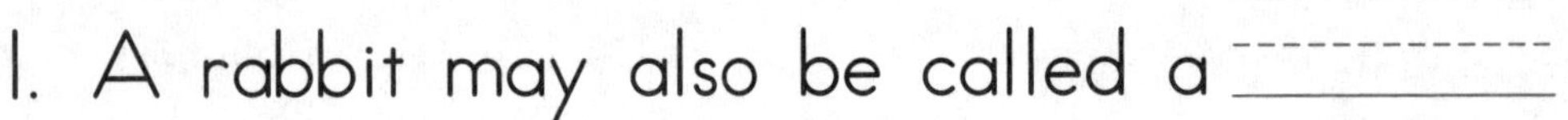

1. A rabbit may also be called a ________ .

2. Barry taught his pet ________ to say some words.

3. We can eat a ________, ________, and ________.

4. Take care so that the cloth will not ________ .

5. The child likes to go up and down the ________ .

Modified Vowels ✎ âr

Review the many ways that you can spell the sound of the **âr** as in **square**: **are** as in **square**, **arr** as in **carrot** , **air** as in **chair**, **err** as in **berry**, **ear** as in **bear**, and **ere** as in **where**.

✔ Choose the correct words from the box at the left and print them in the blanks under their pictures.

marry chariot parrot berry				
	______	______	______	______

✔ Choose the **âr** words from the list above to complete these sentences.
Read the sentences as you print the correct words in the blanks.

1. Ben has a pet ______ that is red and green.
2. Miss Clare can bake ______ pies that taste good.
3. In Bible times some men would ride in a ______.
4. This is a merry affair as Sarah plans to ______.

✔ Choose the letters from the box at the right to answer where you would find the things asked in the questions below. Print the correct letters in the blanks.

1. Where would you find a bear? ___
2. Where will Ben and Sarah marry? ___
3. Where should we carry the pears? ___
4. Where can we go on a stairway? ___
5. Where should this carrot go? ___

a. to the rabbit
b. to our home
c. up and down
d. in the woods
e. in the church

The Sound of ✎ ô

Other lessons have taught that the vowel **o** has several sounds: short **o** as in ŏx, long **o** as in ōak or ōld, o͞o as in spo͞on, and o͝o as in bo͝ok.
The **o** has another sound which may be marked in a dictionary with a caret (**^**) over the **o** like this: dôg.

✔ Underline the **o** sound as in **dôg** as you read these words. Circle the correct word that names the picture next to each list, and write it on the line below.

toss song off	moss boss cloth	strong dog log	frog frost cost	soft moth cloth

✔ Choose the correct words from the box and print them in the blanks below.

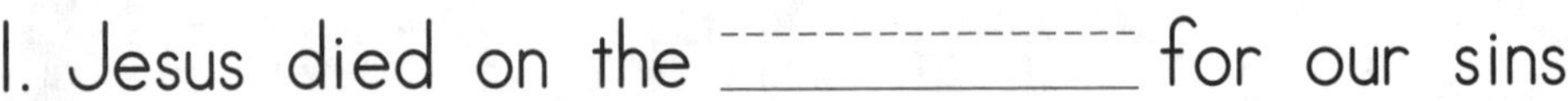

1. Jesus died on the ______________ for our sins.

2. I should love and serve Him as ______________ as I live.

cross
long

The sound of **ô** is also made by the vowel **a** when it is followed by **l**, **w**, or **u**.

✔ Underline the vowel **a** as you read these **ô** words. Circle the correct word that names the picture next to each list, and write it on the line below.

all ball hall	call fall small	raw paw saw	draw straw thaw	lawn dawn fawn
jaw yawn crawl	shawl law awning	Paul Saul auto	laundry pause cause	shawl haul autumn

✔ Choose the **ô** words from the box at the right to complete these sentences.
Print the correct words in the blanks.

1. We saw Paul sip milk with a long ______________.

2. The strong child likes to ______________ in the hall.

crawl
straw

The Sound of ✎ ô

The **ô** sound is also made with the letters augh and ough. NOTE: The letters **gh** are silent.

✔ Choose the correct words from the box at the left and print them in the blanks under their pictures.

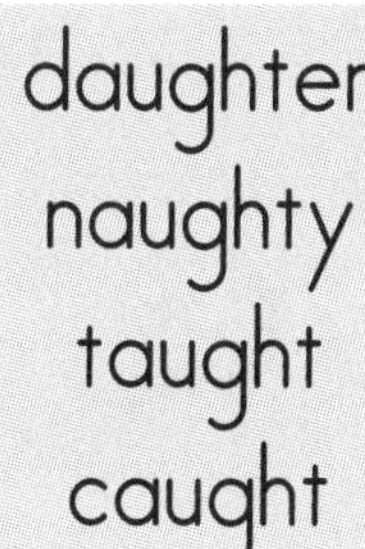

✔ Choose the correct words from the box at the left to complete the following sentences.
Print the correct words in the blanks below.

bought brought thought

1. Bill ______ the boys ought to be kind.
2. Paul ______ a new Bible at the store.
3. He ______ his new Bible to church.

✔ Underline the letters that say the sound of **ô** (**o**, **al**, **aw**, **au**, **augh**, **ough**) in the box below.
Choose words from the box to complete the following sentences. Print the correct words in the blanks.

August	laundry	because	belong	daughter
strong	awning	fought	autumn	talk

1. A ______ wind blew the ______ off of a house.
2. Another name we have for fall is ______.

3. Mrs. Hall taught her ______ to read at home.
4. Dawn helped her mother fold the ______.
5. We ought to help because we ______ to a family.

Review

This lesson will review the vowel digraphs o͞o as in zo͞o and o͝o as in bo͝ok, and the diphthongs **ou** as in **house** and **ow** as in **cow**, and **oi** as in **noise** and **oy** as in **boy**.

✔ Print the words in the columns by using the vowels in the boxes.

oo	oo	ou	ow	oi

	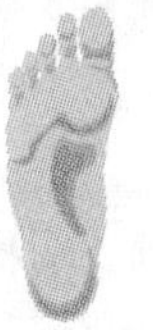	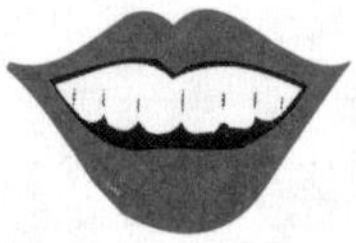		oy 
		 N W E ?		

✔ Print these ***one*** vowel words which have the long **o** or long **i** vowel sounds.

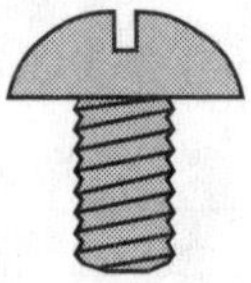

līght
pōst
colt
scroll
roll
grind
right
bolt

? hand

✎ Review

This lesson will review words with vowels that have been modified by the consonant ***r*** as it comes after the vowels: **ar, or, er, ir, ur, ear and (w)or.**

✔ Underline **ar**, **or**, **er**, **ir**, **ur**, **ear** and (w)**or** in the words in the box at the left. Print the correct words under their pictures.

church
shirt
shark
verse
bird
corner
pearls
purse
barn
turtle
words
horn
star
first
corn
turkey

✔ From the list above, choose words that rhyme with the underlined words below to complete the following sentences. Print the correct words in the blanks.

1. How far away God put each ____________!

2. Little Jack Horner sat in a ____________.

3. The nurse put her pearls in her ____________.

Review

Do you remember that the sound of **âr** can be spelled in six different ways?
are as in **square**, **arr** as in **carrot**, **air** as in **chair**,
err as in **berry**, **ear** as in **bear**, and **ere** as in **where**

✔ Underline the letters that make the **âr** sound in the words at the left as you read them. Print the correct words in the blanks below their pictures.

square
pair
error
hare
parrot
chair
bear
carrot

? of shoes

3
+3
7✓

The sound of **ô** as is **dog** also can be spelled in six different ways:
o as in **dog**, **al** as in **call**, **au** as in **haul**, **aw** as in **saw**, **ough** as in **fought**, and **augh** as in **caught**.

✔ Underline the letters that make the **ô** sound as you read the following sentence.

Mr. Fall thought he ought to teach his daughter about God's laws.

frog
moth
taught
laundry
hawk
cloth
cross
salt

✔ Underline the letters that make the **ô** sound in the words at the left. As you read these words, print them in the blanks below their pictures.

2+2=4

✎ Review

The letters **ear** can make three sounds: ēr as in **ear**, ėr as in **earth**, and âr as in **tear**.

✔ Make the correct vowel sound ***marks*** in the words below as in the letters **ear** at the beginning of each row.

ēar	tear	dear	fear	shears	year
ėar	pearl	learn	heard	earn	early
eâr	tear	pear	bear	wear	swear

✔ Print the correct **ear** words in the blanks below their pictures.

tears
bear
earth
pear
ear
learn
pearls
shears

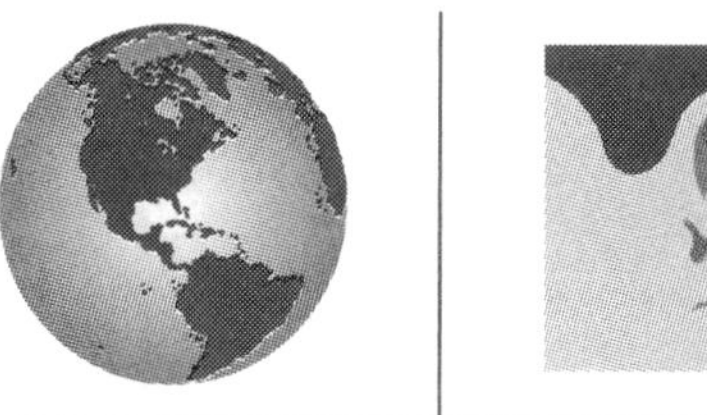
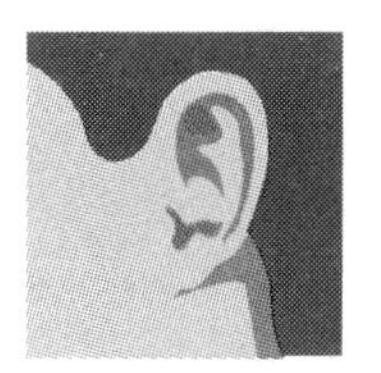

The vowels **ey** usually say the long vowel sound of **e** as in **key**.
They also may say the long vowel sound of **a** as in **they** and **obey**.

Children are happy as <u>they</u> <u>obey</u>.

✔ Choose the words with the **ear** sound from the list above to complete these sentences.
Print the correct words in the blanks.

1. As a person reads to us, our ______ help us to hear.

2. It is good to ______ to say Bible verses.

Trust in the LORD and do good. Psalm 37:3

3. They help us to obey God who made this ______.

4. A little child had ______ when he hurt his foot.

Soft Sound of ✎ c

The consonant **c** makes two sounds. The sound of **c** as in **cat**, **cot**, or **cut** may be called the ***hard*** sound of **c**, which usually is made when the vowels **a**, **o**, or **u** come after the **c**. The **c** has a ***soft*** sound (**s**) when vowels **e**, **i**, or **y** come after the **c** as in **ice**, **city**, and **cymbals**.

✔ Underline the vowels **e**, **i**, or **y** which make the **c** to have the soft sound, as you read these words. Circle the correct word that names the picture next to each list, and write it on the line below.

ice lice nice	mice rice spice	twice city vice	face place grace	brace race lace
bounce ounce fence	pencil glance chance	trace celery space	lettuce dice bicycle	circus circle prince

✔ Choose the words with the soft **c** sound from the box below to complete the following sentences. Print the correct words in the blanks.

juice	bounce	spice	lettuce
bicycle	circus	pencil	rice

1. Vince rode his ____________ in a race in the city.

2. Grace put some ____________ in the cake she made.

3. The class had a nice time at the ____________.

4. Bruce likes to ____________ a basketball.

5. Nancy can trace around a circle with a ____________.

6. The mice ate some of the ____________ in the bowl.

Soft Sound of ✎ g

The consonant **g** makes two sounds. The sound of **g** as in **game**, **go**, or **gum** may be called the ***hard*** sound, which usually is made when the vowels **a**, **o**, or **u** come after the **g**.
The **g** has a ***soft*** sound (**j**) when vowels **e**, **i**, or **y** come after the **g** as in **cage**, **giant**, and **gym**.

✔ Underline the vowels **e**, **i**, or **y** that make the **g** to have the soft sound, as you read these words. Circle the correct word that names the picture next to each list, and write it on the line below.

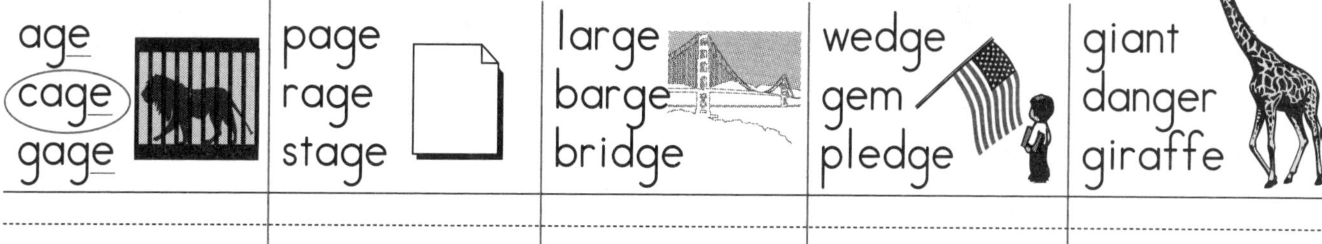

✔ Underline the vowels that make the **g** to have the soft sound, as you read the words at the left. Print them on the line below their pictures.

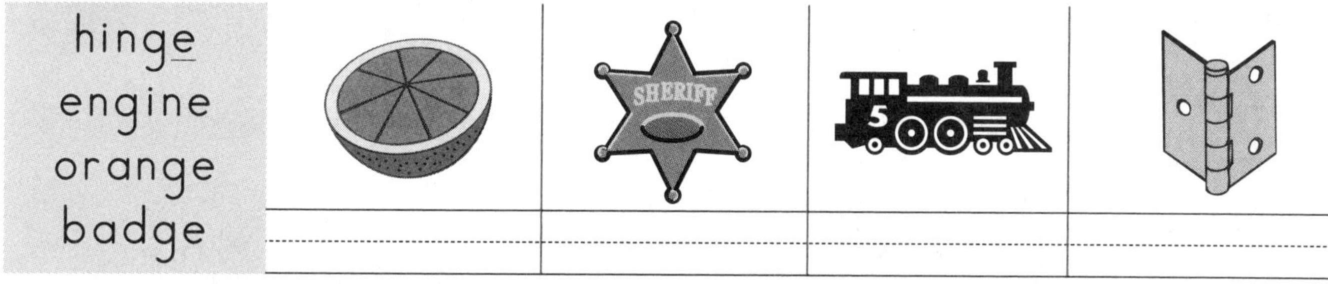

✔ Choose the words with the soft **g** sound from the box below to complete the following sentences. Print the correct words in the blanks.

vegetables	change	charge	hedge
gingerbread	Egypt	manger	gym

1. Mary made a bed in a ______________ for baby Jesus.

2 Joseph had to flee to ______________ with Mary and Jesus.

3. God told the wise men to ______________ their plans.

4 God is in ______________ of all things in our world.

5. It is important to eat ______________ at each meal.

Silent Consonants ✎ kn wr

The *k* is silent when it is followed by **n** as in knot and knee.
The *w* is silent when it is followed by **r** as in write and wrap.

✔ Cross out the silent *k* as you read these words. Print the correct words on the line below their pictures.

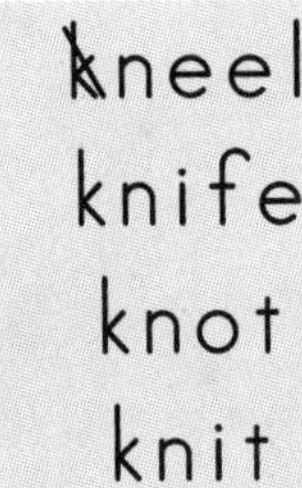

kneel
knife
knot
knit

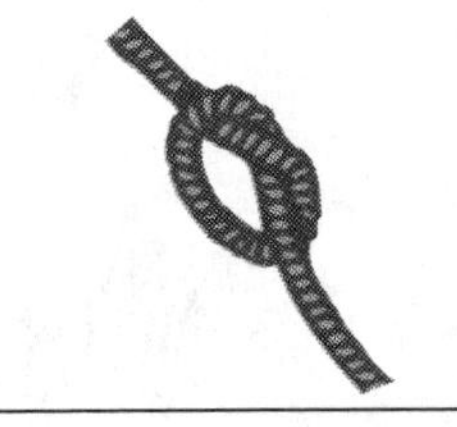   

✔ Cross out the silent **k** in the words at the left. Print the correct words in the blanks below.

knuckles
know
knot
knew

1. Ken ________ how to tie a ________.
2. Kay hit her ________ on the wall.

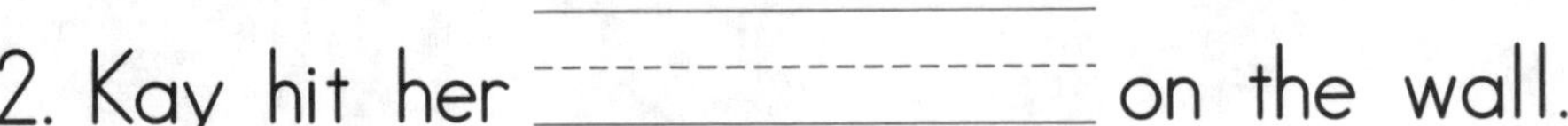

3. Do you ________ how to read the Bible?

✔ Cross out the silent *w* in the words in the box below. Print the underlined words under their pictures. Choose from these words to complete the following sentences. Print the correct words on the blanks below.

wrestle	<u>wrench</u>	wreck	<u>wrong</u>	wrinkle
<u>wreath</u>	wrap	<u>wren</u>	wrist	<u>write</u>

4
+5
7 ✓

1. If we wring out the wet shirt it will ________.

2. Ron will ________ a cloth round his sore ________.
3. The boys do not have wrath as they ________.

✎ Silent Consonants

There are several other sets of letters in which one consonant or vowel may be silent, such as: **gn** as in gnaw, **mb** as in lamb, **bt** as in doubt, **gu** as in guess, **bu** as in build, and **mn** as in hymn.

✔ Cross out the silent letter in each word. Print the correct words that name the pictures below.

thumb	gnat	build	hymn	lamb

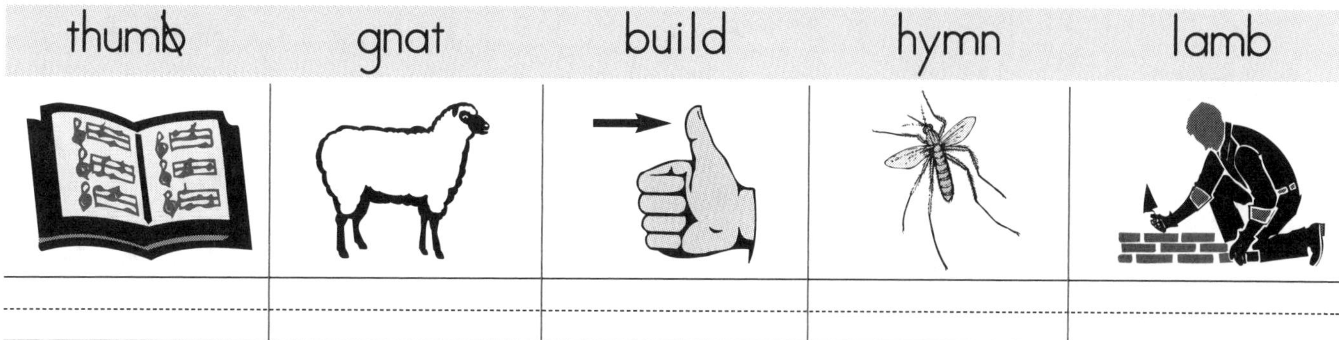

✔ Choose the correct words from the box at the left and print them in the blanks below.

guards	1. Jesus came out from the ________.
climb	2. The ________ became as dead men.
tomb	3. I will need a guide if I ________ a mountain.

✔ Answer these questions by printing **yes** or **no**.

1. Can a gnat tie a knot? no

2. Do you know how to write your name? yes

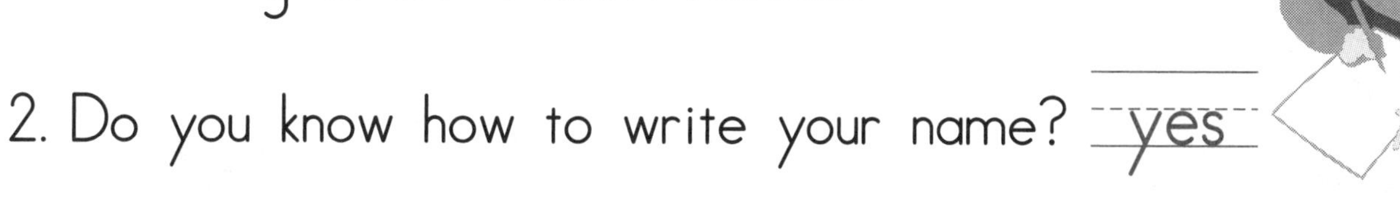

3. Would a wrench help a man build a bridge? ________

4. Does a wren know how to wrap a gift? ________

5. Would you like to pet a soft little lamb? ________

6. Should children know how to obey their parents? ________

Vowel Digraph ✎ ea

You know that the vowels **ea** can make the long sound of **e** as in bēan.
In some words the **ea** may have the short sound of **e** as in hĕad.

✔ Make a short sound mark on the **e** and print the words in the correct blanks.

hĕad	bread	thread	sweater	feather

✔ Choose the correct words from the box at the left and print them in the blanks below.

health
spread
breath
pleasant
read

1. Brett has ________ many books.
2. In cold weather we see our ________.

3. We thank God for our good ________.
4. Hannah ________ jam on the bread.
5. The soft tune is ________ to hear.

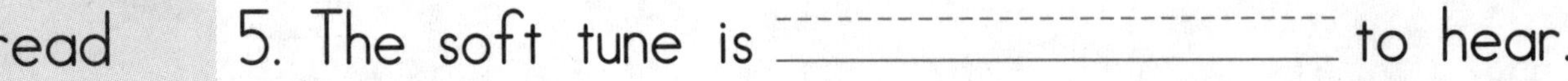

✔ Match the rhyming words.

head	toss	face	health	bread	trap
cross	weather	cage	race	wrap	marry
square	spool	wealth	page	goose	spread
feather	lead	know	night	carry	moose
tears	share	write	thaw	earn	noodle
stool	shears	gnaw	show	poodle	learn

Vowel Digraphs ✎ **ea** and **ou**

You have just learned that the **ea** may have the short sound of **e** as in hĕad.
In a few words the **ea** may also have the long sound of **a** as in stēāk.

✔ Mark the vowels in the list below and choose words to complete the sentences. Print them in the blanks.

steāk
break
great

1. A strong wind may ____________ the kite's string.
2. We have a ____________ and wonderful God.
3. Dan likes to eat ____________ with rice and corn.

Other lessons have taught that the vowels **ou** can make the sounds of **ou** as in **mouse**, **ô** as in **bought**, and **ou** as in **would**. Another sound **ou** makes is the long sound of **u** as in yoū.

✔ Mark the vowels and print the words in the correct blanks.

yoūth	group	wound	soup	cougar

✔ Match the words that rhyme.

great	book	come	coat	bread	light
suit	spot	time	bake	mouse	steak
took	fruit	take	lime	break	house
knot	plate	boat	some	sight	spread
came	tooth	group	page	race	farm
child	same	sleep	soup	charm	more
rake	mild	rage	wheat	store	twist
youth	break	feet	sheep	wrist	face

Compound Words

A compound word is made of two words written together as in **starfish**, **snowman**, and **himself**.

✔ Match the words that could be compound words and print them as one word on the lines below.

blue	milk	her	light	scrap	bell
yard	way	fire	coat	door	not
door	bird	flash	man	can	book
butter	stick	rain	self	ear	plug

bluebird

✔ Divide the ***compound*** words in the box below. Print the correct words under the following pictures.

near-by	homework	teardrop	snowman
sail-boat	baseball	jellybean	paperboy
blue-bird	hairbrush	cookbook	outside
bee-hive	stairway	railroad	fishhook

✎ Compound Words

You have learned that a ***compound*** word is made of ***two*** words written together as in **teapot**.

✔ Match the words that could be ***compound*** words and print them as ***one*** word.

mail	port	moon	book	milk	way
farm	man	note	ball	high	mark
bed	house	snow	bud	book	to
air	room	rose	light	in	man

mailman

✔ Divide these ***compound*** words and print some of them in the correct blanks.

cow-boy	bookmark	newsman	football
some-how	pipeline	oatmeal	flashlight
out-let	cornstalk	housefly	doorknob
him-self	someone	steamship	starfish

Review of Short Vowel ✎ a Words

When a word or syllable has only ***one*** vowel and it comes at the beginning or between two consonants, that vowel usually has the short sound as in **pat**, **man**, and **cap**.

✔ Carefully print these words which have the short vowel sound of **a**.

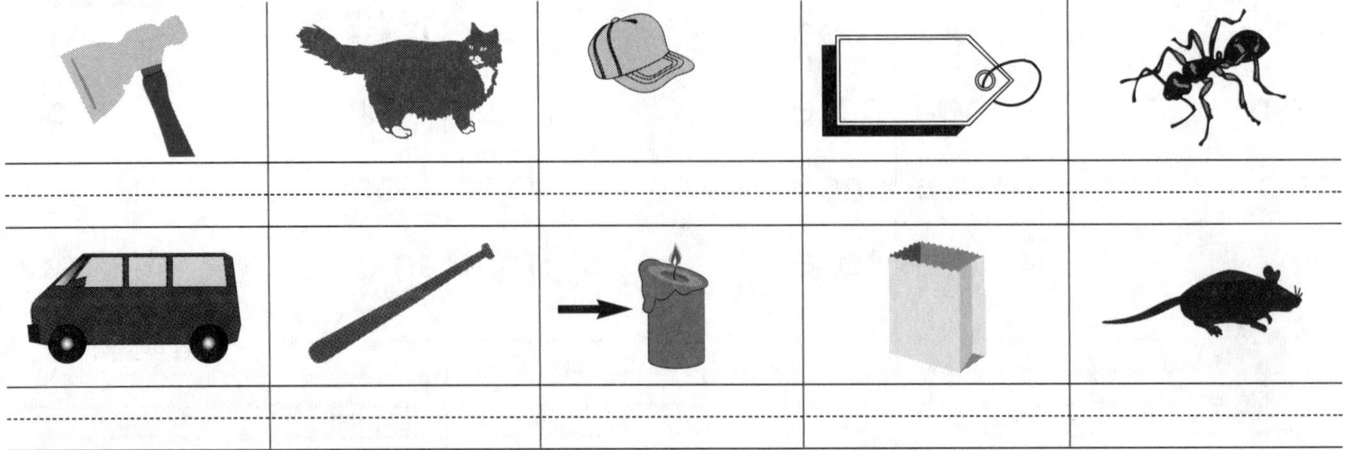

✔ Choose words from the list above to complete these sentences.

1. Dan had on his ________ as he hit a ball with the ________.

2. Jan will go with her dad in his big black ________.

3. The fat ________ ran after a fast ________.

4. Dad has to chop wood with an ________.

5. The bug that went into the lunch ________ is an ________.

✔Rhyming words must have the same vowel sound and ending sound. Match the rhyming words.

ax	tag	nap	sand	tab	fax
pat	stamp	stand	wag	land	glad
can	tax	flag	map	wax	damp
rag	sat	ant	fan	camp	grab
lamp	fan	man	plant	had	band

Review of Short Vowel ✎ a Words

When a word or syllable has only ***one*** vowel and it comes at the beginning or between two consonants, that vowel usually has the short sound as in **jam**, **hat**, and **pad**.

✔ Carefully print these words which have the short vowel sound of **a**.

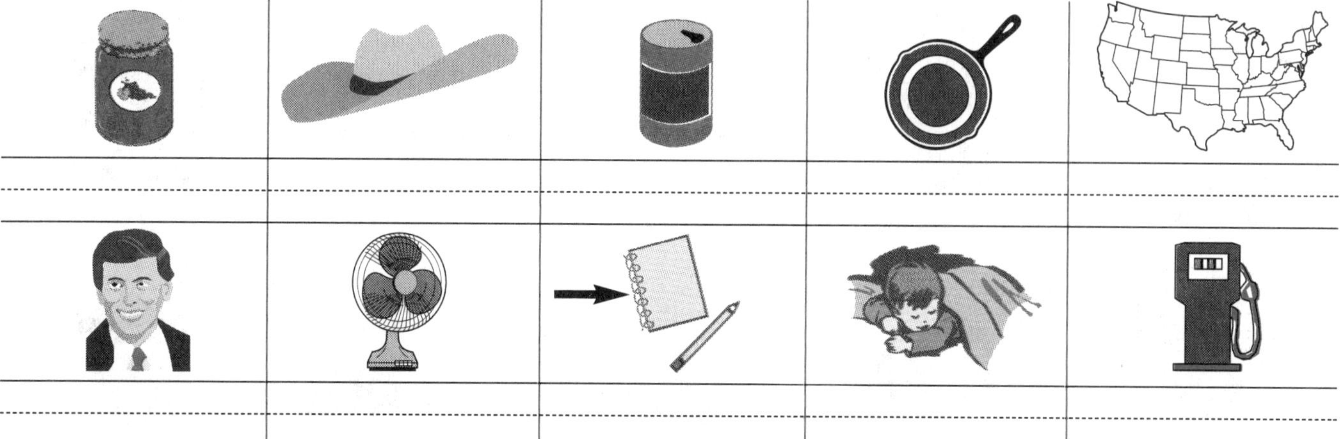

✔ Underline the words that have the short vowel sound of **a**. Answer the questions with **yes** or **no**.

1. Can a flag have a stand? ________ Write yes or no.
2. Can a lamp tag a lad? ________
3. Can hands clap and pat? ________
4. Can a man have a band on his hat? ________

✔ Choose words from the box at the right to complete the sentences. Print the correct words in the blanks.

1. Dan ran as ________ as Sam in the race.
2. Jan has tacks in a ________.
3. A tag is on Jan's new ________.
4. Dad bought a ________ for his ________.
5. Pat could not hold the ________ in her hand.

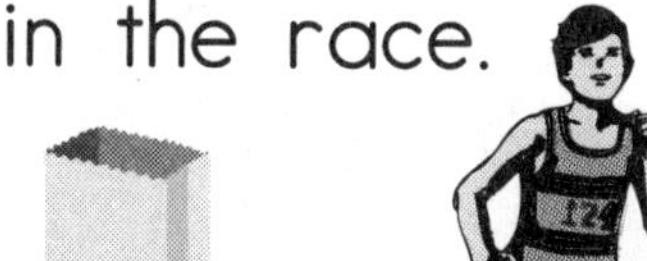

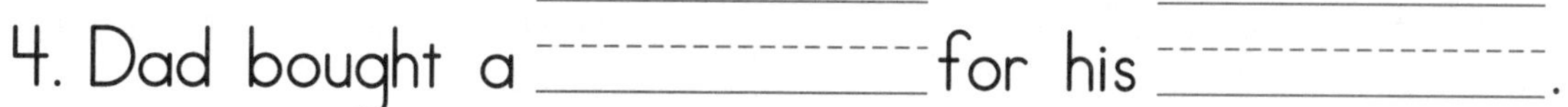

van
sand
map
hat
fast
bag

Review of Short Vowel ✎ e Words

When a word or syllable has only ***one*** vowel and it comes at the beginning or between two consonants, that vowel usually has the short sound as in **pet**, **men**, and **red**.

✔ Carefully print these words which have the short vowel sound of **e**.
See how quickly you can learn this important sound.

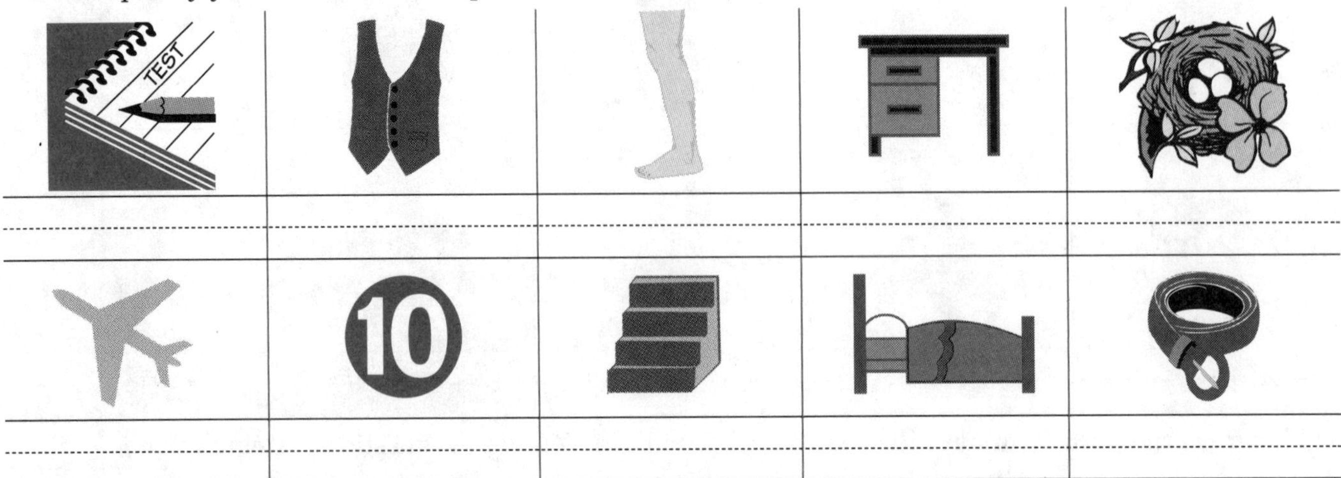

✔ Choose words from above to complete these sentences. Print the correct words in the blanks below.

1. Jed fell on the ________ and cut his left ________.
2. Can Emily see ________ eggs in the hen's ________?
3. Ted sat at his ________ and did his math ________.
4. Nathan has a ________ for his pants and a tan ________.

✔ Rhyming words must have the same vowel sound and ending sound. Match the rhyming words.

bless	leg	peg	step	dress	pen
egg	sell	red	beg	pet	dent
bend	tent	test	spent	swell	wet
fell	stem	spell	well	ten	end
hem	press	pep	led	sent	mess
rent	send	went	pest	mend	smell

Review of Short Vowel ✎ e Words

When a word or syllable has only ***one*** vowel and it comes at the beginning or between two consonants, that vowel usually has the short sound as in **bed**, **met**, and **ten.**

✔ Carefully print these words which have the short vowel sound of **e**.
See how quickly you can learn this important sound.

N
? E
S

✔ You have learned that the vowels **ea** may sometimes have the short sound of **e** as in **head**.
Choose the **ea** words from the box below and print them under their correct pictures.

head	bread	feather	thread	sweater

✔ Complete these sentences with the **ea** words from the list. Print the correct words in the blanks below.

1. It is important to eat __________.
2. Ted read the __________ of the paper.
3. Men found a __________ in a leather bag.
4. Ned will __________ the size of the hall.
5. We will trust in God __________ of worry.

instead
headline
breakfast
measure
treasure

Review of Short Vowel ✎ i Words

When a word or syllable has only ***one*** vowel and it comes at the beginning or between two consonants, that vowel usually has the short sound as in **fit**, **pin**, and **tip**.

✔ Carefully print the correct short vowel **i** words under their pictures.
See how quickly you can learn this important sound.

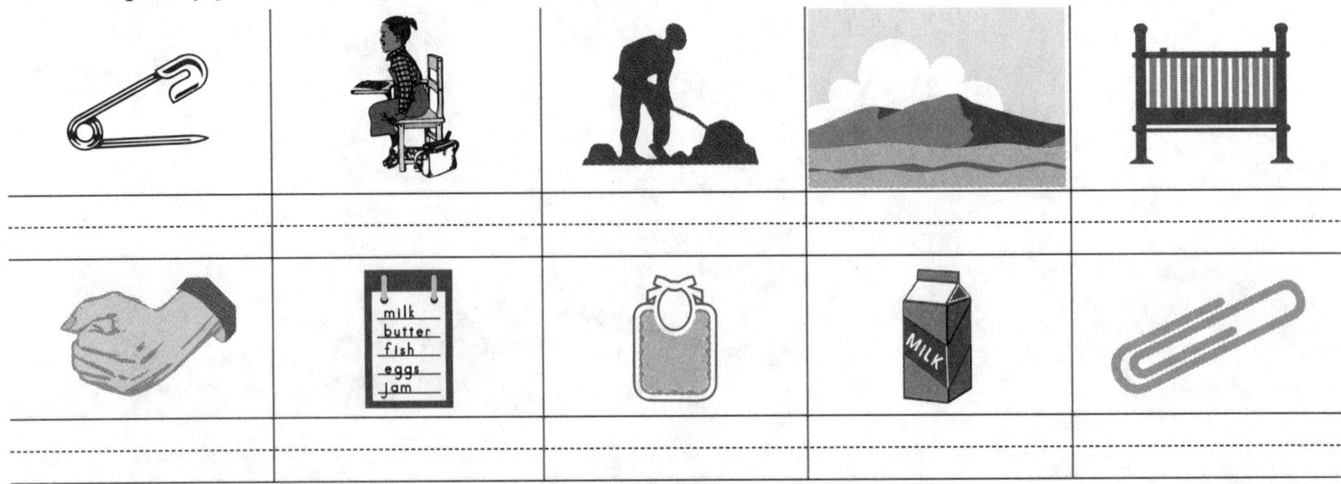

✔ Complete these sentences with the short vowel **i** words from the list. Print the correct words in the blanks.

1. Jill has pink frills on her ________ dress.

2. Tim will ________ and drink his ________.

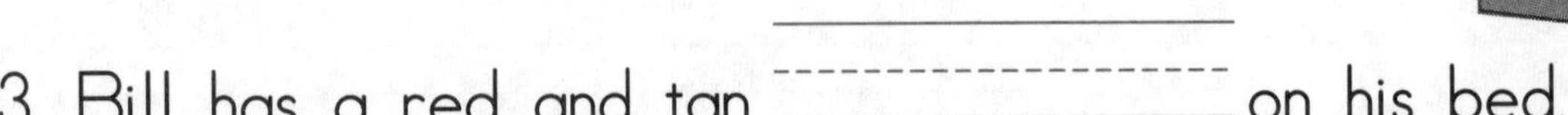

3. Bill has a red and tan ________ on his bed.

4. Dick will ________ his spelling list on a pad.

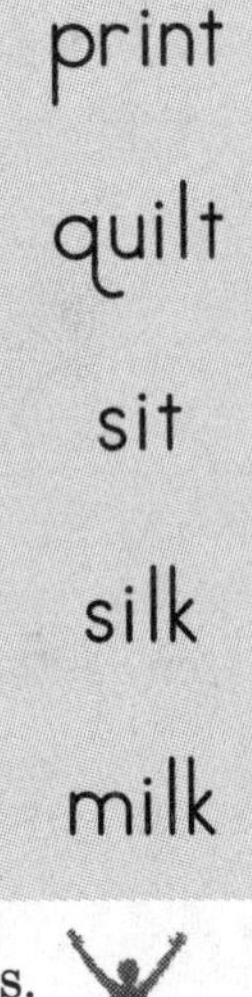

✔ Look and listen for the same vowel sound and ending sound as you match the rhyming words.

bit	rib	milk	is	bill	win
fig	fist	twist	silk	miss	trim
did	dim	dig	kit	sit	fib
him	fit	pill	big	spin	still
crib	hid	his	mist	swim	kiss
list	wig	pit	will	bib	hit

Review of Short Vowel ✎ i Words

When a word or syllable has only ***one*** vowel and it comes at the beginning or between two consonants, that vowel usually has the short sound as in **fit**, **pin**, and **tip**.

✔ Carefully print these words which have the short vowel sound of **i**.

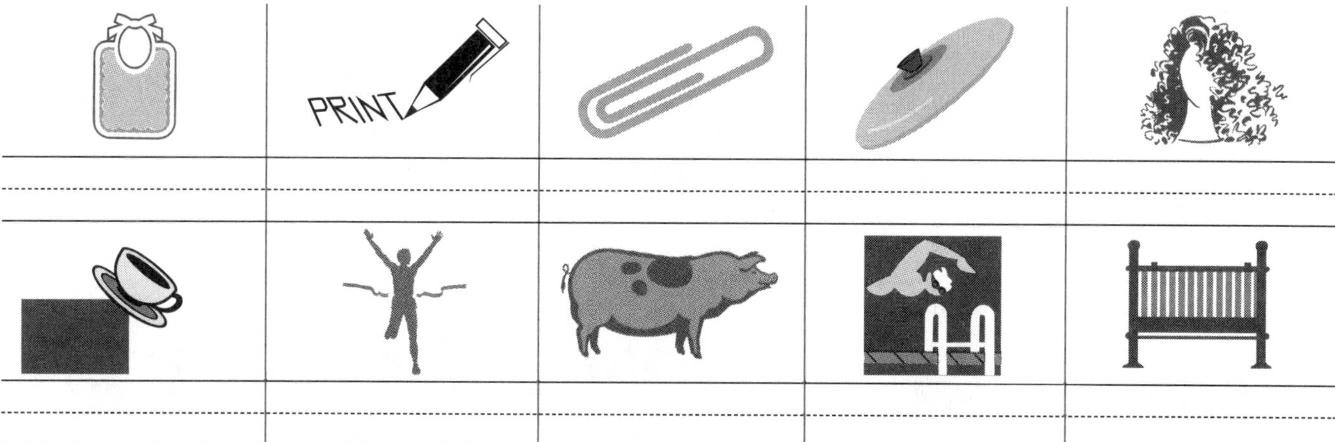

✔ Complete these sentences with the short vowel **i** words from the list. Print the correct words in the blanks.

1. Little Will felt ________ and lay still in his crib.
2. Did the pig dig the ________ in the mud? 
3. Jill will give a ________ and a kiss to her dad.
4. Miss Hill will print with a ________ on the pad.

quill
gift
pit
sick

A compound word has two words written together as in **lifeboat**, **airplane**, **forget**, and **himself**.

✔ Divide these compound words as the example shows.

inside	in–side	tiptoe	
cupcake		sunshine	
beside		milkman	
oatmeal		into	
rowboat		popcorn	

Review of Short Vowel ✎ o Words

When a word or syllable has only ***one*** vowel and it comes at the beginning or between two consonants, that vowel usually has the short sound as in **fox**, **hot**, and **top**.

✔ Carefully print these words which have the short vowel sound of **o**.
See how quickly you can learn this important sound.

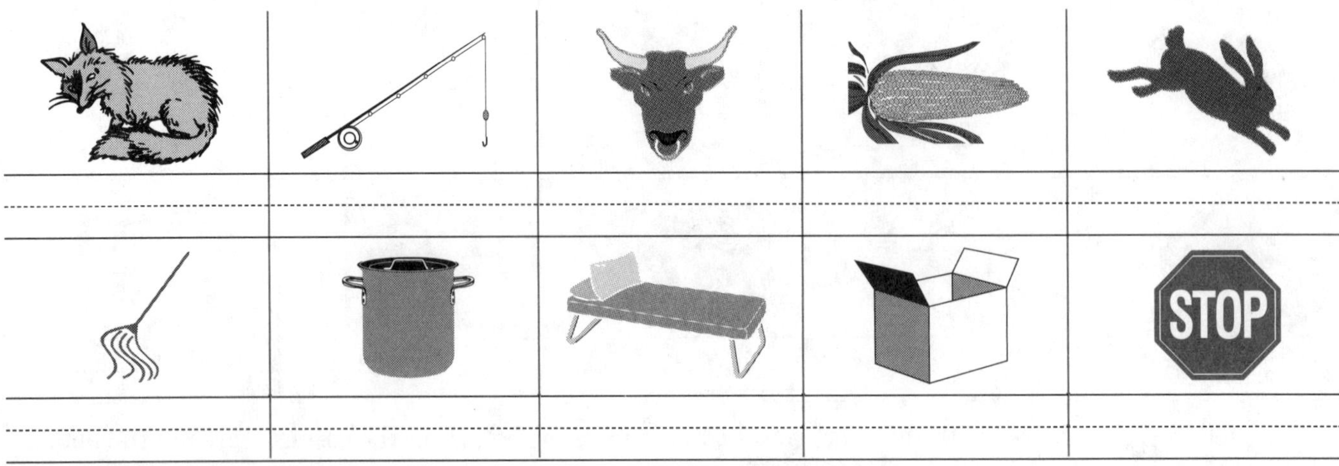

✔ Choose words from the list to complete these sentences. Print the correct words in the blanks below.

1. We are so glad for all of ______ blessings.
2. Scott got a fishing ______ from his dad.
3. Bob must not drop the hot ______ of food.
4. Tom has got a cat with lots of ______.

pot
spots
rod
God's

west
pond
flag
stamp
plant
quill
lamp
stop

✔ The words in the box at the left have consonant blends. Each consonant says its usual sound. Print these words with consonant blends under their pictures.

Review of Short Vowel ✎ o Words

When a word or syllable has only ***one*** vowel and it comes at the beginning or between two consonants, that vowel usually has the short sound as in **fox**, **hot**, and **top**.

✔ Carefully print these words which have the short vowel sound of **o**.
See how quickly you can learn this important sound.

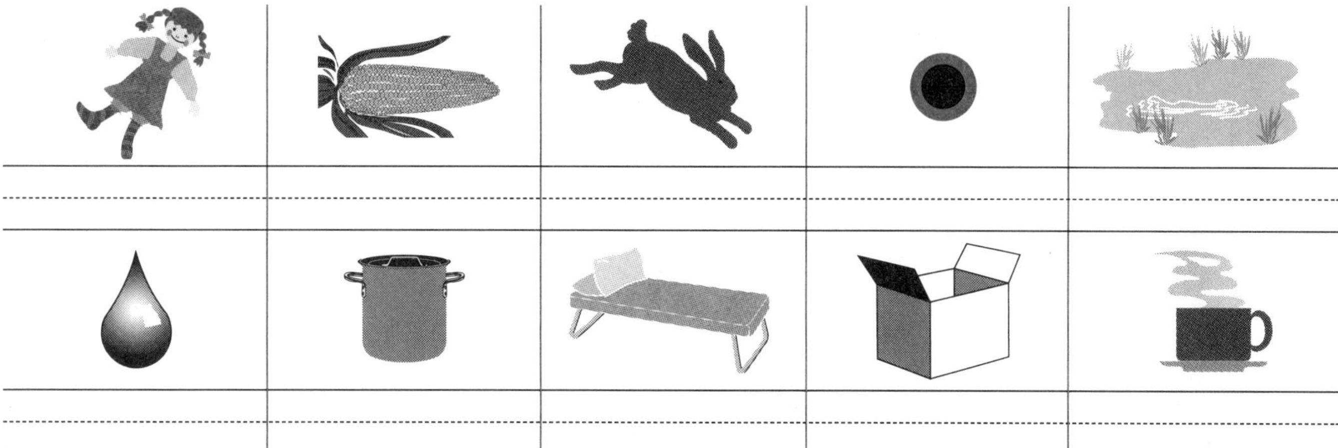

✔ Choose the correct words from the box at the right and print them in the blanks below.

drops	cobs	cot	ox

1. Todd gives the pig lots of ______ to eat.
2. Can Tom hop on the top of an ______?
3. He will sob if he ______ off of its back.
4. Ron has a ______ in his tent.

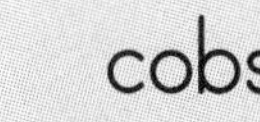

✔ Look and listen as you match these rhyming words.

God	Tom	cot	stop	flop	box
dot	mop	pop	pot	jot	nod
mob	nod	on	cob	fox	flock
hop	tot	rob	Don	rod	blot
Mom	pox	sod	clock	block	slob
ox	sob	lock	rod	glob	drop

Review of Short Vowel ✎ u Words

When a word or syllable has only ***one*** vowel and it comes at the beginning or between two consonants, that vowel usually has the short sound as in **fun**, **hum**, and **tub**.

✔ Carefully print these words which have the short vowel sound of **u**.

✔ Choose compound words from the list to completing these sentences.

1. God made the ______.
2. It is fun to munch on ______.
3. My dad has a bad ______.
4. Bud gave Miss Mund a ______.

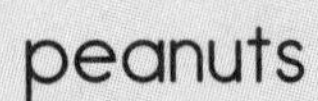

rosebud

sunshine

peanuts

backache

brush

sheep

shirt

fish

dish

ship

shell

shade

REMEMBER! A consonant digraph has ***two*** consonants that make ***one*** sound.

✔ The words in the box at the left have the digraph **sh**. Circle the **sh** in these words. Print the correct words under their pictures.

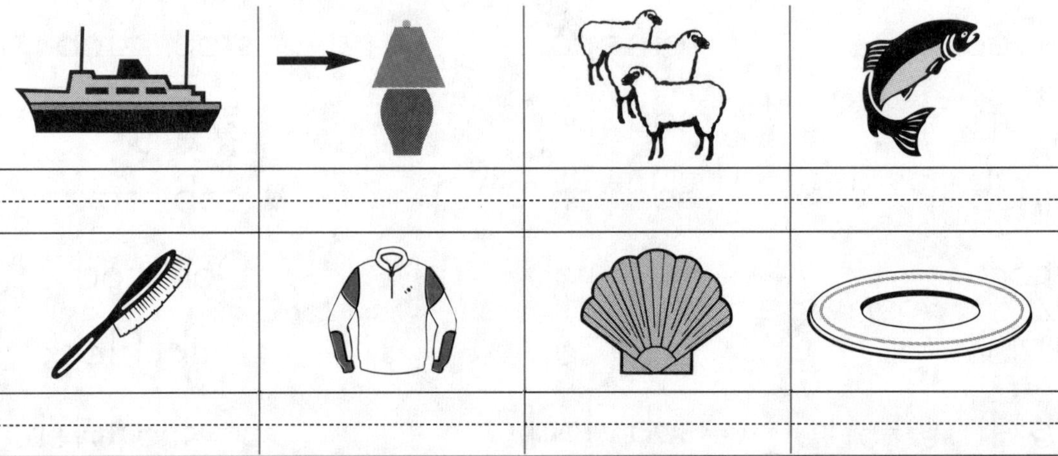

Review of Short Vowel ✎ u Words

When a word or syllable has only one vowel and it comes at the beginning or between two consonants, that vowel usually has the short sound as in **run**, **gum**, and **suds.**

✔ Carefully print these words which have the short vowel sound of **u**.

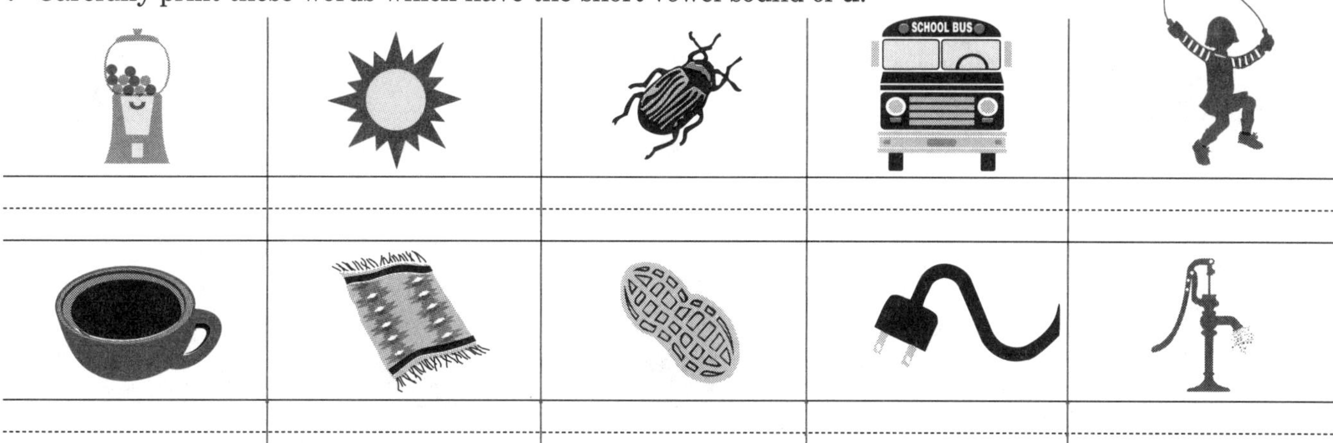

✔ Look and listen as you match these rhyming words.

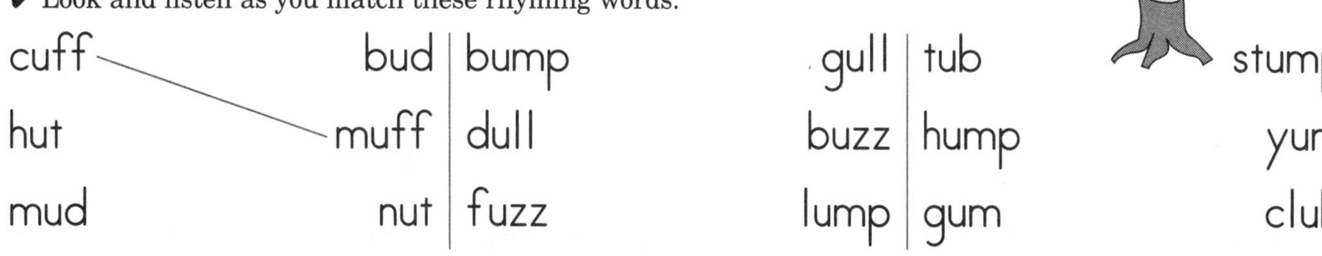

cuff	bud	bump	gull	tub	stump
hut	muff	dull	buzz	hump	yum
mud	nut	fuzz	lump	gum	club

In these words, the **o** makes the short sound of **u** as in **mother**, **love**, and **some**.

✔ Print these words where they belong. Remember that the **o** makes the short sound of **u**.

mother	oven	tongue	dove	money

✔ Choose words from the list to complete these sentences.

1. Today is the first Monday of this ______________.
2. It was three and Tom had done ______________.
3. It is hot if we stand in ______________ of the oven.

front
month
nothing

Review of Short Vowel ✎ Words

When a word has a short vowel sound, usually the consonants **s**, **l**, **f**, and **z** will be doubled. Some exceptions to the doubling rule are **bus**, **gas**, **yes**, **as**, **is**, **has**, **was**, and **his**.

✔ Carefully print these short vowel sound words with doubled consonants.

✔ Look and listen to the short vowel and ending sounds as you match these rhyming words.

fell	muff	bass	sniff	press	buff
buzz	mess	stuff	bliss	boss	dress
bill	bitt	stiff	smell	puff	tell
cuff	class	fizz	lass	cliff	whiff
glass	sell	fuss	muss	dell	grass
bless	fuzz	swell	bluff	will	moss
mitt	still	miss	whizz	brass	spill

✔ Circle the numeral of each sentence that may be true about the picture below.

1. Bill is with his sister.
2. His sister is sad.
3. Nell has a doll.
4. Bill and Nell are glad.
5. Bill will tell a story.
6. You can see grass.
7. Nell has a glass of milk.
8. Nell has on a dress.
9. Bill sits still next to Nell.
10. Bill pets his fluffy cat.

Review of Short Vowel ✎ Words

When a short vowel is followed by a **k** sound, the **k** sound is made by **ck** as in **duck**.

✔ Carefully print these short vowel sound words which end with **ck**.

✔ Look and listen to the short vowel and ending sounds as you print the correct words in the blanks.

quacks
sticks
flock
stack
truck

1. Jack has to pick up a lot of ________.
2. He will ________ the sticks by a brick shack.
3. A big dump ________ will come and get them.
4. He can see a ________ of ducks in the sky.
5. Jack hears the flock as it ________.

✔ Look and listen to the short vowel sounds as you match these rhyming words.

stick	dock	cock	pluck	packet	buck
lack	peck	wick	rock	pickle	stack
tuck	lick	rack	prick	stock	jacket
speck	crack	cluck	deck	duck	sickle
stock	stuck	neck	jack	track	crock

Review of Long Vowel ✎ a Words

When ***two*** vowels are in a word, usually the first vowel says its name, and the second vowel is silent. The letter **y** is a vowel when it is at the end of a word or syllable. The **y** is silent in **ay** words.

✔ Carefully print these long vowel sound words with the vowels **a_e** as in **cake**.

✔ Carefully print these long vowel sound words with the vowels **ai**.

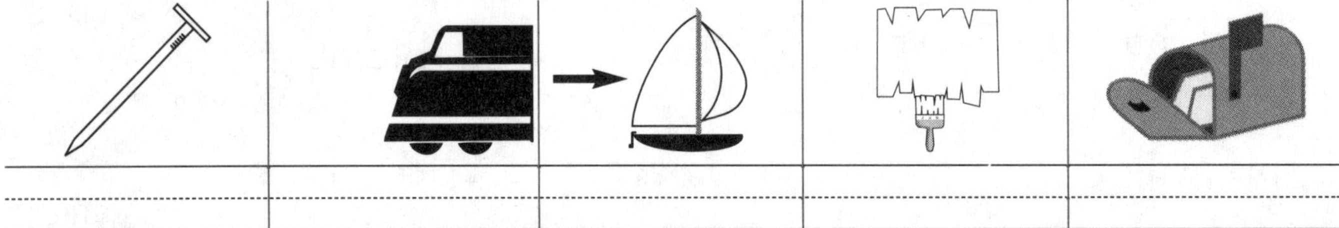

✔ See how quickly you can read up and down the list of the **ay** words in the box below.

bay	Kay	lay	say	fray	tray	stay
day	jay	pay	way	pray	Fay	sway
hay	may	ray	clay	gray	play	stray

✔ Change the pictures above by following these directions.

1. Draw a fox by the cave.
2. Color the paint blue.
3. Draw grass by the gate.
4. Draw tracks for the train.
5. Color the nail gray.
6. Color the grapes green.
7. Draw a flower in the vase.
8. Color the sail red.
9. Draw a tree for the ape.
10. Color the tape yellow.

Review of Long Vowel ✎ a Words

Remember the long vowel RULE: When ***two*** vowels are in a word, usually the first vowel says its name, and the second vowel is silent. These vowels are marked like this:

rāin cāke prāy

✔ Print these long vowel sound words with the vowels **a_e**. Most of the words below are spelled with **ake**.

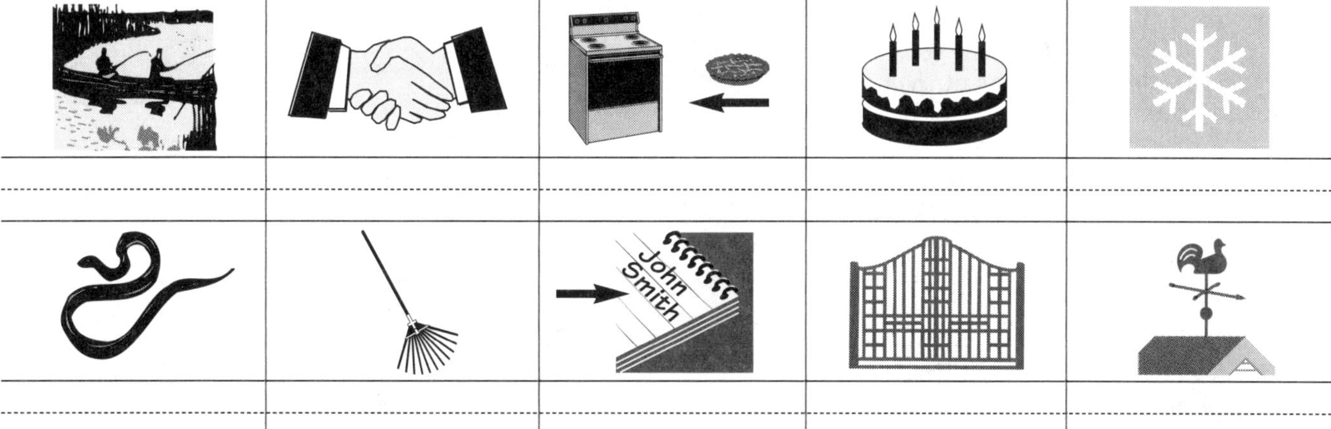

✔ Mark the vowels as you match these rhyming words.

tāil	tray	stray	trail	blame	bait
wake	saint	quail	mane	stale	paste
sway	hāil	lane	brake	wait	strain
brain	take	quake	case	taste	scale
faint	drain	base	gray	gain	shame

✔ Answer these questions with words spelled with **ake**.

1. Kay was still sleepy and did not want to __________ up.

2. When she got up she remembered to __________ her bed.

3. She will help her mother bake a __________.

4. It is polite to __________ hands as you say hello.

5. If a plant is not real it may be a __________ plant.

Review of Long Vowel ✎ e Words

Remember the long vowel RULE: When ***two*** vowels are in a word, usually the first vowel says its name, and the second vowel is silent. The letter **y** is a vowel when it is at the end of a word or syllable. The **y** is silent in **ey** words. These vowels are marked like this:

clēan frēe kēy wē

✔ Carefully print these long vowel **e** words with the vowels **ee** as in **see**. If you need help, you may look in the box at the right.

wheel	**tree**	**heel**	**bee**	**feet**
sheep	**teeth**	**jeep**	**beets**	**sweep**

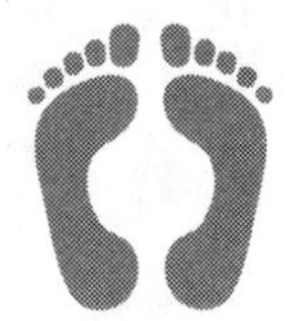				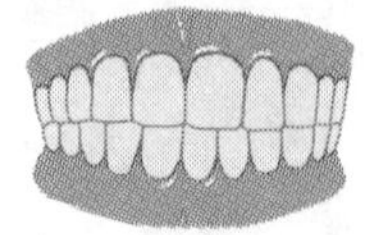

✔ Mark the long vowel **e** sounds in the words below. Print these long vowel **e** words in the correct blanks.

scrēens need greed greet

1. It is polite to shake hands as you ________ people.
2. To keep bugs out, we put ________ on our windows.
3. God is not pleased if we have ________ in our hearts.
4. Greed means that we want much more than we ________.

✔ Mark the long vowel **e** sounds in the words below. Print these long vowel **e** words in the correct blanks.

hē me she we be

1. Steve asked Jean and ________ to ________ on his team.

2. ________ will be glad if ________ play. Jean said ________ will do it.

Review of Long Vowel e Words

Remember the long vowel RULE: When *two* vowels are in a word, usually the first vowel says its name, and the second vowel is silent. The letter **y** is a vowel when it is at the end of a word or syllable. The **y** is silent in **ey** words.

✔ Carefully print these long vowel **e** words with the vowels **ea** as in **sea**. If you need help, you may look in the box at the right.

seal	meal	teach	meat	teapot
beak	seat	wheat	leaf	peas

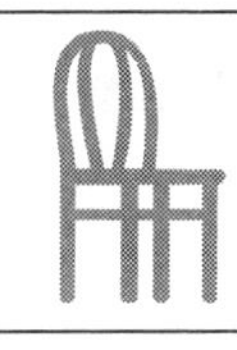				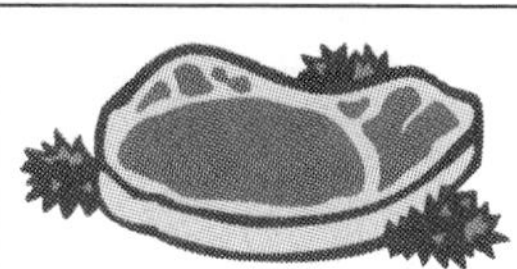

✔ Look and listen to the ending sounds as you match these long vowel sound rhyming words.

breed	seed	beach	leap	greet	flea
tear	lean	heap	peach	meek	meet
weep	peep	seam	tea	steal	seek
mean	near	dear	team	spear	heal
weed	greed	sea	fear	plea	gear

REMEMBER! A consonant digraph has *two* consonants that make *one* sound.

✔ The words in the box at the right have the digraph **ch**. Circle the **ch** and print the word where it belongs.

1. Dick sat on a ________ and ate his ________.

2. We are ________ with God's many blessings.

3. The children saw little ________ at the ranch.

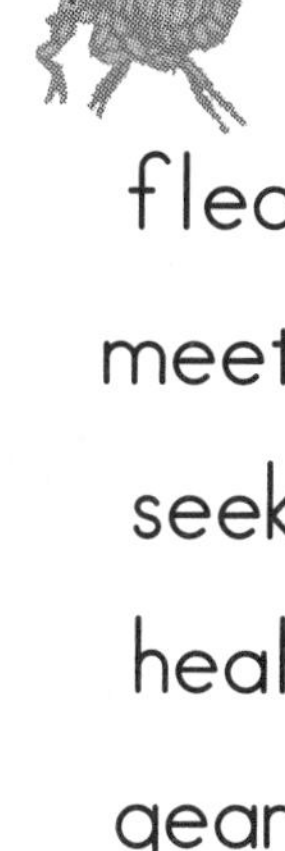

rich
bench
chicks
lunch

Review of Long Vowel ✎ i Words

Remember the long vowel RULE: When ***two*** vowels are in a word, usually the first vowel says its name, and the second vowel is silent. These vowels are marked like this:

fīve̸ tīe̸ flȳ

✔ Carefully print these long vowel sound words with the vowels **i_e**.

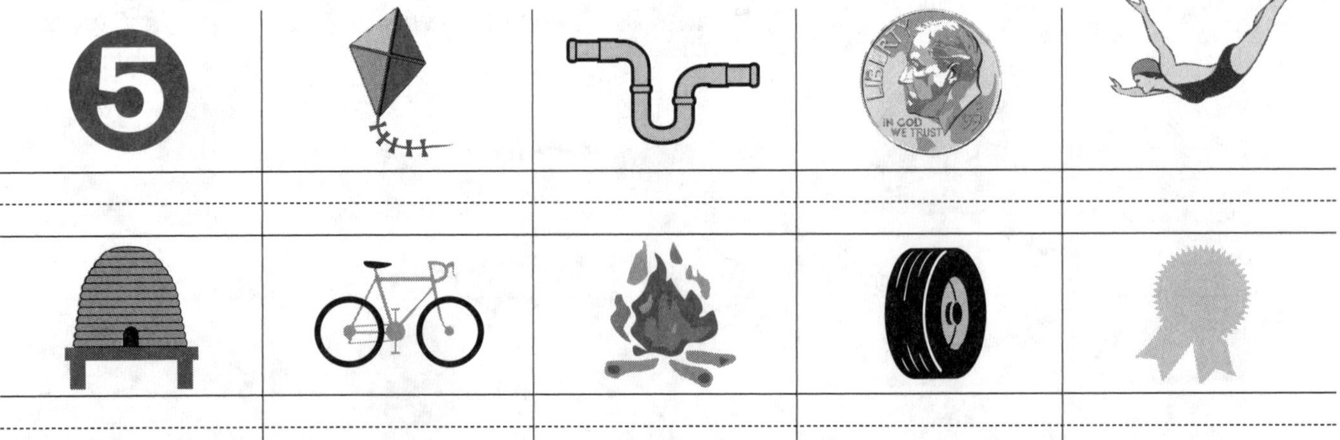

The letter **y** is a vowel when it is at the end of a word.
If it is the only vowel, it has the long **i** sound as in **fly**.

✔ Carefully print these long vowel sound words which end with **y** as in **sky**.

✔ How quickly can you say these words?

by my fry try sly shy spy sty why

✔ Look and listen as you match these rhyming words.

bite	dine	tie	mile	prize	twine
side	site	like	hide	spy	wire
fine	file	time	pie	wipe	sty
try	tide	wide	lime	mine	ripe
tile	cry	smile	dike	hire	size

Review of Long Vowel ✎ i Words

Remember the long vowel RULE: When ***two*** vowels are in a word, usually the first vowel says its name, and the second vowel is silent. These vowels are marked like this:

bīke pīe drȳ

✔ Carefully print the correct long vowel **i**(_**e**) words under the pictures and in the blanks of the sentences below.

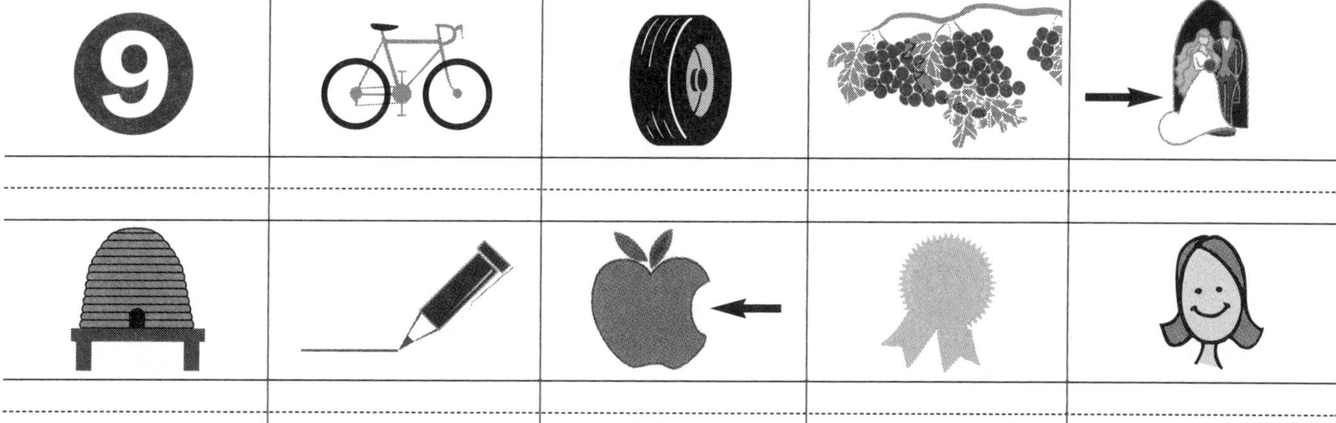

1. The bride had on a ________ dress of fine silk.
2. Dad will ________ the twigs with ________.

white
twine
tie

Usually the vowel **i** is short when it is alone in a word. In these words the vowel is long because it is followed by **ld**, **nd**, or **gh**. REMEMBER: The **gh** is silent. These words are marked like this:

wīld mīnd fīght

✔ Where do these words belong? Use the underlined words in the sentences below.

<u>child</u>	flight	right	fight	light
<u>wind</u>	<u>high</u>	blind	<u>night</u>	grind

1. At ________ my grandfather will ________ his clock.
2. The ________ sat in his ________ chair behind the table.

Review of Long Vowel ✎ o Words

Remember the long vowel RULE: When ***two*** vowels are in a word, usually the first vowel says its name, and the second vowel is silent. These vowels are marked like this:

stōne tōe bōat mōw

✔ Carefully print these long vowel sound words with the vowels **o_e**.

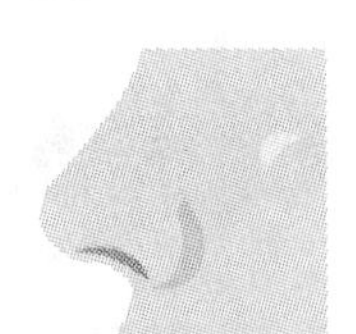
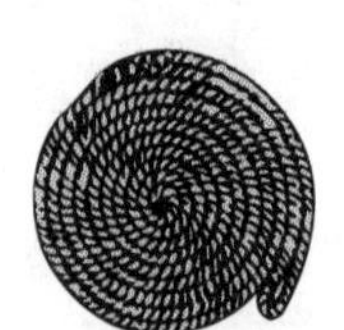
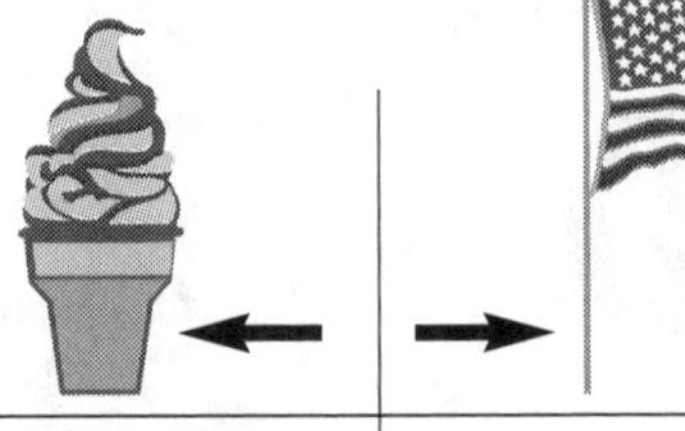

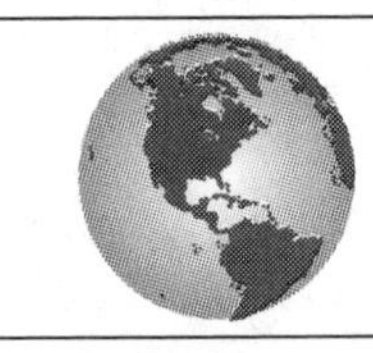

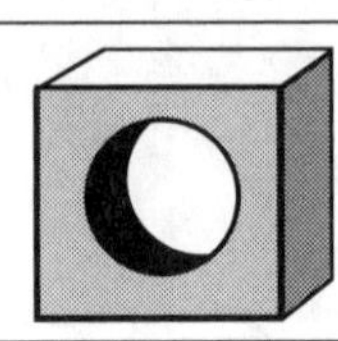
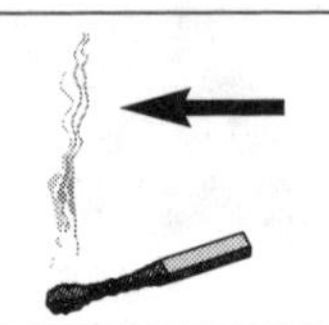

The ***w*** acts as a vowel when it follows another vowel as in **slow**, **low**, and **grow**.

✔ Carefully print these long vowel sound words with the vowels **ow**.

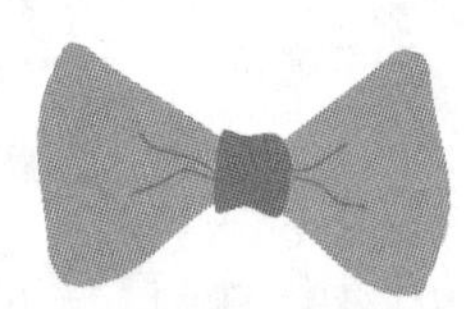

Remember another part of the long vowel RULE: If a word has ***one*** vowel and it comes at the end of the word, that vowel usually has a long sound as in **go**, **no**, **lo**, **so**, **ho**, and **yo-yo**.
The words **do** and **to** are exceptions.

✔ Choose the correct words from the box at the right and print them in the blanks below.

1. Joe has a yellow ________ that glows as it spins.
2. I cannot see the wind ________, but I can feel it.
3. Don sees a ________ snail and a black ________.
4. God makes us ________ as we eat and sleep.

grow
blow
slow
yo-yo
crow

Review of Long Vowel ✎ o Words

Remember the long vowel RULE: When ***two*** vowels are in a word, usually the first vowel says its name, and the second vowel is silent. These vowels are marked like this:

hōpe road show

✔ Carefully print the correct long **o**(**a**) words under the pictures and in the blanks of the sentences below.

1. It is not right when a man ________.

2. An ________ tree is by the ________ near my home.

road
boasts
oak

✔ Look and listen to the ending sounds as you match these rhyming long vowel **o** words.

vote	dome	show	rode	low	moat
lone	quote	woke	stone	oak	hose
hope	rose	roast	flow	stole	bow
pose	rope	code	toast	boat	cloak
home	tone	zone	spoke	close	hole

Usually the vowel **o** is short when it is alone in a word. In these words the vowel is long because it is followed by **ld**, **st**, **th**, **ll**, or **lt**, as in **bold**, **most**, **both**, **toll**, and **jolt**.

✔ Where do these words belong? The underlined words go in the sentences.

colt
post
scroll
bold
stroll
bolt

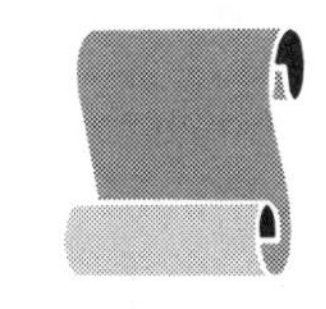	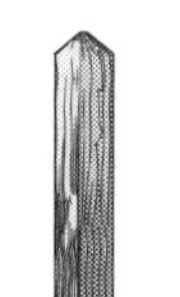	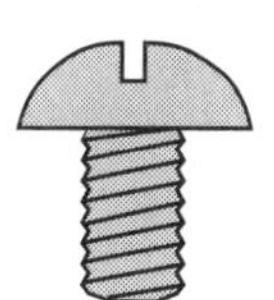	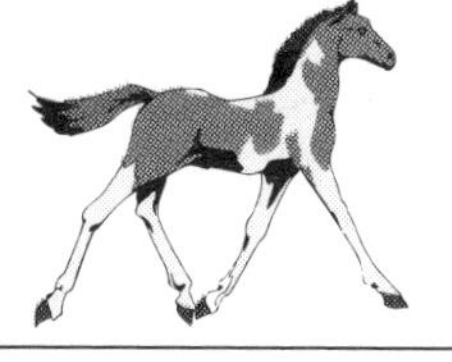

1. The man was brave and ________ as he spoke.

2. Jim holds the child's hand as they ________.

Review of Long Vowel ✎ u Words

Remember the long vowel RULE: When ***two*** vowels are in a word, usually the first vowel says its name, and the second vowel is silent. These vowels are marked like this:

tūbe blūe sūit

flute tune cube suit mule glue tube fruit

✔ Carefully print these long vowel **u** sound words under their correct pictures.

GLUE			

✔ Choose the **ew** (long **u**) words from the list to complete these sentences. Print them in the blanks below.

dew grew drew chew flew blew

1. In June the seeds ____________ into new plants.

2. As the wind ____________ it dried up the ____________.

3. Duke will ____________ his meat so he will not choke.

4. Luke ____________ a map to show the way to his home.

5. A flock of ducks ____________ over the tree tops.

✔ Circle the numeral of each sentence that may be true about the picture.

1. Luke and Drew are glad.
2. You can see a mule.
3. They are playing a game.
4. Luke has a cap on his head.
5. Luke and Drew seem kind.
6. Drew jumps over Luke.

Review of Digraph ✎ oo Words

The vowels **oo** also make the long vowel sound of **u** as in **zoo**, **spoon**, and **goose**.

✔ Carefully print these long vowel **u** sound words made by the vowels **oo**.

✔ Look and listen as you match these rhyming words.

noon	roost	poodle	stoop	tooth	prune
boost	crew	mood	noodle	fruit	proof
grew	fool	groom	pool	roof	zoo
cool	moose	loop	boom	too	suit
loose	soon	cool	food	tune	booth

✔ Use these words to complete the sentences. The words **soup** and **shoe** have the long **u** sound.

balloons rooster soup shoes smooth

1. The class let ______________ with notes go up in the sky.

2. The new road felt ______________ as Luke rode his bike.

3. An old ______________ woke up Sue this morning.

4. Jim put on his ______________ and ate his noodle ______________.

Review of Digraph ✎ oo Words

REMEMBER:! A vowel digraph has ***two*** vowels that make ***one*** sound.
The double vowels **oo** make two sounds: one is o͞o as in zo͞o and the other is o͝o as in bo͝ok.

✔ Choose the correct words from the box below and print them under their correct pictures.

book	football	woods	cookies	hook

ATTENTION! The vowel digraph **oo** makes two sounds: one is o͞o as in zo͞o and the other is o͝o as in bo͝ok.

✔ Carefully mark the vowel digraph **oo** in the following words.

book	moon	tooth	football	rooster
broom	boot	hook	spool	woods

The other ways to spell the o͝o sound are as follows: **u** as in **put**, **o** as in **wolf**, and **ou** as in **should**.

✔ Choose the correct words from the box at the right and print them in the blanks below.

1. Each day we ____________ try to obey God.
2. We would be happy if we ____________ our trust in Him.
3. A wild ____________ would eat a sheep if he could.
4. Dad's dog made the ____________ run into the shed.

wolf
should
bull
put

Review of Digraph ✎ oo Words

REMEMBER:! A vowel digraph has ***two*** vowels that make ***one*** sound.
The double vowels **oo** make two sounds: one is o͞o as in zo͞o and the other is o͝o as in bo͝ok.

✔ Print these words which have one of the two sounds of **oo**

REMEMBER: Other ways to spell the o͝o sound are **u** as in **put**, **o** as in **wolf**, and **ou** as in **should**.

✔ Use these words to complete the sentences.

could
bush
full
pull

1. Ruth likes to __________ the baby on his sled.
2. The child would ride all day if he __________.
3. Cold, white snow is on each tree and __________.
4. This land is __________ of God's goodness.

✔ Match the words that rhyme.

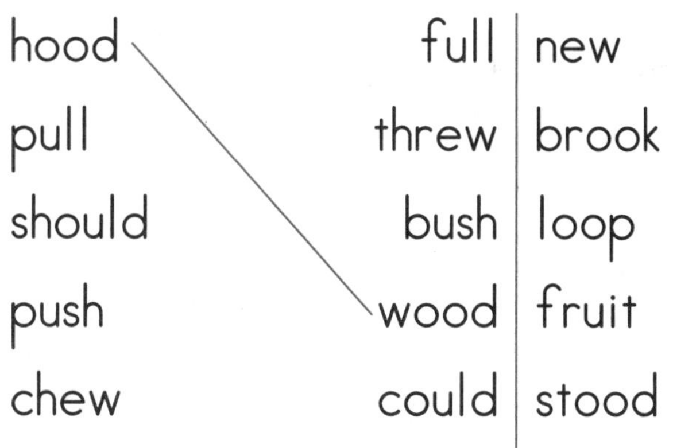

hood	full	new	good	blue	loose
pull	threw	brook	suit	soot	foot
should	bush	loop	flew	look	smooth
push	wood	fruit	coop	goose	took
chew	could	stood	shook	tooth	glue

Review of Diphthong ✎ ow Words

A diphthong is ***two*** vowels sounded so that both vowels can be heard blended together as one. Two sets of vowels make this sound: **ow** is used at the end of words or in words ending with **l** or **n**; **ou** is usually used in other words. REMEMBER: **ow** also says the long **o** sound as in **slow**.

✔ Print these words with the **ow** sound as in **cow**.

a
e
i
o
u

✔ Choose the correct words from the box at the right and print them in the blanks below.

growl
vowels
plow
brown

1. Our class can say the sounds of the ______________.
2. If the cat pounces, the hound will ______________.
3. A man will __________ the ______________ ground.

✔ Circle the numeral of each sentence that may be true about this picture.

1. Jan sat down near her dad.
2. They are not going to town.
3. Her brother is near them.
4. Her father has a book.
5. He has a frown on his face.
6. Jan has on a red blouse.
7. Her dad has brown hair.
8. I think they love each other.
9. They look down at the book.
10. A cow is on the couch.

Review of Diphthong ✎ ou Words

A diphthong is ***two*** vowels sounded so that both vowels can be heard blended together as one. Two sets of vowels make this sound: **ow** is used at the end of words or in words ending with **l** or **n**; **ou** is usually used in other words. REMEMBER: **ow** also says the long **o** sound as in **slow**.

✔ Print these words with the **ou** sound as in **thousand** and **house**.

✔ Choose the correct words from the box at the right and print them in the blanks below.

1. We went downtown to see the __________.
2. At night a __________ lights were put on it.
3. A big crowd stood __________ the fountain.
4. We could hear happy __________ from them.
5. We got back to our house __________ ten o'clock.

about
fountain
sounds
around
thousand

✔ Match the words that rhyme. Remember to listen to the ending letters.

towel	crown	pouch	south	clown	growl
sprout	pound	cloud	ouch	now	wow
mound	power	mouth	pout	fowl	powder
shower	vowel	scout	bounce	mouse	gown
frown	shout	ounce	proud	chowder	grouse

Review of Diphthong ✎ oi Words

Two sets of vowels make this sound: **oi** is used inside of words as in **noise**; **oy** is usually used at the end of words or syllables as in **boy**.

✔ Match the rhyming **oi** and **oy** words.

joint	moist	Floyd	join	royal	spoil
foil	point	voice	Lloyd	coil	loyal
hoist	broil	soil	choice	Roy	annoy
boy	joy	coin	toil	enjoy	toy

REMEMBER! A compound word has two words written together as in **lifeboat**, **airplane**, and **himself**.

✔ Choose the correct compound words to complete the following sentences. Print them in the blanks below.

noisemakers cowboy airplane

1. A person who works on a ranch is a ________.

2. Toys that make noise are ________.

3. They took a long trip in an ________.

three
math
teeth
thick
thin
bath
feather
thumb

REMEMBER! A consonant digraph has two consonants that usually make one sound. The **th** makes two sounds: the soft **th** sound as in **bath** and hard **th** sound as in **the**.

✔ Circle the **th** in the words at the left. Print the words under the correct pictures.

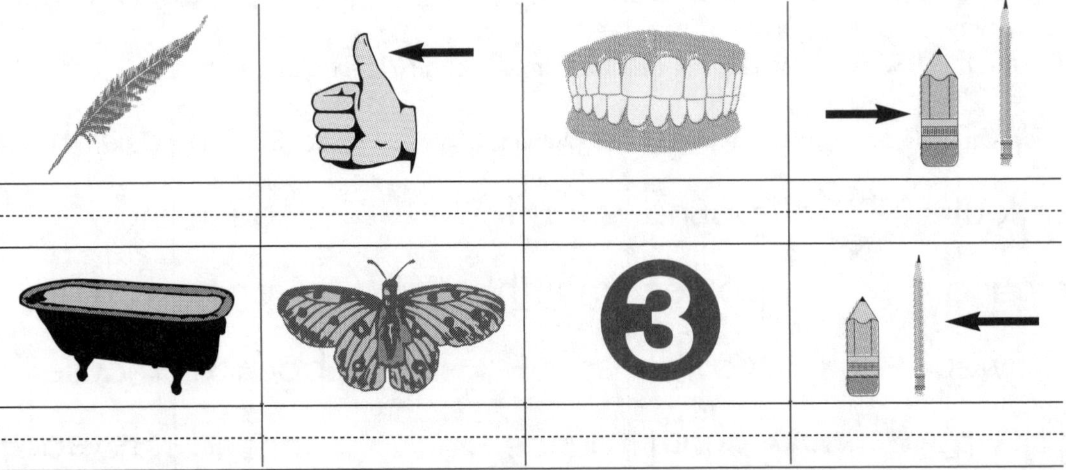

Review of Diphthong ✎ oi Words

A diphthong is ***two*** vowels sounded so that both vowels can be heard blended together as ***one.*** Two sets of vowels make the **oi** sound as in **boil**: **oi** is used inside of words as in **noise**; **oy** is usually used at the end of words or syllables as in **boy**.

✔ Choose the correct words with the **oi** or **oy** sound and print them under their pictures.

boil	boy	point	foil	soil
oil	toys	coins	joints	poison

✔ Choose the correct **oi** or **oy** words from the box at the right and print them in the blanks below.

1. If he sings too loud, it will ______ the tunes.
2. Joy will help her mother ______ some meat.
3. To be faithful means to be ______.
4. The Bible tells us that we should ______ evil.

broil
avoid
loyal
spoil

✔ In which sentences do these digraph **th** words belong? Print them in the blanks below.

thermometer　　weather　　father

1. Beth's ______ put up a new ______.
2. It shows how cold the ______ is each day.

Review of Modified Vowel ✎ **ar** Words

When the consonant **r** comes after a vowel, it changes or modifies that vowel sound. The **ar** sound may be marked like this: **ärk**.

✔ Carefully print these words which have the **ar** sound.

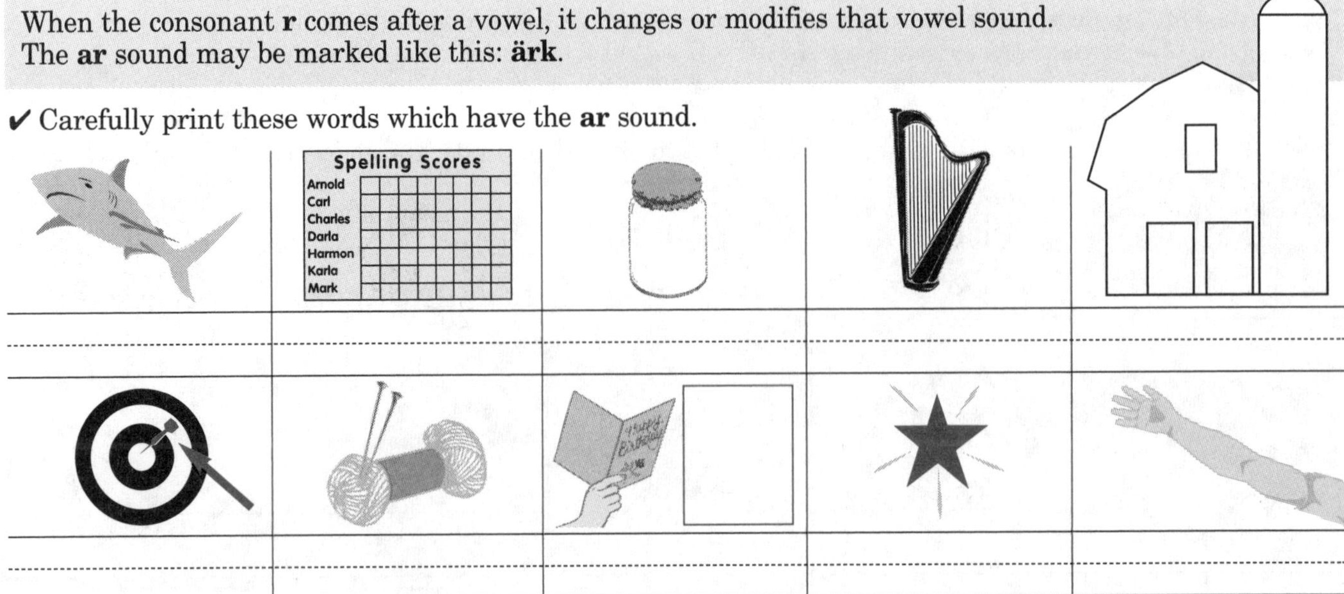

✔ Change the pictures above by following the directions below.

1. Color the sky dark blue around the star.
2. Draw seaweed near the shark.
3. Color the barn red and the silo brown.
4. Color the yarn dark brown.
5. Put grape jam in the jar.
6. Draw a gift in the box next to the happy birthday card.
7. Draw a circle around the harp.

✔ Match the words that rhyme.

hark	tar	start	carp	car	yarn
harm	part	hard	tart	spark	arm
far	dark	sharp	mark	charm	park
art	farm	bark	yard	barn	bar

Review of Modified Vowel ✎ **ar** Words

When the consonant **r** comes after a vowel, it changes or modifies that vowel sound.
The **ar** sound may be marked like this: **ärk**.

✔ Carefully print these words which have the **ar** sound.

✔ Use words from the blanks above to complete these sentences.

1. Noah obeyed God and made an ______ as he was told.
2. Each spring Mark and Carl help to plant a ______.
3. That is when a ______ plows and plants his land.
4. Charles saw a band ______ to the park.

A **suffix** is an ending we sometimes need to add to a ***root*** word as in **farm** to change it.

farm farm<u>s</u> farm<u>ing</u> farm<u>ed</u> farm<u>er</u>

✔ Make new words by adding these suffixes to the ***root*** words. Mark the vowels this way: **därt**.

suffixes ⇨	s	ing	ed	er
därt				
bark				
mark				
start				
park				

Review of Modified Vowel ✎ **or** Words

When the consonant **r** comes after a vowel, it changes or modifies that vowel sound.
The **or** sound may be marked like this: **côrn** and **hôrse**.

✔ Carefully print these words which have the **or** sound. Mark the vowel sound.

W E S ?

✔ Answer these sentences with a word that rhymes with the bold word.

1. Bill **Ford** tries to love and obey the ____________
2. A storm went **forth** and headed up ____________.
3. A boy opened the **door** and sat on the ____________.
4. The man with a **torch** stood on the ____________.
5. Jordan is not too **short** to play in a ____________.

floor
Lord
sport
porch
north

✔ Divide these compound words.

doorway	door–way	postman	
forget		corncrib	
bedroom		airport	
scoreboard		horseshoe	

Review of Modified Vowel ✎ or Words

When the consonant **r** comes after a vowel, it changes or modifies that vowel sound. The **or** sound may be marked like this: **côrn** and **hôrse**.

✔ Mark the vowels in these **ôr** words. Print them in the blanks below to complete the sentences.

ôrgan orange orchard born

1. His family was so happy when Jordan was ________.
2. Mr. Sherman can play the piano and the ________.
3. Fruit trees grow in an ________.

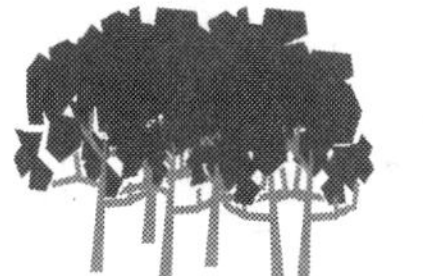

4. Our school colors are blue, white and ________.

short
door
acorn
north

✔ Carefully print these words which have the **ôr** sound under the correct pictures.

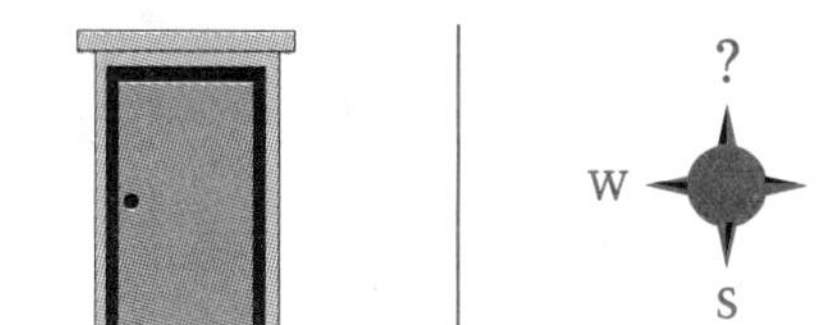

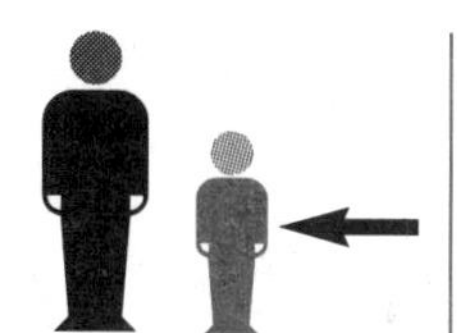

The letters **ness** are a ***suffix*** which help make a word have a certain meaning: **sore + ness = soreness.**

✔ Make new words by adding **ness** to the ***root*** words.

sore + ness = soreness

short + ness = ________

kind + ness = ________

bright + ness = ________

good + ness = ________

sick + ness = ________

dark + ness = ________

cold + ness = ________

blind + ness = ________

glad + ness = ________

Review of Modified Vowels ✎ er ir ur

When the consonant **r** comes after **e**, **i**, and **u**, it changes or modifies those vowels, making the sound of **ur** as in **church**. It may be called the ***schwa*** plus **r** sound: ə**r**.

✔ Carefully print these words which have the ***schwa*** plus **r** sound.

squirrel	nurse	turkey	spider	finger
thirty	verse	turtle	letter	flower

Children, obey your parents in the Lord, for this is right. Ephesians 6:1				
		30		

✔ Complete these sentences with words from the list.

1. Burt set his alarm on ________________ night.
2. He did not want to be late for ________________.
3. He went with his mother, father, and ____________.
4. He had time so he did not have to ____________.
5. The ____________ told a lesson from the Bible.

sister
hurry
preacher
Saturday
church

✔ Print the correct words with the letters **ir** under the pictures.

Review of Modified Vowel ✎ ear wor

You have learned that when **r** comes after **e**, **i**, and **u**, it changes those vowels, making the ***schwa*** plus **r** sound of **er**. Two more ways to spell the **er** sound is **ear** as in **earth** and **(w)or** as in **world**.

✔ Carefully print these words which have the **(w)or** sound.

work	worm	world	worship	words
			work works worked worker	

✔ Choose the correct words from the box at the right and print them in the blanks below.

1. God created the heaven and the ________.
2. It is good if we learn of God ________ in life.
3. Vern ________ about the Lord from his parents.
4. The Bible is ________ more than any other book.
5. We should trust in God and not ________.

worry
worth
earth
early
heard

✔ Match the phrases below to the words with the suffix **er** in the box at the right .

1. When I work, I am a
2. A girl that runs is a
3. A boy that jumps is a
4. A person that thinks is a
5. A man that speaks is a

speaker.
runner.
thinker.
jumper.
worker.

Review of Modified Vowels ✎ âr Words

You know the sound of **är** as in **arm**. The letters **ar** also sound like **âr** as in **square** when it is followed by the vowel **e**. The **âr** sound may be spelled as follows: **are** as in **square**, **arr** as in **carrot**, **air** as in **chair**, **err** as in **berry**, and **ear** as in **bear**.

✔ Carefully print these words which have the **âr** sound.

carrot	bear	stairs	cherry	carry
hare	square	error	pair	chair

5 + 6 12✓				
			? of shoes	

✔ Circle the numerals of the sentences that may be true of the picture below.

1. Larry and Barry are wearing winter jackets.
2. We cannot see their hair under their caps.
3. Larry is going up the stairs to get a cherry.
4. They each have on their pairs of skates.
5. Barry sits on a chair near a bear.
6. Larry is about to hit the puck with his stick.

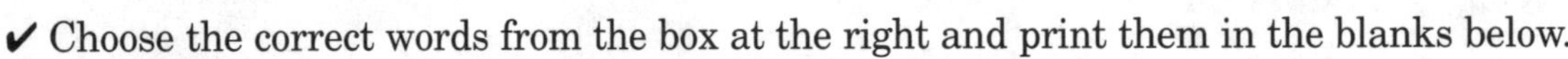

✔ Choose the correct words from the box at the right and print them in the blanks below.

1. On Saturday Sarah and Harry will ______.

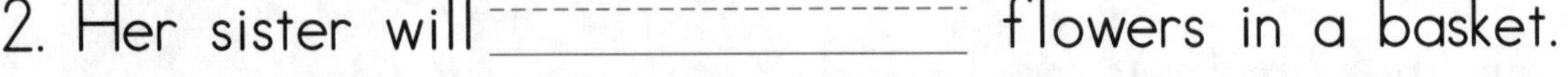

2. Her sister will ______ flowers in a basket.
3. They will ask God for His blessings and ______.

care
marry
carry

Review of Modified Vowels ✎ âr Words

Think again about the ways that the **âr** sound can be spelled:
are as in **square**, **arr** as in **carrot**, **air** as in **chair**, **err** as in **berry**, and **ear** as in **bear**.
In a few words the **âr** sound is spelled like this: **ere** as in **there**, **eir** as in **their**.

✔ Carefully print the correct words which have the **âr** sound under their pictures.

parrot
pear
hair
cherry

✔ How quickly can you read these rhyming words. Use the underlined words in the sentences below.

bare	<u>stare</u>	glare	<u>spare</u>	rare
<u>blare</u>	fare	hare	mare	<u>share</u>

1. Harry had to put on a ______________ tire on his bike.
2. It is kind to ______________ toys with your brother or sister.
3. We could hear the ______________ of a horn.
4. It is not right to ______________ at a person.

✔ Change the picture at the right by following these directions.

1. Color the parrot with bright colors.
2. Put a little brown nut in his beak.
3. Make a white moon and stars in the sky.
4. Draw some green leaves on the gray branch.
5. Make a red berry on the branch for this rare bird.
6. Would you care to carry this parrot to your home? ______________

Review of ✎ ô Words

It is important to review the different sounds that the vowel **o** has:
ŏ as in ŏx, ō as in ōak and ōld, o͞o as in spo͞on, and o͝o as in bo͝ok.
Here is one more sound that **o** has: ô as in crôss and dôg.

✔ Carefully print these words which have the **ô** sound under the pictures and fill in the blanks below.

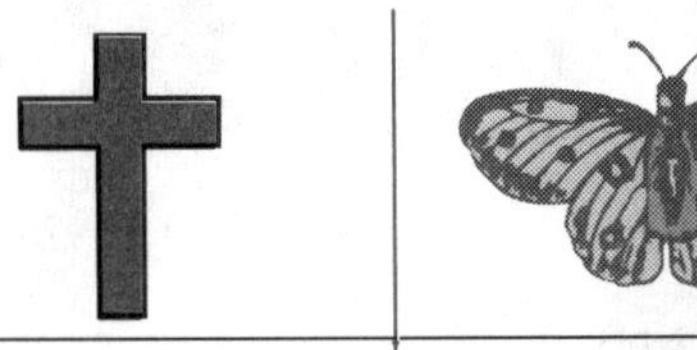

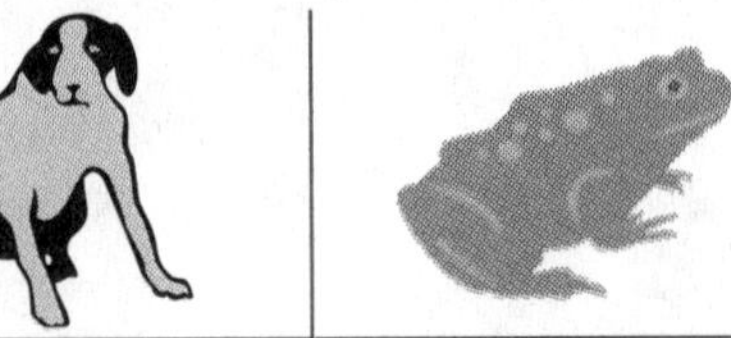

A name for a large pig is ____?

1. A strong dog swam ________ the pond.
2. A green frog jumped off a log in the ________.
3. Jill has a soft cloth that ________ to Jan.

fog
belongs
across

The sound of **ô** is also made by an **a** when it is followed by **l**, **u**, or **w**:
al as in **ball**, **au** as in **auto**, and **aw** as in **paw**.

✔ Match the rhyming words. Be sure to think about the vowel and ending sounds.

yawn	paw	draw	cloth	chalk	fawn
saw	fall	moth	shawl	lawn	toss
pause	cause	salt	malt	thaw	stalk
wall	dawn	crawl	straw	cross	draw

✔ Where do these words need to be printed?

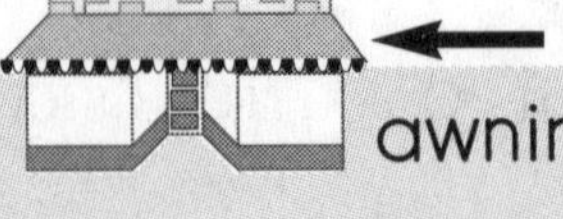

laundry August because awning

1. Dawn has her birthday in the month of ________.
2. Bill put an ________ on his store ________ the sun was hot.
3. Paul helps his mother carry the ________ basket upstairs.

Review of ✎ ô Words

The **ô** sound is also made with the letters augh and ough. The letters **gh** are silent.

✔ How quickly can you read these words? Print the underlined words in the blanks.

caught	taught	daughter	fought	naughty
bought	ought	brought	haughty	thought

1. Mrs. Hall has brought her ______ to a party.
2. Dawn will give a gift that she ______ at a store.

3. She ______ that her pal ought to enjoy it.

✔ Draw lines to the words that answer the questions.

1. What should we always obey? — God's law
2. What has Paul caught with his rod?
3. Where has a dog brought its bone?
4. How can Tom haul some logs?

with his truck
a long fish
to a hole

✔ Underline the letters that say the **ô** sound in the words at the left. Print them under their pictures.

hawk
song
fawn
daughter
draw
jaw
fall
crawl

o al aw au augh ough

Review of Soft Sound of ✎ c Words

Do you remember the two sounds that the letter **c** makes?
1. When **a**, **o**, or **u** follow **c** as in **cat**, **cot**, and **cut**, the **c** may be called the ***hard*** sound.
2. When **e**, **i**, or **y** follow **c** as in **ice**, **city**, and **cymbals**, the **c** may be called the ***soft*** sound.

✔ Underline the vowel **e**, **i**, or **y** that follows the **c** and makes the **c** to have the ***soft*** sound.

pencil	circle	faucet	circus	city
fence	bicycle	lettuce	face	cymbals

✔ Underline the vowel **e**, **i**, or **y** that follows the **c** and makes the **c** to have the ***soft*** sound.

spice celery brace place

1. Cindy sprained her leg and must have a __________ on it.

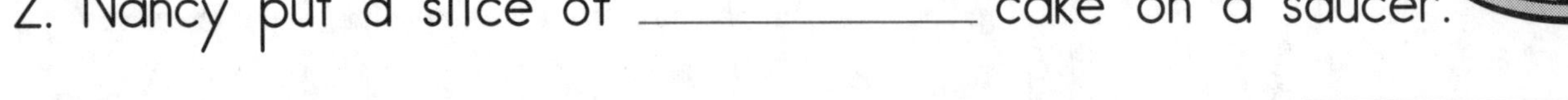

2. Nancy put a slice of __________ cake on a saucer.

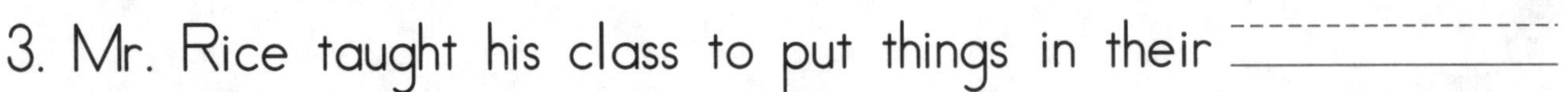

3. Mr. Rice taught his class to put things in their __________.

4. Grace ate a salad with lettuce, carrots, and __________.

✔ Match the words that rhyme.

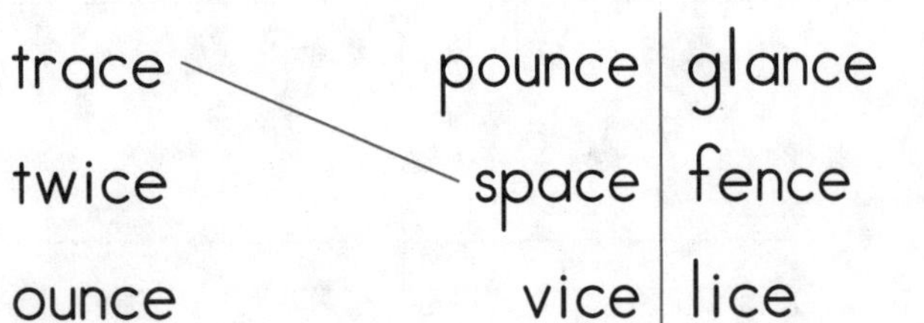

trace	pounce	glance	hence	prince	grace
twice	space	fence	ice	rice	since
ounce	vice	lice	chance	lace	nice

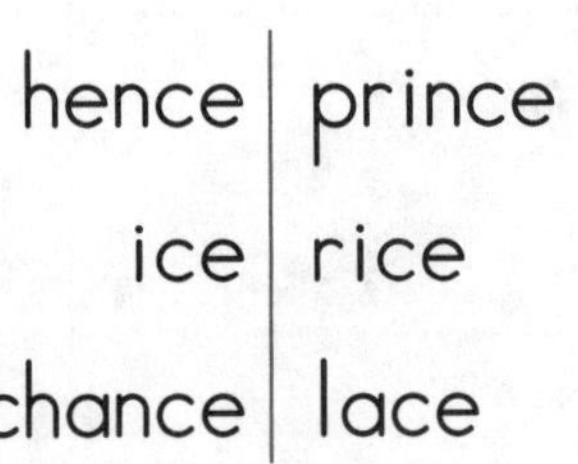

Review of Soft Sound of ✎ g Words

Do you remember the two sounds that the letter **g** makes?
1. When **a**, **o**, or **u** follow **g** as in **game**, **go** and **gum**, the **g** has the ***hard*** sound
2. When **e**, **i**, or **y** follow **g** as in **cage**, **giant**, and **gym**, the **g** has the ***soft*** sound as in **j**.

✔ Underline the vowel **e**, **i**, or **y** that follows the **g** and makes the **g** to have the sound of **j**.

pledge	giraffe	bridge	engine	hinge
page	orange	cage	badge	stage

✔ Choose the correct words from the box to complete the sentences. Print them in the blanks below.

change	giraffe	Vegetables	badge
hinge	pledge	gingerbread	Gerald

1. At the zoo George saw a large ____________.

2. ____________ that God made are good to eat.

3. ____________ helped his father ____________ a tire.

4. A promise is like making a ____________.

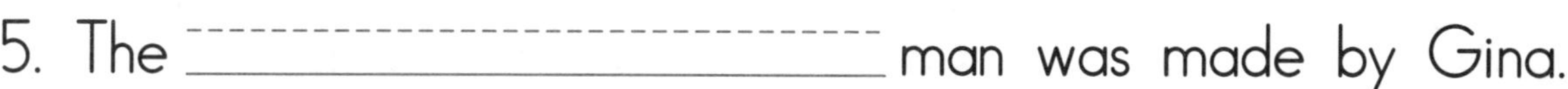

5. The ____________ man was made by Gina.

6. If Bruce learns Bible verses he gets a ____________.

Review of Consonant Digraphs ✎ sh wh

Do you remember that a consonant digraph has ***two*** consonants that make ***one*** sound?
We have reviewed the **th** as in **the** and **think**, and **ch** as in **church**.
This lesson includes words with the consonant digraph **sh** as in **ship** and **wh** as in **whip**.

✔ Circle the **sh** and **wh** in these words as you print them under the correct pictures.

wheel	brush	whale	whip	fish
whiskers	shell	ship	sheep	wheat

cats have ?

✔ Match the words that rhyme. Listen to the vowel sounds!

whip	smash	when	mesh	clash	clock
crash	ship	rash	splash	shock	sleep
rush	crush	fresh	then	sheep	cash

✔ Add the suffix **ing** to the words at the right. Print the words in the blanks as you complete the sentences.

1. Shirley sees her mother ______ as she cooks. — rush
2. She helps her by ______ the potatoes. — mash
3. They will eat the fish he caught while ______. — fish
4. Mother is ______ butter on the fish. — brush
5. Someone is ______ near the door. — whisper

Review of Consonant Digraphs ✎ kn wr

Remember that a consonant digraph has ***two*** consonants that make ***one*** sound.
This lesson includes digraphs that have silent letters: **kn** as in knot and **wr** as in write.

✔ Draw a line through the silent letters in the words below. Print the correct words under their pictures.

knife	wrench	wrist	wreath	wrinkles
write	knee	knob	knuckles	knit

✔ Draw a line through the silent letters in both lists. Print the correct words in the blanks below.

1. The boys like to __________ in gym class.
2. Another word for anger is __________.
3. Jim's father and mother __________ as they pray.
4. Wendy must __________ the dough for bread.
5. James __________ how to say his Bible verses.

kneel
knew
knead
wrestle
wrath

knickknacks knapsack knowledge

1. It is better to have __________ than to have gold.
2. Jill put the __________ into her __________.

Review of Words with Silent Letters

Several sets of letters in which ***one*** consonant or vowel may be silent are:

gn as in gnaw **mb** as in lamb **bt** as in doubt
gu as in guess **mn** as in hymn **bu** as in build

There are only a few words with these sets of silent letters.

lamb
thumb
building
climb
guards
hymn
gnat
gnu

✔ Cross out the silent letter in each word and carefully print the answers.

✔ Choose words from the list above to complete these sentences.

1. A large animal that you may see in Africa is a ________.
2. Tom enjoys seeing men build a ________.
3. The shepherd will climb down a cliff to get the ________.
4. Rachel likes to sing a ________ as she helps her mother.
5. The ________ stood near the castle as they guarded.

✔ Complete these sentences with the correct words in the box to the right.

1. Jesus came out of the ________ and lives in heaven.
2. We need Him to ________ us as our shepherd.

guide
tomb

Review of Words with ✎ Silent Letters

Several more sets of letters in which *one* consonant may be silent are:

lf as in calf **lk** as in walk **tch** as in watch

✔ Draw a line through the silent letters. Print the words under the correct pictures.

psalm
watch
pitch
calf
catch
match
half
palm

The Lord is my shepherd...

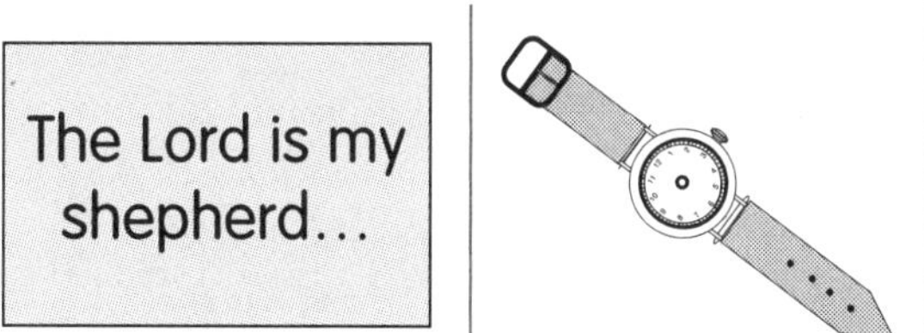

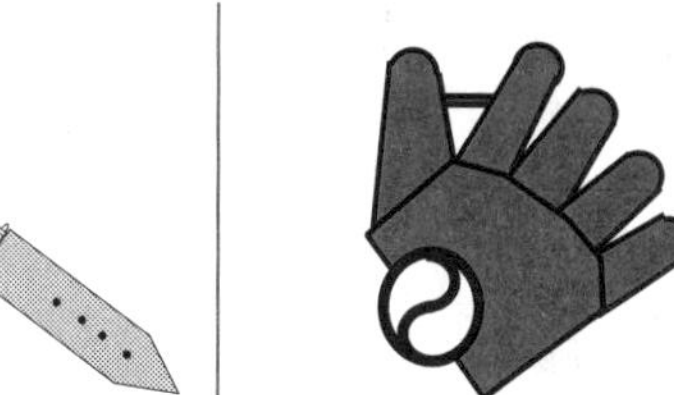

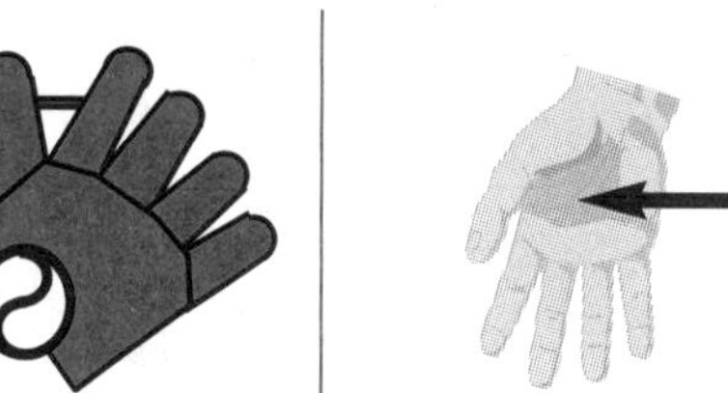

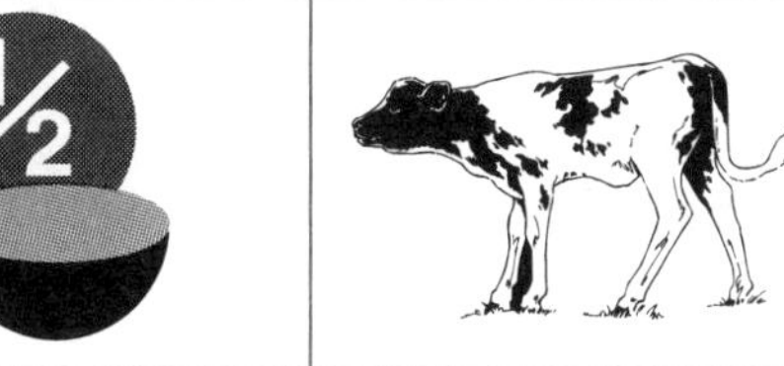

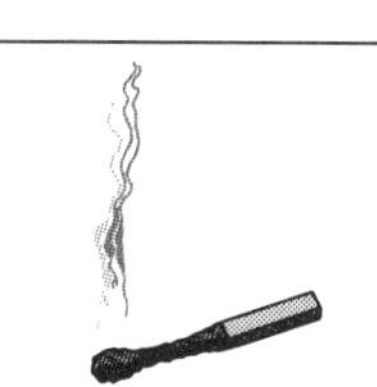

✔ Draw a line through the silent letters in the box at the right. Print the correct words in the blanks below.

1. Grandma and Tim like to ________ on calm days.
2. They saw a nest of eggs that will soon ________.
3. He fell into a ________ as he picked a flower stalk.
4. She had to stitch a ________ on his pants.
5. She made a big ________ of peanut butter cookies.

batch
walk
hatch
patch
ditch

✔ Match the words that rhyme.

chalk	ditch	stalk	scratch	Dutch	calf
pitch	batch	patch	talk	fetch	hutch
match	walk	stitch	switch	half	stretch

Words with ✎ ng nk

When words end with **ng** and **nk**, these letters make a special sound.

king sting thing ink think blink

✔ Add **ng** or **nk** to complete the words in these sentences.

1. David helped Ki____ Saul by using his sli____ to kill Goliath.
2. Kim likes to si____ as she washes dishes in the si____.
3. Do you thi____ to tha____ if someone helps you?
4. Peter tied a stro____ stri____ to his kite.
5. We heard a loud ba____ when Frank dropped his ba____.

MILK

6. Bill would du____ his doughnut before he dra____ his milk.

✔ How do you spell these **ng** and **nk** words?

✔ Add **ing** to complete these words. How quickly can you say them?

br____ fl____ spr____ str____ w____

sw____ sl____ st____ th____ r____

✔ Add **ing** to these words ending with **ff**, **ll**, **ss**, and **zz**.

bless blessing dress ____ buzz ____

call ____ drill ____ roll ____

sniff ____ spell ____ stuff ____

Review of Digraphs ✎ ea and ou

You have learned that **ea** may have the sounds of ēa as in ēat and ĕa as in hĕad.
In a few words the **ea** may have the long **a** vowel sound as in steāk.

✔ Mark the long vowel **a** sounds in the words below. Print these long vowel **a** words in the correct blanks.

breāk breaking great greater

1. Our ______ God created the heaven and earth.

2. There is no one ______ than our Lord.

3. Bill is careful so the point of his pencil will not ______.

4. The wreckers are ______ down an old building.

✔ Print these words in the correct columns.

bread, head, break, great, beak, seat, steak, thread, steal

ēa	ĕa	eā

You have learned that **ou** may have the sounds of **ou** as in **mouse**, **ôu** as in **bought**, and **ou** as in **would**. Another sound **ou** may make is the long vowel sound of **u** as in **you**.

✔ Print these correct words in the blanks below to complete these sentences.

group through soup youth

1. Remember your Creator in the days of your ______.

2. A ______ of students ate ______ and bread for lunch.

3. Tom's dog could jump ______ a hoop and over a gate.

Schwa Sound of ✎ a

Remember that the vowel **o** may have the short vowel **u** sound as in these words:

mother shovel from color wonder love Monday nothing of

Each of the vowels may make the short sound of **u**. A dictionary may show a symbol like this ∂ for that sound which is called a ***schwa*** sound. Some words begin with the letter **a** having this sound as in **arose**.

✔ Read these words and then divide them as you print them.

alike	a-like	ago		alive	
awake		asleep		awhile	
afraid		about		ahead	
away		avoid		astray	
apart		arose		aloud	

✔ Use the underlined words above to complete these sentences. Print them in the blanks below.

1. Long ________ Jesus died on the cross for our sins.
2. Jesus ________ from the tomb and is ________ in heaven.
3. He tells us to trust in Him and not to be ________.
4. The Bible tells us ________ many wonderful lessons.

✔ Divide these compound words.

treetop	tree-top	sailboats	
milkweed		hillside	
playmate		airway	
beehive		beanbag	

Using a and an

When one object is mentioned, the word **an** or **a** may be used when talking about that object.
1. The word **a** is used before a word that begins with a ***consonant***: **a** car, **a** doll, or **a** tack.
2. The word **an** is used before a word that begins with a ***vowel***: **an** ark, **an** egg, or **an** inch.

✔ Notice the beginning letter of each word and think of the rules above about **a** and **an**.

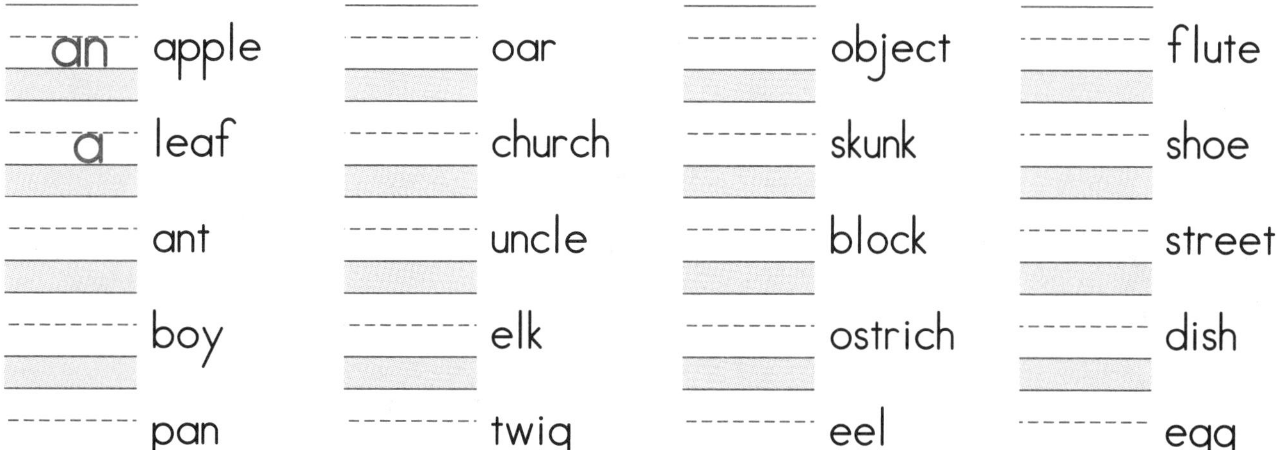

an apple	____ oar	____ object	____ flute
a leaf	____ church	____ skunk	____ shoe
____ ant	____ uncle	____ block	____ street
____ boy	____ elk	____ ostrich	____ dish
____ pan	____ twig	____ eel	____ egg

✔ Think as you print **a** or **an** in the blanks to complete the sentences.

1. Andrew can catch ____ leaf with his hands.
2. He feels ____ east wind is blowing the leaves.
3. His mother put his lunch in ____ brown bag.
4. He has ____ orange, ____ sandwich, and ____ cookie.
5. He saw ____ ant crawl up ____ tree and into ____ hole.

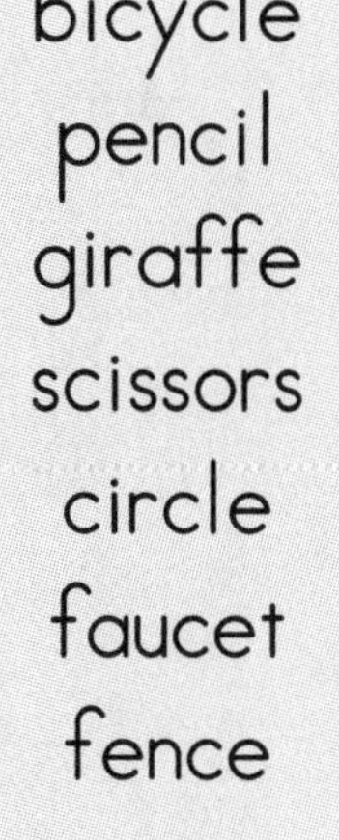

bicycle
pencil
giraffe
scissors
circle
faucet
fence
page

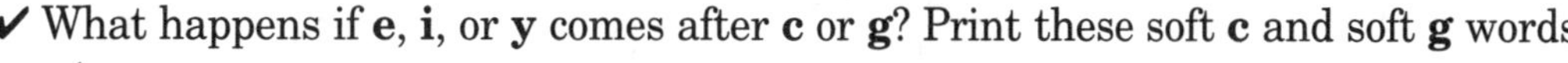

✔ What happens if **e**, **i**, or **y** comes after **c** or **g**? Print these soft **c** and soft **g** words.

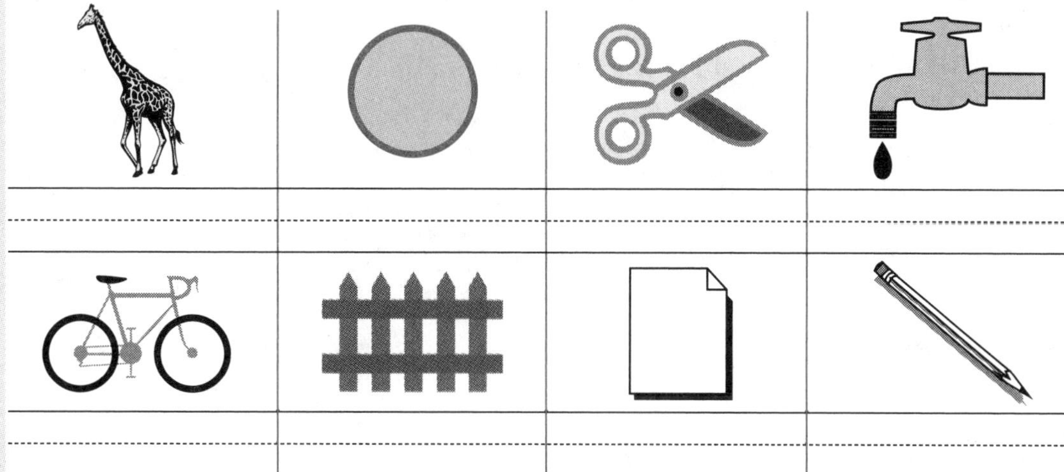

Words Ending With The Vowel ✎ y

1. If the **y** comes after another vowel, it follows the long vowel rule and the **y** is silent as in dāy and kēy.
2. If the **y** is the only vowel in the word, it has a long **i** sound as in flȳ.
3. If a word has more than one syllable, the **y** has the long sound of **e** as in baby (bābē) and lady (lādē).

✔ These words end with **y** and have two syllables. Print them where they belong.

kitty	city	pony	penny	candy
bunny	cherry	puppy	lady	carry

✔ What numbers are these words?

fifty 50 eighty ______ forty ______ thirty ______

twenty ______ ninety ______ sixty ______ seventy ______

✔ The suffix **y** can be added to many words. Add **y** to the ***root*** words and complete the sentences.

1. The cold wind made the air feel ______.
2. Jane went outside and she felt it was ______.
3. It blew her hair so that it was not ______.
4. She is happy even on ______ days.
5. She knows that God makes it sunny or ______.
6. A person is not pleasant if he is ______.

chill
wind
curl
cloud
rain
fuss

Words Ending With The Vowel ✎ y

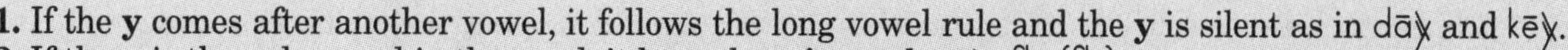

1. If the **y** comes after another vowel, it follows the long vowel rule and the **y** is silent as in dāy and kēy.
2. If the **y** is the only vowel in the word, it has a long **i** sound as in fly (flī).
3. If a word has more than one syllable, the **y** has the long sound of **e** as in baby (bābē) and lady (lādē).

✔ Think of RULES 2 and 3 above as you read these words. Print them in the correct columns.

rocky	sky	chilly	pry	fry
silly	my	why	Mary	needy
try	funny	lady	weary	shy
Sally	windy	cherry	by	happy

y has the long i sound		y has the long e sound		

✔ Think of RULE 1 as you read these sentences. Print a word in the blanks that is spelled with **ay**.

1. Today Ray will ________ with his puppet.
2. Its head is made out of gray ________.
3. It will ________ by Ray and not stray away.
4. The puppet cannot ________ any words.
5. Ray had to ________ lots of money for it.
6. He may soon put him ________ in its box.
7. He will carefully ________ it down.

Plural Words Ending with ✎ y

An **s** is added to the end of many words when *more than one object* is mentioned (***plural***) as follows:

cat ⇒ cats **book ⇒ books** **cake ⇒ cakes**

If a word ends with **y**, two RULES need to be learned:

1. When the **y** follows a vowel, just add **s** as follows: **toy ⇒ toys**, **day ⇒ days**, and **key ⇒ keys**.

✔ Add **s** to make these words plural. Notice the vowel that comes before the ending **y**.

valley	valleys	day		turkey	
toy		way		key	
joy		tray		boy	

The second RULE for words ending with **y** is:

2. When the **y** follows a consonant, change the **y** to **i** and add **es**:

city ⇒ cities **baby ⇒ babies** **pony ⇒ ponies**

✔ Notice the consonant just before the ending **y**. Change the **y** to **i** and add **es** to these words.

lady	ladies	pony		puppy	
copy		lily		city	
story		bunny		duty	
penny		party		candy	
fly		worry		kitty	

✔ Notice if a vowel or consonant comes just before the ending **y**. Think of the two rules above.

1. Brad saw two brown ________ in the yard.
2. He saw them run and play for three ________.
3. He gathered a basket of ________ to eat.
4. Brad picked some ________ for his mother.
5. He knows that God made the green ________.

lily
day
berry
valley
pony

Plural Words Ending With ✎ y

An **s** is added to the end of many words when *more than one object* is mentioned (***plural***) as follows:

cat ⇒ cats **book ⇒ books** **cake ⇒ cakes**

If a word ends with **y**, two RULES need to be learned:

1. When the **y** follows a vowel, just add **s** as follows: **toy ⇒ toys**, **day ⇒ days**, and **key ⇒ keys**.

2. When the **y** follows a consonant, change the **y** to **i** and add **es**:

city ⇒ cities **baby ⇒ babies** **pony ⇒ ponies**

✔ What letter comes before **y**? Think about these RULES as you make the words to become plural.

penny	pennies	lily		cherry	
valley	valleys	fly		tray	
baby		supply		berry	
toy		donkey		key	
turkey		pony		lady	
story		boy		daisy	

✔ Now print these words to be singular or mean ***only one***.

turkeys	turkey	stories		flies	
babies		joys		keys	
bunnies		ladies		cities	

✔ Make the words plural to complete the sentences.

1. A nickel is the same as five ________.
2. The farmer had six cows and ten ________.
3. Jerry had three pears and six ________.
4. Our class has ten girls and ten ________.

turkey
boy
cherry
penny

Plural of Words Ending in ✎ s, x, z, ch, sh

An **s** is added to the end of many words to make them mean *more than one* (**plural**): **cat** ⇒ **cats**.
Remember the RULES for the words ending with **y**:
1. When the **y** follows a vowel, just add **s**: **toy** ⇒ **toys**;
2. When the **y** follows a consonant, change the **y** to **i** and add **es**: **city** ⇒ **cities**.

If a word ends with **s**, **x**, **z**, **ch**, or **sh**, the letters **es** are added to make it plural.
bus ⇒ **buses** **box** ⇒ **boxes** **buzz** ⇒ **buzzes** **lunch** ⇒ **lunches** **dish** ⇒ **dishes**

✔ The "helping hand" tells when to add **es**. If the words end with other letters, just add **s**.

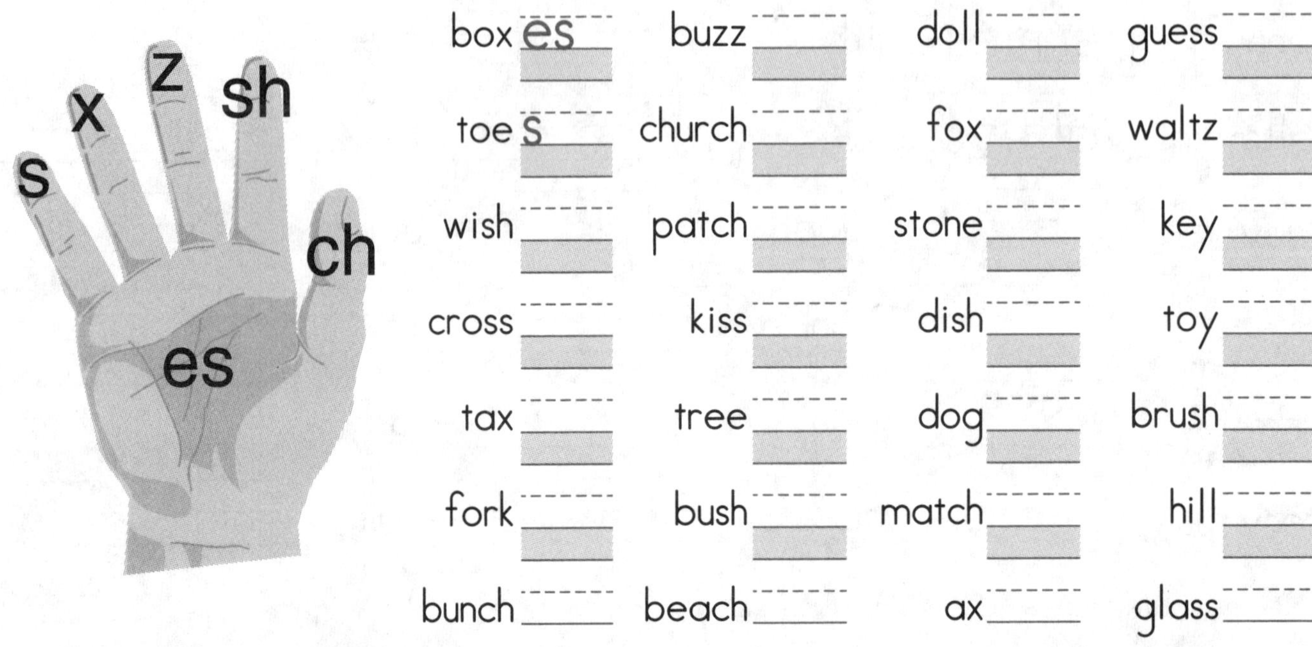

box es	buzz ___	doll ___	guess ___
toe s	church ___	fox ___	waltz ___
wish ___	patch ___	stone ___	key ___
cross ___	kiss ___	dish ___	toy ___
tax ___	tree ___	dog ___	brush ___
fork ___	bush ___	match ___	hill ___
bunch ___	beach ___	ax ___	glass ___

✔ Print the correct words under the pictures. Do you see that some of the pictures are not plural?

✔ Make the words plural in the box at the right. Print them in the blanks to complete the sentences below.

1. Carol's house has two ______________.
2. Jon will clean the ______________ from the fireplace.

ash
porch

Suffixes ✎ -ly and -er

A **suffix** is a word part added to the end of a ***root*** word to change its meaning. You know that **-y** is a suffix when it is added to a ***root*** word such as **wind** ⇒ **windy**. Another suffix is **-ly** as in **soft** ⇒ **softly**.

✔ Add the suffix **-ly** to modify or change the underlined ***root*** words.

1. Cal's school work was neat. He did it ________.
2. Ruth was eager to go with Naomi. She went ________.
3. God made the slow snail. It crawls ________.
4. Peter was quick to see Jesus. He ran ________.
5. Dorcas was kind to people. She treated them ________.
6. Children should be glad to obey. They obey ________.
7. Mr. Brown plays nice music. He plays music ________.
8. The lady has a soft voice. She speaks ________.

✔ Complete these sentences with the following **-er** words as in **work** ⇒ **worker**.

ruler upper lower brighter worker stronger faster

1. A sluggard is one who is lazy and not a good ________.
2. King David tried to honor God by being a good ________.
3. God made Samson to be ________ than other men.
4. Jesus blinded Saul with a light ________ than the sun.
5. Jesus ate supper with the disciples in an ________ room.
6. Men had to ________ a lame man through a roof to Jesus.
7. At times the clock seems to move ________ than we move.

Suffixes and Syllables ✎ er, or, and ar

Suffixes are letters added to the end of a ***root*** word to change its meaning as in **work ⇒ worker**.
A **syllable** is a word or part of a word with a vowel sound which is pronounced with a single sound.
cab ⇒ cabin **rob ⇒ robin** **win ⇒ winter** **late ⇒ later**

✔ Complete these sentences with the following **-er** words. The **er** is part of the last syllable in each word.

answer brother bitter silver winter

1. Thad's little ______ found a ______ coin.
2. We should speak kindly when we give an ______.
3. The weather had ______ winds during this ______.

✔ These words end with **or** and **ar** which make the ər or ***schwa*** plus **r** sound.
Complete the following sentences with the **or** and **ar** words in the box. Print them in the blanks below.

doctor tailor caterpillar cellar
beggar dollar binoculars anchor

1. When our neighbor got sick we called a ______.
2. The sailor uses a pair of ______ to see.
3. Jesus healed the ______ who had been born blind.
4. Bill had a ______ fix the collar on his suit.
5. Jill found a ______ with pretty colors.

✔ Drop the **s** or **es** and add **or** to modify these words. **The One who <u>creates</u> is The <u>Creator</u>.**

1. One who instructs is an ______.
2. One who collects is a ______.
3. One who directs is a ______.
4. One who operates is an ______.

Suffix ✎ -ful

REMEMBER: **Suffixes** are letters added to the end of a word to change its meaning. The suffix -**ful** means ***full of***. The **u** makes a vowel sound, so -**ful** is a syllable.

✔ Carefully add the suffix **ful** and read your new words.

peace	peaceful	fear		shame	
use		care		need	
hope		skill		rest	
watch		truth		pain	

✔ Print these words where they belong to complete the sentences.

cheerful helpful faithful powerful playful careful

1. The little brown puppy was ______.
2. We should be ______ as we help others.
3. Tara tries to be ______ to her mother.
4. We should be ______ as we print.
5. God is always ______ to His people.
6. He is all ______; with Him nothing is impossible.

A good neighbor is

helpful
thoughtful
thankful
useful
careful
truthful
faithful
cheerful

✔ Match the phrases in the left-hand columns with the correct -**ful** words in the right-hand columns.

He who tells the truth is	restful.	One who thanks is	careful.
One who is resting is	truthful.	One who takes care is	cheerful.
One who helps is	fearful.	One who has cheer is	thankful.
Someone who fears is	skillful.	A sore that has pain is	useful.
One who has skill is	helpful.	A thing that is of use is	painful.

Suffixes ✎ -less and -ness

REMEMBER: **Suffixes** are letters added to the end of a word to change its meaning.
The suffix **-less** means ***without*** or ***not***. The **e** makes a vowel sound, so **-less** is a syllable.

✔ Be careful as you add the suffix **-less** and read your new words.

care	careless	worth		bone	
use		blame		tire	
spot		thought		end	

✔ Match these words with opposite meanings.

fearless	careful	painless	useful	faithful	harmful
careless	hopeless	useless	painful	thankful	faithless
hopeful	fearful	helpful	helpless	harmless	thankless

✔ Add **-less** and read the new words.

without faith	faithless	without harm	
without care		without power	
without shame		without hope	

The suffix **-ness** tells about a condition or state of being: **sad** ⇒ **sadness**.

✔ Carefully add the suffix **-ness** as you read your new words. Print the correct words in the blanks below.

quick	quickness	sick		slow	
kind		sweet		sad	
neat		ill		soft	

1. The neighbors showed kindness during Carl's ____________.
2. Miss Ellen's life is full of thoughtfulness and ____________.
3. The opposite of quickness is ____________.

Suffixes ✎ -er and -est

The suffix **-er** is added to words to compare ***two*** things: **fast** ⇒ **faster**.
The suffix **-est** is added to words to compare ***more than two*** things: **tall** ⇒ **taller** ⇒ **tallest**.

✔ Neatly add the suffixes **-er** and **-est** to form new words.

	-er	-est		-er	-est
kind	kinder	kindest	wild		
long			high		
short			tall		
clear			old		
thick			cold		
slow			fast		
small			quick		

✔ Add the suffixes **-er** or **-est** to complete these sentences.

1. An elephant is one of the ____________ animals. (strong)
2. Judy is ____________ than her older brother and sister. (short)
3. A giraffe is one of the ____________ animals God created. (tall)
4. Nathan runs ____________ than any of the boys on the team. (fast)
5. Pat's kite flew the ____________ of all the children. (high)
6. Summer is the ____________ time of the year. (warm)
7. God made the hummingbird ____________ than the wren. (small)
8. The turtle is one of the ____________ animals in the world. (slow)

Sounds of Suffix -ed

The suffix **-ed** can make three different sounds:
d as in **cheered** and **called**; **t** as in **fixed** and **worked**; and ∂**d** as in **printed** and **handed**. PRINT

Conrad called his father. The man worked hard. Tom printed neatly.

✔ As you read these words, underline the **-ed** sound. Print the sound **-ed** makes in the blanks: **d**, **t**, or **ed**.

turned	d	squirted		jumped	
fixed	t	finished		climbed	
handed	ed	asked		hunted	
served		scolded		pushed	
rushed		weeded		groaned	
called		learned		planted	

Every syllable has a vowel sound. When the **-ed** sounds like ∂**d**, it makes another syllable as in **handed**.

✔ Listen to the suffix **-ed** and print how many syllables each word has.

pulled	1	searched		called	
handed	2	carted		folded	
thanked		finished		greeted	
cheered		walked		burned	

✔ Circle the numeral for the sentences that may be true.

1. Jeff and his sister do not like to read.
2. He is reading a book on plants.
3. He enjoys reading in his home.
4. A horse is reading a big book about hay.
5. Renee is reading about pretty flowers.

✎ Adding Suffixes

If a one-syllable word with a short vowel ends with ***one*** consonant, ***double*** the consonant before adding a suffix that begins with a vowel: **hop** ⇒ **hopped** ⇒ **hopper** ⇒ **hopping** ⇒ **hoppy**.

✔ Remember to double the ending consonant as you add these suffixes to the short vowel words.

	-ed	-ing
nap	napped	napping
shop		
rub		
drip		
scrub		
step		
tap		

	-er	-est
hot		
mad		
big		
thin		
fat		
dim		
wet		

✔ Read the rule again before you add suffixes to these short vowel words. REMEMBER: **y** may be a vowel.

swim + ing = swimming

scrub + er =

jump + ing =

shag + y =

flat + er =

trim + ing =

fill + ed =

stick + y =

fog + y =

stiff + est =

pick + ing =

stamp + ed =

win + er =

drip + ing =

✔ Underline the suffixes in the following sentence.

A fluff<u>y</u> squirrel jumped and hopped while gathering nuts.

Suffixes and Words Ending with ✎ e

When a word ends with a silent **e**, drop the **e** before adding a suffix that begins with a vowel: **skate ⇒ skating**, **use ⇒ used**, **bake ⇒ baker**, **cute ⇒ cutest**, **shine ⇒ shiny**.

✔ Add these suffixes to the words ending with a silent **e**.

	-ed	-ing		-er	-est
wave	waved	waving	tame		
hope			late		
scrape			cute		
sneeze			fine		
paste			ripe		
smile			close		

✔ Add the suffixes **-ed**, **-er**, **-est**, or **-ing** to these words as you complete the sentences.

1. Miss White ________ the class to her home.
2. The boys are ________ their hands to answer.
3. I think that Chris is the best ________ in school.
4. Tom is always ________ with his father.
5. Mr. Hill's dog had the ________ puppies.
6. It was fun when the children ________ books.
7. Jim's home is the ________ to church.

invite
raise
write
joke
cute
trade
close

✔ Underline the suffixes and print the ***root*** word.

raised	raise	skater		smiling	
finest		bony		shiny	

✎ Review of Suffixes

When adding a suffix beginning with a <u>vowel</u> (**-ed**, **-er**, **-ing**, **-est**, or **-y**) remember two RULES:
1. If a one-syllable word with a <u>short vowel</u> ends with ***one*** consonant, ***double*** that consonant before adding a suffix: **nap** ⇒ **napped**, **tap** ⇒ **tapping**, **fat** ⇒ **fattest**, **wet** ⇒ **wetter**, and **mud** ⇒ **muddy**.
2. If a word ends with a silent **e** drop the **e** before adding a suffix: **wave** ⇒ **waving** and **late** ⇒ **later**.

✔ Add the suffixes **-er** and **-est** to these short vowel words as you complete the sentences.

1. My cat is fat, Jan's is ____________, but Ted's is ____________.
2. Levi is tall, Ben is ____________, but Sam is ____________.
3. Ed's cup is full, Al's is ____________, but mine is ____________.
4. My dog is big, Jill's is ____________, but Kay's is ____________.
5. Jay is kind, Glen is ____________, but Mike is ____________.

✔ Add the suffixes **-er** and **-est** to these words which end with **e** as you complete the sentences.

1. Jon came late, Will came ____________, but Todd came ____________.
2. The pear is ripe, the apple is ____________, but the plum is ____________.
3. Our bird is tame, our cat is ____________, but our dog is ____________.
4. Tim lives close, Gail lives ____________, Don lives ____________.
5. Dirt is fine, sand is ____________, but flour is ____________.

✔ Add the suffix **-y**, which is a vowel, to these words. REMEMBER the rules above.

flop	flop-py	drip	____________
bug	____________	rose	____________
sun	____________	stone	____________
grease	____________	taste	____________

✎ Review of Suffixes

When adding a suffix beginning with a vowel (**-ed**, **-er**, **-ing**, **-est**, or **-y**) remember these RULES:
1. If a one-syllable word with a short vowel ends with ***one*** consonant, ***double*** that consonant before adding a suffix: **nap** ⇒ **napped**, **tap** ⇒ **tapping**, **fat** ⇒ **fattest**, **wet** ⇒ **wetter**, and **mud** ⇒ **muddy**.
2. If a word ends with a silent **e** drop the **e** before adding a suffix: **wave** ⇒ **waving** and **late** ⇒ **later**.

✔ Add these suffixes which begin with vowels to these words. Print the **RULE NUMBER** in the column.

Word		Suffix		Answer	Rule	Word		Suffix		Answer	Rule
save	+	ing	=	saving	2	win	+	er	=		
mop	+	ed	=	mopped	1	tug	+	ed	=		
spin	+	er	=			sun	+	y	=		
wide	+	est	=			quote	+	ed	=		
waste	+	ed	=			type	+	ing	=		
mud	+	y	=			thin	+	est	=		
bake	+	er	=			write	+	ing	=		

Two more suffixes that begin with a vowel are: **-en** as in **glad** ⇒ **gladden**, **-able** as in **like** ⇒ **likable**.
When adding a suffix beginning with a vowel (**-ed**, **-er**, **-ing**, **-est**, **-en**, **-able**, or **-y**) remember these RULES:
1. If a one-syllable word with a short vowel ends with ***one*** consonant, ***double*** that consonant before adding a suffix: **nap** ⇒ **napped**, **tap** ⇒ **tapping**, **fat** ⇒ **fattest**, **wet** ⇒ **wetter**, and **mud** ⇒ **muddy**.
2. If a word ends with a silent **e** drop the **e** before adding a suffix: **wave** ⇒ **waving** and **late** ⇒ **later**.

✔ Add these suffixes which begin with vowels to these words. Print the **RULE NUMBER** in the column.

Word		Suffix		Answer	Rule	Word		Suffix		Answer	Rule
sad	+	en	=	sadden	1	dine	+	ing	=		
like	+	able	=	likable	2	glad	+	en	=		
dig	+	ing	=			run	+	er	=		
wise	+	er	=			wide	+	est	=		
size	+	able	=			wave	+	ing	=		
flop	+	y	=			fat	+	est	=		

✎ Review of Suffixes

When adding a suffix beginning with a vowel (**-ed**, **-er**, **-ing**, **-est**, **-en**, **-able**, or **-y**), remember these RULES:

1. If a one-syllable word with a short vowel ends with ***one*** consonant, ***double*** that consonant before adding a suffix:
nap ⇒ napped

2. If a word ends with a silent **e**, drop the **e** before adding a suffix beginning with a vowel:
wave ⇒ waving

3. If a short vowel word ends with ***two*** consonants just add the suffix beginning with a vowel:
jump ⇒ jumping

4. If a word has a long vowel sound just add the suffix beginning with a vowel:
rain ⇒ rained

✔ Add these suffixes which begin with vowels to these words. Print the **RULE NUMBER** in the column.

Word		Suffix		Answer	Rule	Word		Suffix		Answer	Rule
brave	+	est	=	bravest	2	bump	+	ing	=		
shop	+	ed	=	shopped	1	run	+	er	=		
camp	+	er	=	camper	3	like	+	able	=		
snow	+	ed	=	snowed	4	fill	+	ing	=		
plan	+	ed	=			paint	+	ing	=		
rose	+	y	=			sad	+	en	=		
pose	+	ing	=			crisp	+	y	=		

To add a suffix beginning with a consonant (**-less**, **-ness**, **-ly**, or **-ful**), usually no change is needed.

✔ Add the suffixes **-less**, **-ness**, **-ly**, or **-ful** to these words. Remember the rule above.

Word		Suffix		Answer	Word		Suffix		Answer
lone	+	ly	=	lonely	cup	+	ful	=	
kind	+	ness	=		glad	+	ness	=	
cheer	+	ful	=		slow	+	ly	=	
care	+	less	=		doubt	+	less	=	
pain	+	ful	=		red	+	ness	=	
bone	+	less	=		joy	+	ful	=	

Words Ending With ✎ y

Why does the "y" need special attention?

1. If a word ends with a **y** next to a <u>consonant</u>, we usually change the **y** to **i** and add the suffix: **try** ⇒ **tried**, **carry** ⇒ **carrier**, **story** ⇒ **stories**, **beauty** ⇒ **beautiful**, and **penny** ⇒ **penniless**.

2. DO NOT change the **y** when a <u>vowel</u> comes before it: **play** ⇒ **played**, **gray** ⇒ **grayest**.

3. DO NOT change the **y** when adding the suffix **ing**: **carry** ⇒ **carrying**, **play** ⇒ **playing**.

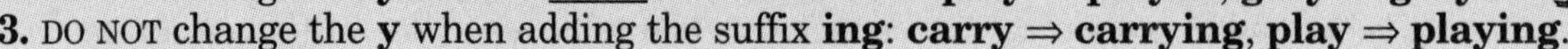

✔ Add these suffixes to the words which end with a **y**.

heavy + ness =	heaviness	copy + er =	
happy + est =		cry + es =	
merry + ly =		plenty + ful =	
marry + ed =		cozy + er =	
dry + est =		sorry + est =	
busy + ness =		hurry + ed =	

✔ Add these suffixes to the words. Remember! DO NOT change the **y** if a vowel comes before it.

play + ful =	playful	joy + ful =	
pray + er =		obey + ed =	
gray + est =		pay + able =	
plenty + ful =		cry + es =	

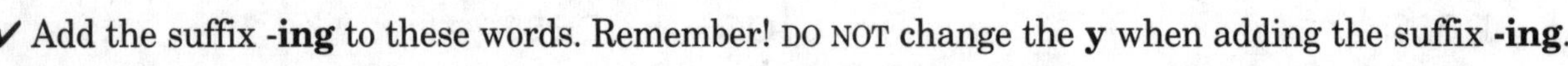

✔ Add the suffix **-ing** to these words. Remember! DO NOT change the **y** when adding the suffix **-ing**.

stay	staying	obey		cry	
pray		carry		say	
try		worry		hurry	
marry		play		copy	

Words Ending With ✎ y

How do you add a suffix to a word ending with a "y"?

1. If a word ends with a **y** next to a consonant, we usually change the **y** to **i** and add the suffix: **try** ⇒ **tried**, **carry** ⇒ **carrier**, **story** ⇒ **stories**, **beauty** ⇒ **beautiful**, and **penny** ⇒ **penniless**.
2. DO NOT change the **y** when a vowel comes before it: **play** ⇒ **played**, **gray** ⇒ **grayest**.
3. DO NOT change the **y** when adding the suffix **ing**: **carry** ⇒ **carrying**, **play** ⇒ **playing**.

✔ Add the suffixes to these words ending with **y**. Print the **RULE NUMBER** in the column.

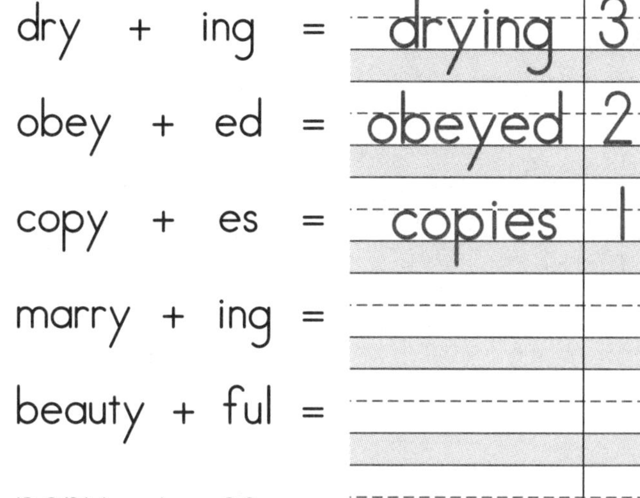

dry + ing =	drying	3	fly + ing =		
obey + ed =	obeyed	2	handy + est =		
copy + es =	copies	1	tiny + est =		
marry + ing =			study + ed =		
beauty + ful =			delay + s =		
pony + es =			play + ful =		

✔ Think carefully as you use the words and the suffixes to complete the sentences.

happy + ly	study + ing	missionary+es	worry + es
copy + ed	pray + ing	joy + ful	

1. Karen ____________ goes to church with her parents.
2. She ____________ some Bible verses on a pad of paper.

3. The people are ____________ about the book of Job.
4. They are ____________ for some friends in Korea.
5. Their friends are ____________ in that country.
6. They also pray to the Lord about some ____________.
7. Going to church is a ____________ time for Karen.

✎ Review of Words with Suffixes

A **suffix** is a syllable in itself if it has a vowel sound as in **fly-ing**, **bone-less**, **land-ed**, and **lunch-es**.

✔ Divide these words into syllables. Do you hear the vowel sound that is in each of these suffixes?

praying	pray–ing	kindness	
newest		speaker	
helpful		painting	
sadly		thoughtful	
slower		softest	
harmless		darkness	
tested		wisely	

A **suffix** is a syllable in itself if it has a vowel sound as in **fly-ing**, **bone-less**, **land-ed**, and **lunch-es**. Never divide a combination of letters that are pronounced as one syllable as in **jumped** or **looks**.

✔ Divide these words into syllables. Watch for words with suffixes that should not be divided.

treated	treat–ed	helper	
feared	feared	smallest	
reading		trusted	
careful		greedy	
works		called	

✔ Underline the words in these verses that have suffixes.

- Blessed is the man who always fears the Lord. (Proverbs 28:14a)
- A foolish son is his father's ruin. (Proverbs 19:13a)

- A faithful man will be richly blessed. (Proverbs 28:20a)

✎ Review of Words with Suffixes

A **suffix** is a syllable in itself if it has a vowel sound as in **fly-ing**, **bone-less**, **land-ed**, and **lunch-es**.

✔ Each of the sentences have ***two*** words with **suffixes**. Underline the words and divide them as you print them. Watch for words with suffixes that should not be divided.

	1 Syllable Words	2 Syllable Words
1. Chuck wants to be helpful to dad.	wants	help–ful
2. He thinks about the Bible teaching.		
3. He is blessed when he is praying.		
4. They will be watching his good works.		
5. You will be thinking about her deeds.		
6. He knows a lying word will hurt them.		

REMEMBER! If a word ends with **s**, **x**, **z**, **ch**, or **sh**, add **es** to make it plural:
bus ⇒ **buses**, **box** ⇒ **boxes**, **buzz** ⇒ **buzzes**, **lunch** ⇒ **lunches**, and **dish** ⇒ **dishes**.

✔ The **e** makes a vowel sound which makes **es** to be a syllable. Divide these words.

catches catch–es

mixes

dishes

reaches

marches

taxes

dresses

buzzes

✔ Divide these compound words.

footprints foot–prints

highway

tonight

something

stairway

popcorn

necktie

beanbag

Prefixes ✎ un- and dis-

A **prefix** is a syllable placed before a ***root*** word to change its meaning as in **unhappy** and **disagree**. The prefixes **un-** and **dis-** are usually opposite the meaning of the ***root*** word.

✔ Underline the ***root*** word and draw a ring around the prefix. Print the root word on the line.

disappear	appear	unfair	
unscrew		displease	
dislocate		unwilling	
unkind		unsafe	
unhappy		disobey	
dishonest		unknown	
untrue		dislike	

✔ Match the words which have the opposite meaning.

agree	unjust	order	unpin	screw	untrue
certain	unhappy	known	dishonest	please	dislocate
just	unfold	fair	disobey	willing	unsafe
happy	dislike	pin	unknown	true	unscrew
fold	disagree	honest	disorder	locate	displease
like	uncertain	obey	unfair	safe	unwilling

✔ Print the word with a **prefix** which has the meaning of the underlined words.

1. Jim was <u>not willing</u> to be dishonest.
2. It is wrong when a person is <u>not kind</u> to his pet.
3. The Lord is <u>not happy</u> if we disobey our parents.
4. God is just; He is angry if people are <u>not fair</u>.

Prefixes ✎ **re-**, **de-**, and **pre-**

A **prefix** is a syllable placed before a ***root*** word to change its meaning as in **retype**, **defrost**, and **prefix**. The prefix **re-** usually means ***do again***. The prefix **de-** usually means ***from***. The prefix **pre-** usually means ***before*** or ***ahead***.

✔ Divide these words which have prefixes.

defrost	de–frost	rebuild	
reread		preview	
detour		remake	
preschool		detest	
depart		retell	
refile		replant	
rewash		prewar	

These words also begin with the syllables **re-**, **de-**, and **pre-** as in **remind**, **decide**, and **prevent**.

✔ Read this list and use the underlined words to complete the sentences.

prepares	recess	pretend	present	delicious
rejoice	receive	decides	remind	depend

1. Conrad can smell the ______ food in the kitchen.
2. He is happy that his mother ______ such tasty meals.
3. His father never has to ______ him to wash his hands.
4. He does not need to ______ that he is hungry.
5. His family always thanks God for the food they ______.
6. After dinner he ______ to do homework before playing.

Prefixes ✎ **ex-**, **fore-**, and **for-**

A **prefix** is a syllable placed before a ***root*** word to change its meaning as in **exit** and **forenoon**.
The prefix **ex-** usually means ***from*** or ***out of*** as in **ex-tent** and **ex-it**.
The prefix **fore-** usually means ***before*** in time or place as in **fore-noon**.
The prefix **for-** usually means ***away***, ***apart***, or ***off*** as in **for-bid**.

✔ Read and divide these words into syllables.

forefinger	fore-finger	forefather	
expand		excuse	
foretell		forbid	
forgive		forehead	
exclaim		explain	
forward		express	
exchange		forget	

✔ Circle the prefixes as you read these words. Use the underlined words to complete the sentences below.

expel	foreknow	extend	forewarn	forearm
forever	foreground	forecast	extract	explode

1. We will be happy as we live in heaven with God ________.
2. Only our great Lord can ________ the future.
3. When Kevin fell he got a cut on his left ________.
4. Our family heard the weather ________ on the radio.
5. The vet had to ________ a broken tooth from a monkey.
6. The policeman had to ________ the rude boy from the store.

Prefix ✎ be- Suffix and Prefix Review

A **prefix** is a syllable placed before a ***root*** word to change its meaning.
A **suffix** is a letter or group of letters added to the end of a ***root*** word to change its meaning.

✔ Read aloud the following words which begin with the syllable or prefix **be-**.
Divide these words into syllables and use them in the sentences below.

be–low	believe	belongs	behave	beware
be–gins	behind	beneath	beside	before

1. Everyone should ____________ in God and the Bible.
2. I kneel ____________ my desk to pray as school ____________.
3. The duck flew ____________ or ____________ the clouds.
4. We honor our parents when we ____________ as we should.
5. A rabbit ran ____________ the shed before Wag could get it.
6. We should ____________ of being a lazy person.
7. We should not take anything that ____________ to others.

✔ These words have **prefixes** and **suffixes**. Read and divide these words into syllables.

preschooler	pre–school–er	replanted	
untruthful		departed	
remaining		unfairly	
retested		explaining	
unpacking		unscrewing	
unwisely		defrosted	
previewing		rereading	

✎ Rules One and Two For Dividing Words

Rule One: A one-syllable word must never be divided.

✔ Try to print these one-syllable words without looking at the list. They should never be divided.

deer	cross	clock	mouse	square
heart	wrench	check	goose	write

Rule Two: Divide a compound word between the words that make the compound word.

✔ Divide these compound words. Try to print the names of the pictures without looking at the list.

foot-ball	windmill	textbook	barnyard
hair-cut	tiptoe	homework	bluebird
footprint	into	baseball	clipboard
snowflake	stairway	workman	quicksand
sailboat	sidewalk	outlet	fishbowl

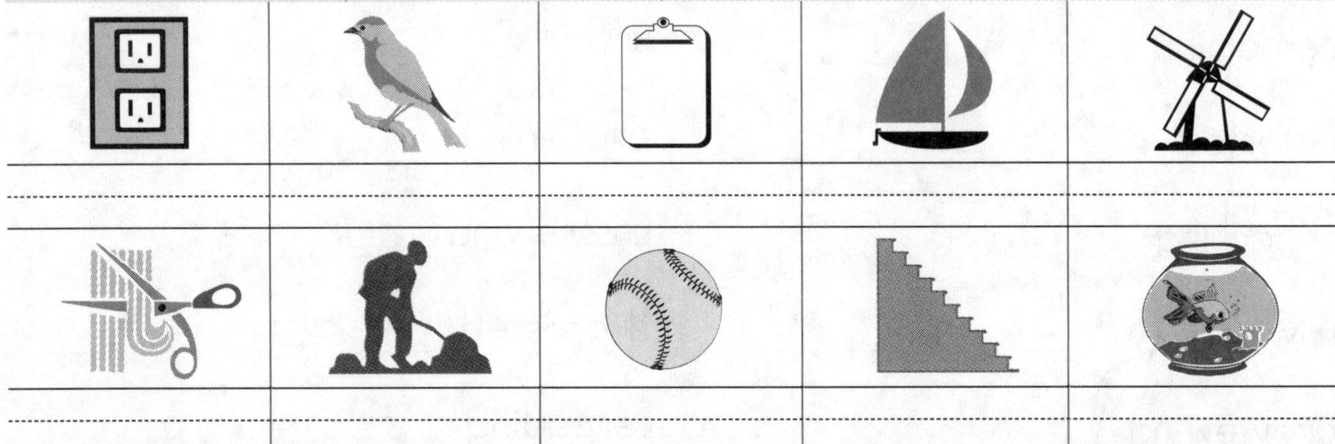

✎ Rules Three and Four For Dividing Words

Rule Three: When a word has a suffix that makes a vowel sound, divide the word between the ***root*** word and the **suffix**.

✔ Divide these words with suffixes. See how quickly you can read them.

thoughtful	thought–ful	throwing	
parting		helper	
kindness		careless	
wisely		thinking	
joyful		faithful	
jumping		highest	
smallest		sweetness	

Rule Four: When a word has a prefix that makes a vowel sound, divide the word between the **prefix** and the ***root*** word.

✔ Divide these words with prefixes. See how quickly you can read them.

unsafe	un–safe	explode	
displease		depart	
derail		unchain	
rebuild		explore	
forenoon		around	
prepaid		forehead	
beside		preview	

Review of Prefixes ✎ **un-**, **dis-**, **ex-**, and **re-**

REMEMBER: A **prefix** is a syllable placed at the beginning of a ***root*** word to change its meaning.
Rule Four: Divide a word with a prefix between the **prefix** and the ***root*** word.

The prefixes **un-** and **dis-** usually give the ***root*** word the ***opposite*** meaning.
The **ex-** usually means ***out of*** or ***from***. The prefix **re-** usually means ***do again***.

✔ Divide these words and use the underlined words to complete the sentences below.

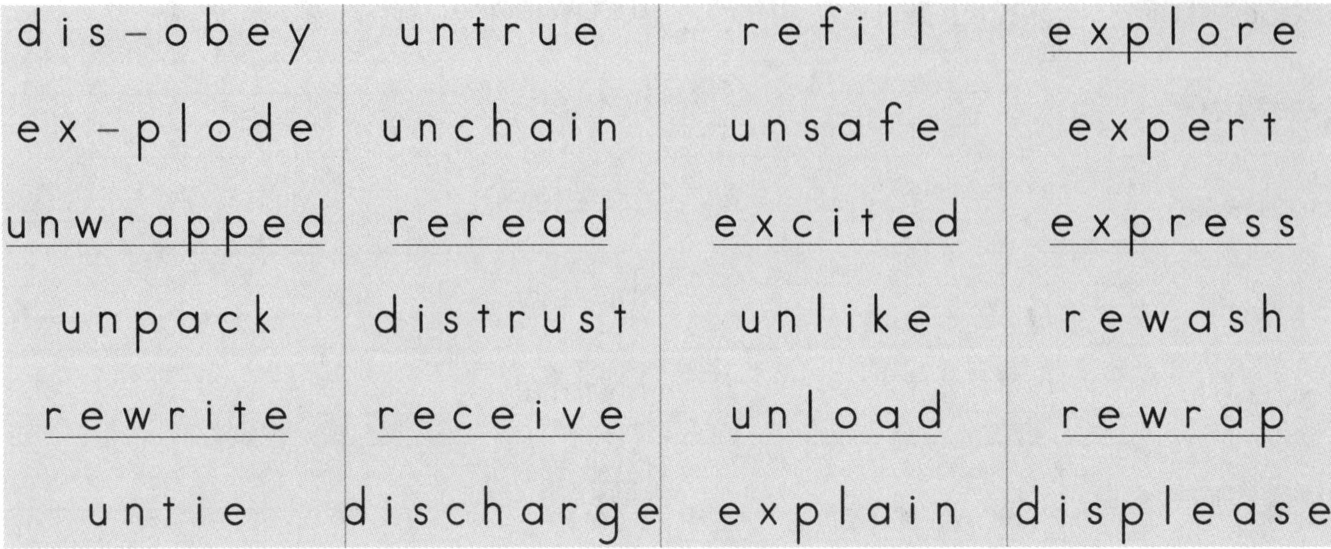

dis–obey	untrue	refill	explore
ex–plode	unchain	unsafe	expert
unwrapped	reread	excited	express
unpack	distrust	unlike	rewash
rewrite	receive	unload	rewrap
untie	discharge	explain	displease

1. Ted was happy to ______________ a letter from his Uncle Jim.
2. Right away he ______________ the letter to his parents.
3. He was ______________ that his parents let him go to visit him.
4. Tim wrote a note to his uncle, but he had to ______________ it so it would be neater.
5. Mother had to ______________ Uncle Jim's gift which their baby had ______________.
6. Ted took an ______________ train to his uncle's town.
7. His uncle helped him ______________ his luggage from the train.
8. After Ted unpacked, he went to ______________ his uncle's farm.

Review of Prefixes ✎ **pre-**, **fore-**, and **for-**

REMEMBER: A **prefix** is a syllable placed at the beginning of a ***root*** word to change its meaning.
Rule Four: Divide a word with a prefix between the **prefix** and the ***root*** word.

The prefix **pre-** usually means ***before*** or ***ahead***. The prefix **de-** usually means ***from***.
The prefix **fore-** usually means ***before in time or place***. **For-** usually means ***away***, ***apart***, or ***off***.

✔ Divide these words and use the underlined words to complete the sentences below.

de–part	predict	detour	forward
pre–fix	because	delay	around
prepare	derail	forenoon	between
prepaid	defrost	forget	again
prevent	awoke	forever	became
preview	depress	forehead	before

1. Pam told Ann a big secret ______________ she went to her home.
2. At night she could not ______________ about the secret.
3. It would ______________ Ann from falling asleep quickly.
4. As Ann ______________ in the morning, she became excited again.
5. She went ______________ her room putting her things away.
6. She helped ______________ breakfast and told her family the secret.
7. Then she asked if she may be excused ______________ she wanted to run and see Pam's new baby sister.

✔ Add the beginning syllable or prefix **in-** to completes these words. See how quickly you can read them.

___form	___side	___crease	___deed	___stead
___to	___land	___vite	___vent	___dent

✎ Accented Syllables

As you say words with more than ***one*** syllable, you can hear that one syllable is pronounced ***stronger*** than the others as in **hap´ py**, **read´ ing**, **un fold´**, **dis please´**, and **thought´ ful**.
The little mark (´) after the syllable shows that it is the ***stronger*** or ***accented*** syllable.

✔ Read these words and put an ***accent*** mark (´) after the syllable that is ***stronger*** or said with force.

pan´ da	scis sors	be tween	un wrap
kan ga roo´	ta ble	fish ing	chil dren
snow´ flake	po lice	un fold	talk ing
foot prints	let ter	pen cil	re fill
en gine	ap ple	re pair	care less
sail boat	a wake	un kind	think ing
re turn	hair cut	kind ness	faith ful

✔ Here are some children's names. Mark the ***accented*** syllable that is stronger or said with force.
You will notice that the ***first*** syllable of each of these names is the ***accented*** syllable.

Nan´ cy	Con nel	Al len	Ra chel
Peg´ gy	Jan et	Da vid	Con rad
Na´ than	Bet ty	Han nah	Pe ter

✔ Find these words in this lesson and print them in syllables. Mark the ***accented*** syllable.

✎ Schwa Sound

The last syllable of these words is the ***unaccented*** syllable. The vowel has the ***schwa*** sound (ə) which sounds like a short vowel **u**. This sound may be made by any of the vowels.

comma agent pencil second focus

✔ Listen for the ***schwa*** sound (ə) as you say these words. Print the words under their pictures below.

camel	ribbon	lion	squirrel	lemon
button	seven	melon	bushel	period

				This sentence ends with a period. ←

✔ Print the correct words from the box above to complete the following sentences.

1. A ripe ______ is much sweeter than a yellow ______.
2. God gave Samson strength so he was able to kill a ______.
3. Terry and Jerry carried a ______ of apples for mom.
4. Jill sewed a ______ on her coat.

✔ Circle the prefixes **re-**, **de-**, **pre-**, **dis-**, and **un-** and print the ***root*** words on the lines.

uncertain	certain	preview		unlock	
rework		refill		unfold	
defrost		prewash		dislike	
unjust		reread		replace	
rebuild		unpack		unkind	
disobey		prewar		displease	
unwrap		refile		remake	

Review of Schwa Sound ✎ **a** Words

The letter **a** at the beginning of these words is the first syllable. It is the ***unaccented*** syllable and has the ***schwa*** sound as in **ago**, **away**, and **around**. A dictionary may show it this way: ∂ **go**.

✔ Read the words and divide them into syllables. The ***accent*** mark belongs on the second syllable.

afraid	a-fraid′	along	
ahead		alone	
again		amount	
apart		awake	
around		aside	
awhile		alike	
ago		alive	

✔ Choose words from the list to complete these sentences.

1. Al was ______ all day, but then he fell asleep.
2. Mr. Sherman told us ______ many Bible stories.
3. Jesus ______ from the grave after three days.
4. We should obey Him as we ______ His coming.
5. We should ______ being foolish in all things.
6. The Bible says to stay ______ from wicked people.

avoid
about
away
awake
await
arose

✔ Double the last consonant and add **y** to these short vowel words. Divide them into syllables.

mud	mud-dy	pup		fog	
fun		drip		shag	
crab		snap		flop	

Schwa Sound ✎ le Words

These words have ***two*** or ***three*** syllables and end with **le**. The first syllable is ***accented***. In the last syllable the **e** has the ***schwa*** sound as in **ta´ ble**, **bu´ gle**, **cat´ tle**, and **puz´ zle**.

people
eagle
bugle
bicycle
apple
triangle
circle
turtle

✔ Carefully print the correct words under the following pictures.

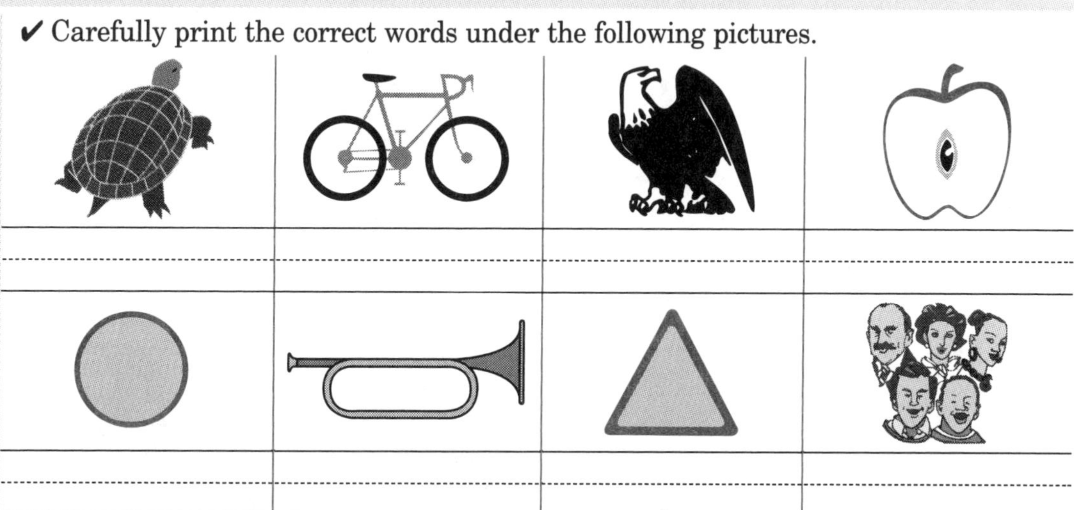

✔ Choose **le** words from the box at the right to complete these sentences. Print them in the blanks below.

ankle
apple
castle
candle
saddle
bottle
stable
bridle

1. Ted had pizza and a ________ of juice to eat.
2. After Hannah fed an ________ to her pony, she put a ________ and ________ on him.
3. She led him from the ________ to ride him.
4. Jenny put a pretty ________ on the table for light.
5. It would be nice to visit an old English ________.
6. Tom hurt his ________ as he slipped in the puddle.

When words ending with **le** are divided, the consonant just before the **le** is usually part of the last syllable as in **ta´ ble**, **bu´ gle**, **cat´ tle**, and **puz´ zle**.

✔ Divide these words into syllables.

gentle	gen–tle	jungle		tumble	
dimple		middle		little	
riddle		single		purple	

Schwa Sound ✎ le Words

It is fun to learn about the many words that end with **le**. Here is another lesson with them.

✔ Match the phrases with the pictures. NOTE: The underlined words end with the ***schwa*** plus **l** sound of **le**.

1. a little turtle in a puddle
2. a single apple on a table
3. a child with a dimple
4. a needle and a thimble

5. a candle on a table
6. a star with a twinkle
7. a ruffle on a cradle
8. a bundle of purple socks

✔ Print the correct words under the following pictures.

handle	ankle	middle	bridle	castle
saddle	bottle	paddle	needle	bubbles

REMEMBER! The consonant just before the **le** is usually part of the last syllable as in **sin´ gle** and **ta´ ble**.

✔ Divide these words as you say them. Do you notice that the first syllable follows the vowel rules?

grumble	grum–ble	pebble		sparkle	
wiggle		bundle		jumble	
tangle		giggle		temple	

Schwa Sound ✎ ckle Words

These words have the consonant digraph **ck** followed by **le** as in **pick´ le**.
The consonant **ck** must never be divided. The **ck** stays with the short vowel in the first syllable, so the **le** does not have another consonant in the last syllable as in **buck´ le**. The **le** stands alone.

✔ Do you see the **ck** in these words? Divide the words right after the **ck** as in **chuck´ le**.

p i c k – l e	c r a c k l e	b u c k l e	t r i c k l e	s h a c k l e
t i c k – l e	c h u c k l e	t a c k l e	f r e c k l e	s p e c k l e

buckle
cradle
rattle
pickle
cattle
freckles
fiddle
puddle

✔ Where do these words belong?

REMEMBER! When a **ck** is in a word, divide the word right after the **ck** as in **tack´ le**.
If there is no **ck** in the word, a consonant is usually part of the **le** as in **ta´ ble** and **tur´ tle**.

✔ Divide these words.

needle	nee–dle	bundle		turtle	
prickle	prick–le	sprinkle		middle	
snuggle		jungle		struggle	
ripple		speckle		rumble	
chuckle		cable		fumble	
people		steeple		stumble	
eagle		tackle		crackle	

Review of Sounds of ✎ **a** Words

The vowel **a** has several sounds.
This lesson talks about three of these sounds. | căt | cāke | ago (ə)

✔ As you read these words, listen to the sound of the **a** and mark it correctly. DO NOT mark the other vowels.

ănd	alike	along	asleep	stay
chāin	stable	ago	about	sandal
around (ə)	cattle	apple	cradle	stamp
afraid	ask	shade	alone	amount

✔ Match these words with the phrases that describe them.

a. candle	___ a leather seat on a horse		g. people	___ a little laugh	
b. bugle	a a form of wax with a wick		h. chuckle	___ persons	
c. saddle	___ like a small trumpet		i. pebble	___ jerky motions	
d. crumple	___ little spots on the skin		j. cattle	___ to fall or trip	
e. freckles	___ land with trees and vines		k. stumble	___ farm animals	
f. jungle	___ to crush into wrinkles		l. wiggle	___ a little stone	

ap–ple
tack–le
people
pickle
steeple
bubbles
bicycle
circle

✔ Divide the words into syllables and print them under the correct pictures.

Words Ending with Silent ✎ e

These words end with the vowel **e**. Words ending with soft **c** (*s*) or **g** (*j*), usually have a final silent **e**. Usually a silent **e** follows words ending with the letters **s**, **r**, or **v**.

✔ Read the following words with a silent **e** and print them under the correct pictures.

nurse	geese	fence	bounce	hinge
store	blouse	purse	mouse	glove

✔ Read the following words with a silent **e** and print them in the correct blanks below.

plunge	loose	more	have
choice	ounce	since	give

1. The ring felt light ________ it weighed only one ________.
2. We saw the man ________ into the lake to save the child.
3. Our teacher will ________ us a ________ of books to read.
4. Ed's shoes were ________, so he tied the laces once ________.
5. We ________ many wonderful ways to serve our great Lord.

✔ Add the suffix **-ing** to these words which end with a silent **e** by dropping the **e** and adding **ing**.

serve serving plunge ________ have ________

bounce ________ give ________ store ________

Review of Long ✎ i and o Words

Usually the vowels **i** and **o** have the short sound when they are alone in a word. In some words they have the long vowel sound as in chīld and cōld.

✔ Read the following long vowel **i** and **o** words. Print them under the correct pictures.

flight	high	colt	child	night
light	post	cold	bolt	grind

✔ Use words from the box at the right to complete the following sentences.

1. You will find the frisky colt ______ the barn.
2. Mother told Sue that she may ______ the baby.
3. We should be kind as we ______ our parents.
4. When we visited Mr. Holt, he was a kind ______.
5. In the ______ Testament of the Bible we read that to get wisdom is far better than to get ______.

Old
hold
behind
gold
host
mind

✔ Add **-ing** to these words and divide them. NOTE: just add the suffix **-ing** to words that end with **w**, **x**, or **y**.

throw	throw–ing	fix		play	
mix		try		wax	
pray		draw		snow	

Review: Modified Vowels ✎ er Sound

REMEMBER: When the consonant **r** comes after **e**, **ea**, **i**, **(w)o** and **u**, it modifies those vowels by making the **er** sound as in **verse**, **earth**, **bird**, **world**, and **church**. It is the ***schwa*** (ə) plus **r** sound.

✔ Carefully print the following words with the **er** sound under the correct pictures.

earth	squirrel	turtle	words	church
letter	skirt	giraffe	thirty	finger

(church)	work works worked working	(envelope)	(turtle)	(giraffe)
(squirrel)	30	(skirt)	(finger)	(earth)

✔ Choose the words with the **er** sound from the box at the right to complete the following sentences.

1. Kurt got up early as he ______ the birds singing.
2. Today he will ______ with his ______.
3. After breakfast he will read some Bible ______.
4. Kurt has ______ the words from his lessons.
5. He will wear his white and ______ jacket today.

father
verses
heard
learned
purple
work

When adding **-ing** to short vowel words ending in a ***single*** consonant, ***double*** the consonant and add **-ing**.

✔ Add the suffix **-ing** to these words. Divide them as you print the correct answers in the blanks below.

ship	ship-ping	tag	______	bat	______
cut	______	hem	______	sled	______
mop	______	tug	______	win	______

Review: Modified Vowels ✎ ear Sound

The letters **ear** can make three different sounds as in **ear**, **earth**, and **peâr**.

✔ Make the correct vowel sound ***marks*** in the following words: **ear**, **earth**, and **peâr**.

dēar	clear	hear	year	gear
ėarn	pearl	learn	search	heard
peâr	bear	wears	tearing	wearing

✔ Choose the **ear** words from the box at the right to complete the following sentences. Print the correct words in the blanks below.

ears
search
hear
wears
early
earth
learn
earn

1. Tim ________ his coat during the winter every year.
2. Anne will ________ for her pencil near her desk.
3. Phil is thankful he has good ________ so he can ________.
4. From the Bible we ________ that God created the heavens and the ________.
5. Jeff wakes up ________ in the morning for his paper route so that he can ________ some money.

✔ How do you make these words ending with **s**, **x**, **z**, **ch**, and **sh** to be plural? Divide them.

wash	wash–es	branch	________	waltz	________
brush	________	tax	________	patch	________
buzz	________	march	________	quiz	________
box	________	bush	________	cross	________
dress	________	glass	________	mix	________

Review: Three Sounds of Digraph ✎ ea

Letters **ea** makes three different sounds: **ea** = ē as in ēach, **ea** = ā as in greāt, and **ea** = ĕ as in brĕad.

✔ Make the correct vowel sound ***marks*** over the **ea** in the following words as in ēach, greāt, and brĕad.

tēase	peanut	weapon	greater	peas
hĕad	leather	deaf	bean	squeal
steāk	bleach	flea	leaf	breath
heaven	speak	teach	preach	health
feather	breaking	beak	beach	break

✔ Use the words in the box at the right to complete the following sentences.

heavy, pleasant, meadow, treasure, stream, dreams, please, yeast

1. We say "__________" and "thank you" to be polite.
2. Joseph had __________ about his older brothers.
3. The bread will rise because it has __________ in it.
4. A piano is too __________ for one person to move.
5. The nice weather made our walk __________.
6. The Bible, God's Word, is a great __________.
7. The cows graze in the __________ and get water from a __________.

✔ Where do these words belong?

fishbowl | necktie | snowman | mailbox

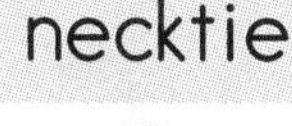

Words Ending with Long Vowel ✎ e o

A vowel at the end of a one-syllable word usually has the long vowel sound as in hē and nō. Remember the rules for dividing words into syllables: **RULE ONE:** Never divide a one-syllable word.

✔ Form words by adding the vowel to the consonants in each column.

o	e	y		
g	b	b	sl	sk
l	h	m	cr	fr
n	m	sh	fl	sp
s	w	wh	tr	dr

✔ Match these rhyming words.

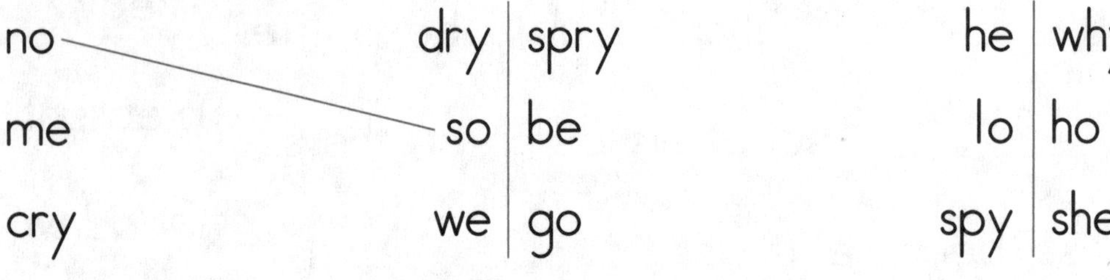

no	dry	spry	he	why	fry
me	so	be	lo	ho	we
cry	we	go	spy	she	no

✔ Use words from the lists above to complete these sentences.

1. Would you like to ________ to the zoo with ________?
2. ________ would see ________ many animals that God made.
3. We will see birds that cannot ________ in the ________.
4. ________ mother said we will ________ to go today.

✔ Complete the words below by adding the ending vowels **ea**, **ee**, **ie**, **oe**, and **ue**. The first vowel says its name, and the second vowel is silent. How quickly can you read them?

ea	ee	ie	oe	ue
t	b	d	f	d
s	fr	l	d	tr
fl	tr	p	t	bl

Vowels **ie** Make the Long ✎ **e** Sound

The vowels **ie** in these words make the long vowel sound of **e** as in ch\ēf and f\ēld.

✔ Circle the letters **ie** and practice reading each word. Use the underlined words in the sentences below.

believe	field	shriek	relieve	relief
shield	brief	niece	yield	belief
fierce	grieve	grief	piece	Chief

1. The Pilgrims were thankful that God sent an Indian friend named ________ Massasoit.

2. Some of the Indians were dangerous, ________ fighters.

3. They had some trouble and ________ during the first winter.

4. Some of the children made a frightened ________ when they first saw the Indian Samoset.

5. It was hard to ________ he could speak English to them.

6. It was a ________ to know that Samoset was friendly.

✔ Use these compound words in the sentences below.

farmhouse	butterfly	shoelaces	baseball
herself	schoolwork	basketball	ladybug

1. Caleb likes to play ________ and ________.

2. In the ________, he does his ________.

3. He reads about the ________ and a ________.

4. He taught Sue to tie her ________ by ________.

Review of ✎ ô Words

Do you remember the different sounds that the vowel **o** has?

o as in **ox** | ō as in ōak | ōō as in spōōn | ŏŏ as in bŏŏk | ô as in crôss

✔ Match these words with their meanings. Use the underlined words in the following sentences.

1. gloss	____	angry
2. toss	____	throw
3. cross	____	green plant
4. <u>moss</u>	1	shine

1. lost	____	frozen dew
2. frost	____	the price
3. cost	____	not on
4. <u>off</u>	____	not found

1. <u>log</u>	____	a large pig
2. fog	____	hopping animal
3. <u>frog</u>	____	clouds near land
4. hog	____	part of tree

1. moth	____	not hard
2. broth	____	an insect
3. <u>cloth</u>	____	used for clothes
4. <u>soft</u>	____	thin soup

1. Al sees a ________ on a log that is covered with ________.
2. He put a brown ________ that is ________ over the frog.
3. He will try to catch it before it jumps ________ of the ________.

When the vowel **a** is followed by an **l**, it usually has the **ô** sound. as in **hall**, **walk**, and **salt**.

✔ Match these words with their meanings.

1. all	____	little
2. halt	____	tumble over
3. fall	____	stop
4. small	1	everything

1. walk	____	a plant stem
2. stalk	____	a passageway
3. hall	____	speak or yell
4. call	____	move on foot

Review of ✎ ô Words

The sound of **ô** is often made with the letters **aw** as in **law** and **claw**.

✔ Match these words with their meanings.

1. jaw	____	chews	1. hawk	____	begins to melt
2. paw	____	part of mouth	2. dawn	____	grassy yard
3. straw	____	animal's foot	3. lawn	____	large bird
4. gnaws	____	dried grain stalk	4. thaws	____	early morning
1. crawl	____	terrible	1. awning	____	not cooked
2. claw	____	young deer	2. yawn	____	cutting tool
3. fawn	____	bird's sharp nail	3. raw	____	cover for shade
4. awful	____	move like baby	4. saw	____	deep breath

The sound of **ô** may also be spelled with the letters **ough** as in **bought** and **augh** as in **caught**.

✔ Print these words next to their meanings. Use the underlined words in the sentences below.

<u>taught</u> caught <u>daughter</u> brought | <u>thought</u> naughty <u>bought</u> ought

did teach	____	did think	____
a parents' girl	____	to not behave	____
did catch	____	did buy	____
did bring	____	should	____

1. Mrs. Smith ____ a toy bear for her ____.
2. Anne ____ that it was tired and ought to sleep.
3. Her mother ____ her how to sew a blanket.

Review of ✎ ô Words

REMEMBER: The sound of **ô** may be spelled with the letters **ought** as in **bought** and **aught** as in **caught**.

✔ After you have read these words, print them in the correct sentences.

1. Tim did buy gum. ______ daughter
2. We should do it. ______ fought
3. A girl is a... ______ bought
4. He did fight. ______ ought

1. She did catch. ______ brought
2. Dad did teach. ______ sought
3. To bring means... ______ taught
4. To search means... ______ caught

✔ After you have read these words, print them in the correct sentences.

daughter	taught	bought	ought
caught	thought	fought	naughty

1. Tim ______ a fish with a rod that he had ______.
2. Someone who does wrong is ______.
3. They ______ to be punished.
4. Mr. Hall ______ his ______ how to drive their car.
5. We ______ it was nice when Tom brought treats.
6. God helped David as he ______ against Goliath.

✔ How do you divide these words which end with a suffix?

colder	cold–er	stillness	______	helpful	______
landed	______	newest	______	useless	______
singing	______	started	______	gladly	______
joyful	______	careful	______	louder	______

Review of ✎ ô Words

The sound of **ô** may also be spelled with the letters **al** as in **call** and **aw** as in **hawk**.

✔ Print the words in the blanks below next to their meanings.

talk	jaw	halt	fall	stalk	hawk	small
ball	stall	walk	hall	draw	dawn	paw

part of mouth jaw

to speak

move on foot

round object

stop STOP

place for cow

tumble over

early morning

animal's foot

large bird

passageway

plant stem

little

make a picture

mall	gnaw	raw	fawn	lawn	crawl	malt
awful	straw	saw	yawn	thaw	claw	call

shopping place mall

terrible

dry grain stalks

to chew

cutting tool

young deer

deep breath

not cooked

to speak or yell

move like baby

grassy yard

bird's sharp nail

food flavoring

to melt

Review Lesson of ✎ ew Words

Words ending with the long vowel **u** sound often end with the spelling **ew**. The ***w*** is used as a vowel.

✔ Match these words with their meanings. Use the underlined words to complete the sentences below.

drew	knew	threw	flew	hew	pew	brew
crew	grew	blew	chew	new	stew	dew

group of workers	crew	thick soup	
did draw		water on lawn	
eat with teeth		did fly	
wind that moved		row of seats	
did grow		to carve or cut	
did throw		prepare tea	
did know		not old	

1. The boys sat quietly in the first ______ of their ______ church.
2. They had seen the ______ of men working hard to build it.
3. They ______ they should be quiet and listen each time they come to worship the Lord.
4. If the wind ______, it would strew papers around.
5. The bird ______ down to drink some ______ on the grass.

✔ Add **-es** to make the following words ***plural***. NOTE: These words end with **sh**, **ch**, **s**, **x**, or **z**.

church	dish	brush	lunch
bus	cross	patch	box

Review Lesson of ✎ âr Words

Words that have the letters **air** make the sound of **âr** as in **stair**.

✔ Print the correct **air** words under their pictures. Use the underlined words in the sentences below.

hair	airmail	chair	repair	airfield
pair	stairway	dairy	fair	airliner

		? of shoes		

1. Jane saw the crew quickly ________ the tire on the airplane.
2. We sent letters ________ to children in Russia.
3. Our class enjoyed the field trip to the ________ farm.

REMEMBER: When a short vowel word ends in a ***single*** consonant, that consonant is usually ***doubled*** before adding a suffix which begins with a vowel as in **cut ⇒ cutting** and **hop ⇒ hopping**.

✔ Underline the ***root*** words as they were before **-ing** was added. Divide the words into syllables. BE CAREFUL! If the ***root*** words end with **ll**, **ss**, **ff**, or **zz**, DO NOT divide those double letters.

tap-ping	tipping	puffing	hopping
will-ing	jumping	chopping	fluffing
reading	hitting	fussing	rolling
buzzing	filling	winning	sunning

✔ The letter **e** was taken off before adding the suffix **-ing**. Write the ***root*** words of these words.

making	make	baking		poking	
coming		sharing		taming	
giving		wasting		piling	

Review Lesson of Soft ✎ c Words

When **c** is followed by **e**, **i**, or **y** the **c** usually has the ***soft*** sound of **s** as in **cent**, **city**, and **cycle**.

✔ Print these words with the ***soft*** sound of **c** under the correct pictures.

ice	slice	necklace	mice	pencil

✔ Print these words with the ***soft*** sound of **c** in the blanks to complete the sentences below.

rice	prince	spice	cymbals
princess	cement	price	citizen

1. Dad put some ________ on the ________ before he ate it.
2. The king's children are ________ and ________.
3. Nancy's father became an American ________.
4. The men made a ________ sidewalk through the park.
5. Cindy saw a fancy dress, but the ________ was too much.
6. Vince played the ________ in the marching band.

✔ Think carefully as you add **-er** and **-est** to these ***root*** words. Divide the words into syllables.

	–er	–est		–er	–est
old	old–er	old–est	wet	wet–ter	wet–test
quick			sad		
slow			thin		
fast			hot		

Review Lesson of Soft ✎ c Words

When **c** is followed by **e**, **i**, or **y** the **c** usually has the ***soft*** sound of **s** as in **cent**, **city**, and **cycle**.

✔ Print these words with the ***soft*** sound of **c** under the correct pictures.

face	circle	city	faucet	bicycle

✔ Print these words to complete the sentences.

glance	space	lettuce	trace
lace	ceiling	bounce	circus

1. Jill had a salad made of ________, tomatoes, and celery.
2. Tracy's ball can ________ as high as the ________.
3. To look at something means to notice it or ________ at it.
4. Joy will sew some ________ on the ________ of the torn cloth.
5. Do you like to draw or ________ pictures?
6. Sam thought it was fun to go to the ________ with Dad.

✔ Divide these words with prefixes into syllables.

un–tie	awake	depart	prepaid
ex–plode	preview	forehead	unpack
refill	unchain	around	rewrite
distrust	explain	displease	beside
forward	rebuild	unsafe	refill

✎ Rule Five For Dividing Words

When ***two or more*** consonants come between ***two*** vowels, the word is usually divided between the first two consonants as in **but´ ter** and **hun´ gry**. A consonant usually follows a short vowel sound.

✔ Divide these words into syllables and print them under the correct pictures.

let-ter	basket	squirrel	balloon	engine
rab-bit	panda	scissors	hippo	finger

✔ Reread RULE FIVE above before you divide and match these rhyming words. Listen to the vowels.

puz-zle	fellow	kitten	bunny
yel-low	Jenny	butter	mitten
Ben-ny	muzzle	jello	gutter
bug-gy	muggy	funny	hello

✔ Circle the numeral if the sentence may be true about the picture. Divide the underlined words.

1. Ben-ny is holding two bal-loons.
2. His sister is crying.
3. Jenny wants a balloon.
4. She has a ribbon in her hair.
5. She is holding a yellow pillow.
6. Jenny is happy with Benny.

✎ Review of Five Rules For Dividing Words

✔ Read these FIVE RULES and divide the words correctly

RULE ONE: A one-syllable word must never be divided.

seal	star	shears	drink	gift

RULE TWO: Divide a ***compound*** word between the words that make the compound word.

s u n – s e t	t o d a y	l a d y b u g	b a s e b a l l
h i m – s e l f	b l a c k b i r d	c o r n s t a l k	n e c k t i e

RULE THREE: When a word has a **suffix** that makes a vowel sound, divide the word between the ***root*** word and the **suffix**.

cooking	cook–ing	helper		careless	
joyful		tested		faithful	
tallest		softness		going	

RULE FOUR: When a word has a **prefix**, divide the word between the **prefix** and the ***root*** word.

rework	re–work	dismiss		prepaid	
unsafe		become		asleep	
depart		export		misuse	

RULE FIVE: When ***two or more*** consonants come between ***two*** vowels, the word is usually divided between the first two consonants.

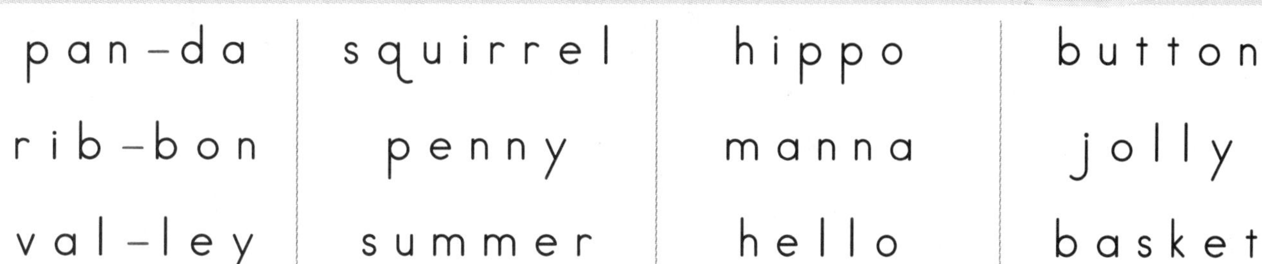

p a n – d a	s q u i r r e l	h i p p o	b u t t o n
r i b – b o n	p e n n y	m a n n a	j o l l y
v a l – l e y	s u m m e r	h e l l o	b a s k e t

✎ Rule Six For Dividing Words

Rule Six: When a ***single*** consonant comes between ***two*** vowels, the word is usually divided after the consonant if the first vowel sound is ***short*** as in **cab´ in**, **heav´ en**, and **moth´ er**.

✔ Divide these words into syllable and print the words under the pictures. If the vowel has a ***short*** sound, a consonant stays with it.

cam–el cabin wagon seven robin

✔ Divide these words into syllables. Listen for a short vowel. Do not divide consonant digraphs **th**.

liz–ard	radish	travel	pedal
heav–y	metal	heaven	visit
mel–on	finish	level	model
chap–el	lily	lemon	shadow

Do you remember learning about words ending with **le**? You have already learned how to divide them. **Rule 10 a**: When a word ends in **le**, the consonant just before the **le** is usually part of the last syllable as in **bu´ gle** and **cat´ tle**. Divide these words into syllables and print them under the pictures.

ap–ple tumble turtle bottle people

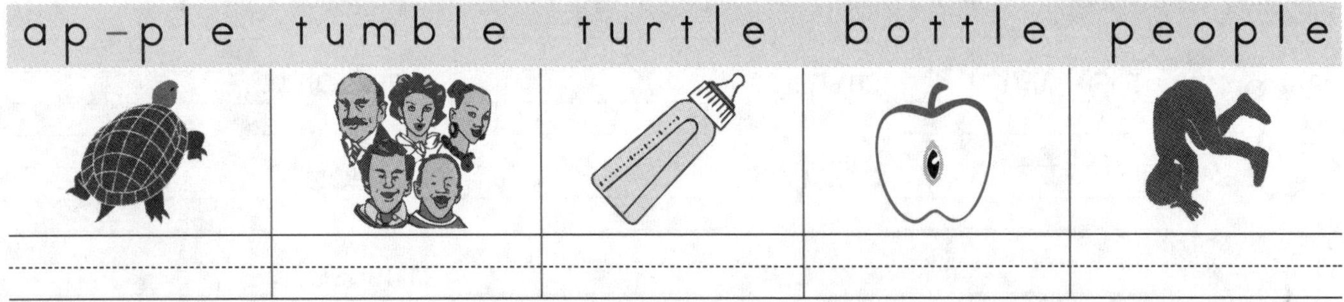

Rule 10 b: Words ending with **ckle** are divided after the **ck**, making **le** the last syllable as in **pick´ le**.

tickle	tick–le	trickle		speckle	
buckle		freckle		crackle	
tackle		shackle		chuckle	

✎ Rule Seven For Dividing Words

When a ***single*** consonant comes between ***two*** vowels, the word is usually divided before the consonant if the first vowel sound is ***long*** as in **mu´ sic**, **ze´ bra**, **co´ zy**, and **tu´ lip**.

✔ Divide these words into syllables. Divide right after the vowels that make the long vowel sound.

dai-sy	lady	paper	student	tiger

✔ Divide these words into syllables. Listen for a long vowel.

la-zy	legal	David	police	locate
co-zy	odor	moment	climate	zebra
la-bel	protect	pupil	spider	music
ba-sin	lady	rider	cable	tulip
si-lent	nature	pilot	secret	hotel

✔ Do you remember that the suffix **-er** modifies or changes a word? The **-er** has the ***schwa*** plus **r** sound. Take off the **s** or **es** from the underlined word and add the suffix **er** as you print what each person does.

1. A person who paints is a painter.
2. A person who pitches is a ________.
3. A person who teaches is a ________.
4. A person who preaches is a ________.
5. A person who sings is a ________.
6. A person who farms is a ________.
7. A person who bakes is a ________.

eigh Usually Has the Long Vowel ✎ a Sound

The letters **eigh** make the long vowel sound of **a** as in **eight** (**8**).

✔ Print the correct **eigh** words in the blanks below.

eighteen	sleigh	eight	eighth	eighty
8	18	80	8th	

✔ Use these words to complete the following sentences.

weighed weightless neighbors freight neighs

1. Joe worked hard to move the ______________ from the truck.
2. Each box ______________ many pounds.
3. When Nancy's horse ______________, she feeds him.
4. The Bible teaches us to love our ______________.
5. A feather is so light that it is almost ______________.

REMEMBER: When a word ends with a consonant and **y**, change the **y** to **i** when you need to add the suffixes **-er** and **-est** as in **easy** ⇒ **easi<u>er</u>** ⇒ **easi<u>est</u>**.

✔ Add the suffixes **-er** and **-est** to the following words.

pretty	prettier	prettiest
dirty		
shady		
sunny		
happy		
sandy		

Review of Digraphs ✎ kn wr

In the digraph **kn**, the ***k*** is silent as in know. In the digraph **wr**, the ***w*** is silent as in wrap.

✔ Print the correct words with the digraphs **kn** and **wr** under their pictures.

knob	wreath	knit	wrist	knot
knee	wren	knife	wrench	write

✔ Use the letters **eigh** to spell words that fit the meanings below. REMEMBER: **eigh** makes the long **a** sound.

1. It is the number that is one more than seven.
2. It is what we call someone who lives near us.
3. It is something to ride in as a horse pulls us.
4. It is the sound that horses make.
5. It is what trucks, trains, and airplanes carry.
6. It is the answer to forty plus forty. 40 +40 ?

✔ Where do these words belong?

beard	earth	shears	pearls	pear

Review Lesson of Soft ✎ g Words

When **g** is followed by **e**, **i**, or **y**, the **g** usually has the ***soft*** sound of **j** as in **cage**, **giant**, and **gym**. Some exceptions to this rule are as follows: **get**, **gift**, and **give**.

✔ Print the correct words with the ***soft*** sound of **g** under their pictures.

cage	pledge	orange	bridge	pigeon
wedge	giraffe	engine	badge	hinge

✔ Choose the correct words to complete the following sentences. Print them in the blanks below.

Judge	danger	village	manger	Egypt

1. Jesus Christ was born in the little ______ of Bethlehem.
2. Mary laid Him in a ______ because there was no bed.
3. Jesus was in ______ of being killed by evil King Herod.
4. God told Joseph to take Him to safety in ______.
5. Jesus Christ is our Creator, Saviour, King, and ______.

A vowel before the letters **dge** usually has the ***short*** sound as in **bridge** and **wedge**.
A vowel before the letters **ge** or **nge** usually has the ***long*** sound as in **cage** and **manger**.

✔ Print the ***first*** vowel on the line and mark it to show if it has a ***short*** or ***long*** sound.

age $\bar{a}$	badge ___	stage ___	budge ___	dodge ___
danger $\bar{a}$	ridge ___	huge ___	page ___	angel ___

Making Plural Words Ending in ✎ f or fe

When a word ends in **f** or **fe**, change the **f** or **fe** to **v** and add the suffix **-es** to make the word ***plural*** as in **calf** ⇒ **calves** and **knife** ⇒ **knives**. Two exceptions are as follows: **belief** ⇒ **beliefs** and **chief** ⇒ **chiefs**.

✔ Use the RULE above to make the following **f** and **fe** words ***plural***, except for **chief**.

leaf leaves wife

calf scarf loaf

wolf half knife

shelf chief life

✔ Print the singular ***root*** words for these ***plural*** words.

wolves wolf thieves knives

lives shelves leaves

loaves calves wives

Do you remember? Often we just add an **-s** to make words ***plural***.
1. If a word ends with **y** and a vowel is right before it, just add **-s** as in **boys** and **monkeys**.
2. Change the **y** to **i** and add **-es** when the **y** comes after a consonant as in **babies** and **ladies**.
3. If a word ends with **s**, **x**, **z**, **sh**, or **ch**, add **-es** as in **buses**, **boxes**, **buzzes**, **dishes**, and **lunches**.

✔ Make the following words ***plural***.

valley valleys turkey

fly box church

brush bench tax

pencil dress pony

city beach lily

joy lady ranch

splash table ax

The Apostrophe ✎ ’ For Possession

The little mark called the ***apostrophe*** (’) is used in two ways. The first way is as follows:
Rule 1: To show that someone or something owns or possesses something, usually an ***apostrophe*** and an **s** (**’s**) are added to the end of the word. (**Rule 2**, concerning contractions, is covered in a later lesson.)

the cat’s dish the lady’s purse the man’s hat a friend’s home Dan’s car

✔ Add an ***apostrophe*** and an **s** (**’s**) to show possession or ownership.

jacket of Luke	Luke’s jacket	dog of John	
coat of Anna		shoe of Jay	
book of Greg		dress of Ruth	
doll of Jessica		truck of Ben	
desk of Levy		Bible of Paul	

✔ Add an ***apostrophe*** and an **s** (**’s**) to show possession or ownership as you complete these sentences.

1. Grace gave Janelle a pencil, so it is Janelle’s pencil.
2. If Connel owns a sailboat, it is ____________.
3. Her father gave Kelsey a gift, so it is ____________.
4. Eric was given a rabbit, so it is ____________.
5. Because God created our world, it is ____________.
6. If a pen belongs to Mr. Sherman, it is ____________.
7. Hannah owns a scissors, so it is ____________.

✔ Make these words ***plural*** by changing the **f** or **fe** to **v** and adding **-es**, except for **belief**.

leaf	leaves	wolf		scarf		half	
life		shelf		knife		thief	
calf		loaf		belief		wife	

Syllables ✎ Rules Six and Seven

Rule Six: When a ***single*** consonant comes between ***two*** vowels, the word is usually divided after the consonant if the first vowel sound is ***short*** as in **cab´ in**, **heav´ en**, and **moth´ er**.
The short vowel needs a consonant.

Rule Seven: When a ***single*** consonant comes between ***two*** vowels, the word is usually divided before the consonant if the first vowel sound is ***long*** as in **mu´ sic**, **ze´ bra**, and **co´ zy**.
The long vowel can stand alone.

✔ Divide these words according to the RULES above.

finish	fin–ish	heavy			
robin		cover		tiger	
radish		metal		tulip	
cabin		legal		pony	
chapel		story		label	
wagon		paper		cozy	
river		lazy		motor	

✔ Think carefully of the RULES as you listen to the first vowels, and then divide the words.

7

lady	la–dy	seven			
travel		legal		zebra	
metal		river		model	

✔ Do you remember how to use an ***apostrophe*** and **s**? The **cap** that belongs to **Sam** is written: **Sam's cap**.

1. When William eats an apple, it is ______.
2. If a kangaroo has food, it is the ______.
3. If a squirrel found a nut, it is the ______.
4. Tom got a letter in the mail, so it is ______.

The Apostrophe ✎ ' With Contractions

A ***contraction*** is a short way of writing two words. They are written together, but ***one or more*** letters are left out. This lesson gives the second way in which the ***apostrophe*** is used.
RULE 2: An ***apostrophe*** is used to replace the missing letters. Usually the first word is not changed.

do not ⇒ don't they will ⇒ they'll he is ⇒ he's you are ⇒ you're

✔ Write these words as ***contractions***. Take out the underlined letters as in **do not ⇒ don't**.

do not	don't	he will	______	he is	______
has not	______	she will	______	she is	______
have not	______	we will	______	it is	______
should not	______	they will	______	here is	______
were not	______	it will	______	we are	______
was not	______	you will	______	they are	______

✔ Write the words below the blanks as ***contractions***. Take out the underlined letters as in **is not ⇒ isn't**.

1. Jim ______ (was not) in school today, because he ______ (did not) feel well.
2. Jesse ______ (could not) reach the top shelf; he ______ (is not) tall enough.
3. ______ (We will) go to lunch as soon as ______ (we are) finished with math.
4. Angela ______ (is not) sure that ______ (she will) be able to eat all her pizza.

✔ See how nicely you can draw pictures of these words ending with **le**.

turtle	candle	bubbles	table	apple

The Sound of **z** Made by ✎ **s**

Sometimes an **s** can sound like a **z** as in **rose** and **teams**.

✔ Print **s** or **z** on the lines to show the sound made by the **s**.

mouse	s	peels		gates		needless	
obeys		six		has		wheels	
horse		arise		nose		rains	

Apostrophe* Rule 1:** To show that someone or something owns or possesses something, usually an ***apostrophe and an **s** (**'s**) are added to the end of the word as in **Charles Spurgeon's son**.

✔ Add **'s** to the underlined words to show ownership, and print the phrases to complete the sentences.

1. The white hat on Naomi is Naomi's hat.
2. The bow on the bear is the ________.
3. The dress on the bunny is the ________.
4. The sail on the boat is the ________.
5. The shirt belongs to Jay; it is ________.
6. The pen belongs to Jill; it is ________.

Apostrophe* Rule 2:** An ***apostrophe is put in the place of the missing letters which are removed when forming a ***contraction***. Usually the first word is not changed.
Contractions can also be written with the word **have** as in **we have ⇒ we've**.

✔ Print these words as ***contractions*** by taking out the underlined letters and adding an ***apostrophe***.

we have	we've	has not		you have	
would not		they have		let us	
we are		she is		he is	
they are		should not		could not	

✎ More Plural Forms of Words

Some words form their ***plurals*** in an unusual way as in **ox** ⇒ **oxen** and **mouse** ⇒ **mice**.

✔ Print these ***plural*** words where they belong. Use these words to complete the sentences below.

feet children women teeth men geese

tooth ______ foot ______ woman ______

child ______ man ______ goose ______

1. As the ______ smiled, their missing ______ showed.
2. The ______ screamed when they saw the two mice.
3. The ______ chased the two noisy ______ into the barn.
4. The baby's ______ were perfectly formed by our Creator.

REMEMBER the following RULES for making words ***plural***:

1. To make many words ***plural***, just add **-s** as in ***cats***.
2. To make words ***plural*** that end with **sh**, **ch**, **s**, **x**, or **z**, add **-es** as in **dishes**.
3. To make words ***plural*** that end with **y** follow the next two RULES:
   - **a.** Add **-s** if **y** comes after a vowel as in **boys**.
   - **b.** Change the **y** to **i**, and add **-es**, if y comes after a consonant as in **city** ⇒ **cities**.

✔ Think of the RULES above as you make these words plural.

peach peaches toy ______ turkey ______

frog ______ box ______ fly ______

sky ______ jacket ______ injury ______

girl ______ tax ______ valley ______

tray ______ waltz ______ watch ______

glass ______ bush ______ ash ______

patch ______ berry ______ ax ______

✎ Review of Plural Words

When a word ends in **f** or **fe**, change the **f** or **fe** to **v** and add the suffix **-es** to make the word ***plural*** as in **calf** ⇒ **calves** and **knife** ⇒ **knives**. Two exceptions are: **belief** ⇒ **beliefs** and **chief** ⇒ **chiefs**.

✔ Think of the above RULES as you make these words plural.

belief	beliefs	scarf		wolf	
calf	calves	half		knife	
life		loaf		leaf	
thief		chief		shelf	

REMEMBER the following RULES for making words ***plural***:

1. To make many words ***plural***, just add **-s** as in ***cats***.
2. To make words ***plural*** that end with **sh**, **ch**, **s**, **x**, or **z**, add **-es** as in **dishes**.
3. To make words ***plural*** that end with **y** follow the next two RULES:
 a. Add **-s** if **y** comes after a vowel as in **boys**.
 b. Change the **y** to **i**, and add **-es**, if y comes after a consonant as in **city** ⇒ **cities**.

✔ Think of the above RULES as you make these words plural.

church	churches	table		brush	
fox		dress		boy	
turkey		lunch		fly	
match		box		city	
girl		cherry		valley	
tray		track		tax	

A few words become ***plural*** in special ways as in **man** ⇒ **men**.

✔ Match the following words to their unusual ***plurals***.

man	women	child	mice	goose	workmen
tooth	teeth	mouse	feet	ox	geese
woman	men	foot	children	workman	oxen

✎ Rule Eight for Dividing Words

Rule Eight: If a vowel is sounded alone in a word, it forms a syllable by itself as in **a´ rose** and **o´ bey**.

✔ Listen to your voice as you read these words. Think about RULE EIGHT as you divide them.

animal an–i–mal

alarm

open

about

ocean

uniform

unit

agree

catalog

away

imitate

alike

melody

above

obey

idol

✔ How should you divide these long words? Here is an example: **man-u-fac-ture**.

magazine mag–a–zine

gasoline

electric

telephone

eternal

education

✔ Use the words in the list below to complete the following sentences.

amuse apart ashore avoid among anoint

1. The Pilgrims came ______ to America thanking God.
2. The few toys ______ their things did ______ them.
3. Each Sunday is set ______ to worship the Lord.
4. We should ______ making friends with naughty children.
5. God told Samuel to ______ David as king of Israel.

✎ Rule Nine for Dividing Words

RULE NINE: When ***two*** vowels come together and are sounded separately, divide the word between the two vowels as in **po´ et, ri´ ot**, and **pi-a´ no**.

✔ Listen to your voice as you read these words. Think of RULE NINE as you divide them.

violin	vi–o–lin			trial	
poem				annual	
giant		radio		diaper	
idea		rodeo		quiet	
ruin		violet		science	
lion		ideal		create	
cruel		real		usual	

✔ Carefully divide these long words. Use the underlined words to complete the following sentences.

creation	cre–a–tion	warrior	
radiator		period	
guardian		graduate	
pioneer			

1. Terry's school has one ________ for studying the Bible.
2. The ________ helped to make our room warm and cozy.
3. Joshua was a godly, brave ________ for the Lord.
4. In seven years, you should ________ from eighth grade.
5. Did you realize that a ________ lived a dangerous life?

✎ Final Review of Rules for Dividing Words

Rule One: A one-syllable word must never be divided. Print the words under the correct pictures.

point	wash	mouse	heart	cross

Rule Two: Divide a ***compound*** word between the words that make the ***compound*** word.

dish–pan	dollhouse	snowflake	doorman
tip–toe	sunshine	birthday	anything

Rule Three: When a word has a **suffix** that makes a vowel sound, divide the word between the ***root*** word and the **suffix**.

quickly	quick–ly	smallest		hopeful	
kinder		fearless		rested	
walking		softest		taller	

Rule Four: When a word has a **prefix**, divide the word between the **prefix** and the ***root*** word.

preview	pre–view	rejoice		unfair	
mislead		forecast		depart	
distrust		express		rebuild	

Rule Five: When ***two or more*** consonants come between ***two*** vowels, the word is usually divided between the first two consonants.

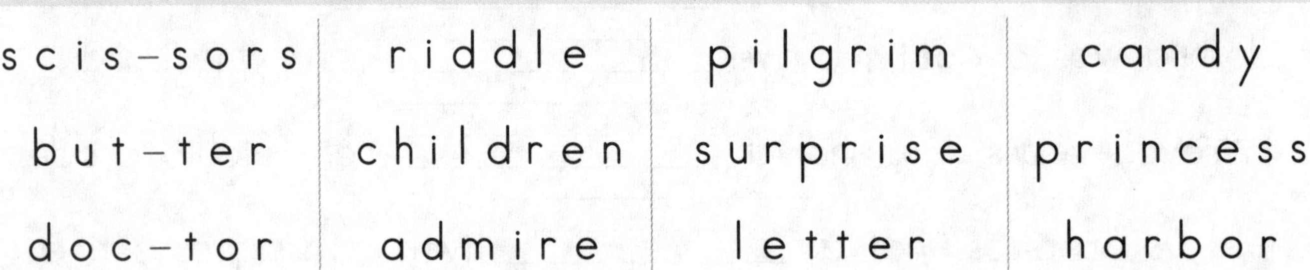

scis–sors	riddle	pilgrim	candy
but–ter	children	surprise	princess
doc–tor	admire	letter	harbor

Final Review of Rules for Dividing Words

Rule Six: When a ***singular*** consonant comes between ***two*** vowels, the word is usually divided <u>after the consonant</u> if the first vowel sound is **short** as in **cab´ in**. Divide the words and print them under the correct pictures.

liz–ard	present	cabin	seven	city

Rule Seven: When a ***singular*** consonant comes between ***two*** vowels, the word is usually divided <u>before the consonant</u> if the first vowel sound is ***long*** as in **co´ zy**. Divide the words and print them under the correct pictures.

stu–dent	lady	zebra	tulips	tiger

Rule Eight: When a vowel is sounded alone in a word, it forms a syllable by itself as in **o-bey**.

o–bey	idol	unit	ocean	animal
o–pen	alike	ago	awake	arose

Rule Nine: When ***two*** vowels come together and are sounded separately, divide the word between the two vowels as in **gi´ ant**, **po´ et**, and **di´ et**.

di–al	cruel	diet	giant	radio
li–on	ruin	poem	quiet	fluid

Rule Ten: **a.** If a word ends in **le**, the consonant before the **le** is usually part of the last syllable as in **rat´ tle**. **b.** If a word ends in **ckle**, the **ck** stays with the short vowel in the first syllable, and the **le** stands alone as in **pick´ le**, **tack´ le**, and **freck´ le**.

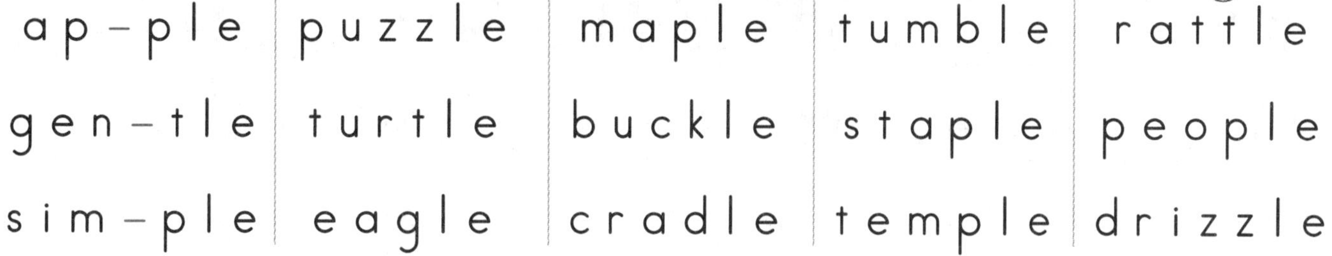

ap–ple	puzzle	maple	tumble	rattle
gen–tle	turtle	buckle	staple	people
sim–ple	eagle	cradle	temple	drizzle

✎ Synonyms

Synonyms are words that have the ***same or similar*** meaning as in **small** ⇒ **little** and **happy** ⇒ **glad**.

✔ Match the following **synonyms**.

thankful	close	raise	home	woods	ships
happy	gift	stay	still	close	forest
fix	glad	told	lift	pretty	near
near	grateful	quiet	remain	funny	comical
present	repair	house	spoke	boats	beautiful

✔ Use the words above as you print **synonyms** of the words that are underlined in the sentences below.

1. The Bible class gave a gift or ____________ to the missionary.
2. He was very grateful or ____________ for their thoughtfulness.
3. He did not remain or ____________ here very long.
4. The missionary left his house or ____________ to go overseas.
5. God sent him to preach near or ____________ to a small village.
6. He told or ____________ about how Jesus died for our sins.

✔ Choose the correct **synonyms** from the following box and print the words in the blanks below.

shout	skip	fowl	village	tired
insects	lad	woman	pal	rabbit

lady ____________

friend ____________

bugs ____________

boy ____________

town ____________

sleepy ____________

yell ____________

hop ____________

hare ____________

bird ____________

Synonyms

Synonyms are words that have the ***same or similar*** meaning as in **quick** ⇒ **fast** and **speak** ⇒ **talk**.

✔ Match the following **synonyms**.

fall	little	glisten	shop	crawl	fast
fall	even	postman	sparkle	child	infant
small	autumn	strike	unhappy	fearful	inform
level	tiny	store	hit	report	creep
small	drop	sad	mailman	swift	afraid

✔ Use the words above as you print **synonyms** of the words that are underlined in the sentences below.

1. The happy child or ______ likes to crawl or ______.
2. In the fall or ______ the leaves drop or ______.
3. Wag barks if the mailman or ______ knocks on our door.
4. Tim bought a small or ______ ball at the shop or ______.
5. Our family likes to look at the stars glisten or ______.
6. We are not fearful or ______ because God cares for us.

✔ Choose the correct **synonyms** from the following box and print the words in the blanks below.

shut	injure	large	trip	polite
happy	pretty	silly	wonderful	listen

glad ______

beautiful ______

huge ______

courteous ______

journey ______

hear ______

great ______

hurt ______

close ______

funny ______

✎ Antonyms

Antonyms are words that have the ***opposite or almost opposite*** meaning as in **up ⇒ down**.

✔ Match the following **antonyms**.

strong	absent	many	thin	bright	spend
happy	far	loose	dry	cool	dull
repair	weak	wet	few	large	warm
near	break	thick	dark	sick	small
present	sad	light	tight	save	well

✔ Use the words above as you print **antonyms** of the words that are underlined in the sentences below.

1. The sad little lady did not feel ________.
2. The pipe had a break, so the man had to ________ it.
3. His sickness made the strong boy feel ________.
4. Carol hung the wet sheets in the sun so now they are ________.
5. Tim will not spend all of his money, but will ________ some of it.
6. Cal's new shoes were tight, but now they are ________.

✔ Choose the correct **antonyms** from the following box and print the words in the blanks below.

hot	light	build	open	long
many	fat	over	speak	love

heavy	________			hate	________
close	________			listen	________
short	________	destroy	________	few	________
thin	________	under	________	cold	________

✎ Antonyms

Antonyms are words that have the ***opposite or almost opposite*** meaning as in **day** ⇒ **night**.

✔ Match the following **antonyms**.

asleep	enemy	young	quiet	sharp	cold
slow	soft	noisy	go	hot	wrong
friend	awake	win	old	full	slowly
hard	under	come	difficult	swiftly	dull
over	fast	easy	lose	right	empty

✔ Use the words above as you print **antonyms** of the words that are underlined in the sentences below.

1. On hot days it is nice to have a ________ drink of juice.
2. As Al turned off the noisy music, the room became ________.
3. The full bowl of popcorn soon became ________.
4. Jon said the test was difficult, but Bill said it was ________.
5. The sharp knife became ________ when it was used to cut wood.
6. A fawn leaped over the fence and a rabbit ran ________ it.

✔ Choose the correct **antonyms** from the following box and print the words in the blanks below.

unkind	sadly	thankful	displeased	harmless
careful	disobey	unwilling	swiftly	hopeful

pleased ________

obey ________

gladly ________

kind ________

thankless ________

careless ________

slowly ________

harmful ________

willing ________

hopeless ________

✎ Review of Synonyms and Antonyms

Synonyms are words that have the ***same or similar*** meaning as in **small ⇒ little**.
Antonyms are words that have the ***opposite or almost opposite*** meaning as in **up ⇒ down**.

✔ In the blanks between the words, print an **S** if the words are **synonyms**, words that have the ***same*** meaning, or print an **A** if the words are **antonyms**, words that have the ***opposite*** meaning.

good	A	bad	foolish		wise	report		tell
quiet	S	still	big		large	hate		love
inside		outside	joy		sadness	high		low
tall		short	idea		plan	in		out
over		under	quick		swift	go		leave
rush		hurry	hot		cold	sick		ill
under		below	protect		guard	happy		unhappy
shut		close	up		down	kind		mean

✔ Complete these sentences with these **synonyms** and **antonyms**.

wise beautiful outside kindly ascend sparkle

1. If you are not inside your home, you are ________ of it.
2. The pretty dress looked ________ on the little girl.
3. The stars look like they glisten or ________ in the sky.
4. The way of a fool seems right to him, but a ________ man listens to advice. (see Proverbs 12:15)
5. We should not speak evil but ________ toward others.
6. Andy likes to watch planes climb or ________ into the sky.

✎ Homonyms

Homonyms are words that ***sound alike***, but have ***different*** meanings and spellings as in **deer** ⇒ **dear**.

✔ Match the following **homonyms**.

1. maid	___ sent	1. weak	___ won	1. bee	___ seam
2. blew	___ rode	2. through	___ beet	2. meet	___ would
3. cent	1 made	3. one	___ week	3. seem	___ do
4. road	___ write	4. eight	___ threw	4. dew	___ be
5. right	___ blue	5. beat	___ ate	5. wood	___ meat

✔ Choose the correct **homonym** from the box at the right to complete each of the following sentences.

1. Al helped his mother ________ apples for a pie.
2. The wind ________ some sand into our faces.
3. Some sand got into Tim's left ________.
4. Bill's ________ has gone up ten pounds.
5. Bob hiked to the ________ of the mountain.
6. His ________ got red from the sunshine.
7. He was happy as he ________ down in a car.

peal	peel
blue	blew
I	eye
wait	weight
peak	peek
nose	knows
road	rode

✔ Match the following **homonyms**.

1. our	___ read	1. or	___ wrap	1. pain	___ lead
2. red	___ flour	2. ring	___ knot	2. led	___ sale
3. fare	___ hour	3. rap	___ oar	3. feet	___ pane
4. flower	___ fair	4 not	___ wring	4. sail	___ feat

Three Sounds of Digraph ✎ ch

The digraph **ch** can make three sounds: **ch** as in **chair**, **k** as in **Christ**, and **sh** as in **chef**.

✔ Print the underlined **ch** words in the correct columns below: **ch** for the sound as in **check**, **k** for the sound as in **choir**, and **sh** for the sound as in **chef**.

1. The choir sang in church.
2. They sang praises to Christ.
3. The orchestra also played.
4. Cheryl has a new Bible.
5. The chef is a good cook.
6. The chiffon pie is sweet.
7. Timothy sat in a chair.
8. Ed likes chocolate ice cream.

ch	k	sh

✔ Choose the correct **ch** words from the list below to complete the following sentences.

chrysalis   Christian   champion   parachute

1. Stephen was the first ______ to be killed for his faith.
2. He was a ______ of the Christian faith.
3. The hard pupa of a butterfly is called a ______.
4. Would you be brave enough to jump with a ______?

✔ Correctly add the suffix **-ed** to these words. Think of the sound **-ed** makes and print it in the column.

tap	tapped	t	dip			pat		
pin			sob			rub		
pad			sin			beg		

Digraphs ✎ gh and ph

The digraphs **gh** and **ph** can make the sound of **f** as in **digraph**, **phrase**, **laugh**, and **tough**.

✔ Print the **gh** and **ph** words under their correct pictures.

telephone	cough	photo	dolphin	elephant

Review the following digraphs: **ch**, **sh**, **th**, **wh**, **kn**, **gn**, **wr**, **ph**, **gh**, and **ck**.

✔ Circle the **digraphs** in these words. Use the underlined words to complete the sentences below.

Christ	parachute	which	knock	chef
rough	telephone	shepherd	chocolate	Philip
birthday	thick	sign	church	champion
Phyllis	together	chorus	thermometer	whisper
tough	brother	sheep	knowledge	laugh

1. The Lord is the ____________ of his people.
2. The girls' ____________ sang about the birth of ____________.
3. Mom used a ____________ to see if I had a fever.
4. Grandpa called the twins ____________ and ____________.
5. They like to talk ____________ on the ____________.
6. The twins each got a big ____________ candy bar.
7. Charlie knows that it is wrong to ____________ in church.

Words Ending with ✎ -tion

The letters **tion** make the sound of ***shun*** as in **nation** and **vacation**.

✔ Add **-tion** to these words and read them. Use the underlined words to complete the sentences below.

afflic tion	elec	na	informa
frac	rela	mo	resurrec
inven	crea	auc	introduc
educa	vaca	cau	celebra
forma	injec	sta	circula

1. We praise the Lord for His wonderful ______.
2. The book had ______ on the ______ of radios.
3. We are praying for Al who has a serious ______.
4. In the spring we have a week's ______ as we have a ______ of Jesus Christ's ______.

A **syllable** is made up of ***one or more*** letters pronounced together as a ***single*** sound with a vowel. Each **syllable** has a vowel sound as in **strong´**, **neigh´ bor**, **in-ven´ tion**, **stee´ ple**, and **tel´ e-phone**.

✔ Write the number of syllables that are in these words. Listen and think as you say each word.

trust	1	invitation		forgiving		thoughtful	
scrubbing	2	slept		buckle		truthful	
spring		kind		battle		education	
telephone		knocked		careful		vacation	
splashed		warning		steeple		resurrection	

Words Ending with -sion

The letters -**sion** make the sound of ***shun*** or ***zhun*** as in **discussion** and **division**.

✔ Add -**sion** to these words and read them. Use the underlined words to complete the sentences below.

colli sion	admis ______	conclu ______	televi ______
discus ______	exclu ______	inva ______	confu ______
divi ______	revi ______	excur ______	fu ______

1. You have had many hours of talking or ______.
2. It is better to read a book than to watch ______.
3. Terry was glad that the story had a happy ______.
4. There was ______ as the children looked for their shoes.
5. We prayed for a friend who was in a car ______.
6. Children under ten paid no ______ to the fair.

Do you remember that sometimes digraphs **gh** and **ph** make the sound of **f as** in **laugh** and **telephone**? Do you also remember that the digraph **ch** makes three different sounds as in **chip**, **chef**, and **choir**?

✔ Use the words in the list below to complete the following sentences.

elephant　chauffeur　phonics　spinach　rough

1. A ______ came to take the bride to church.
2. God made something like a finger at the end of the trunk of an ______. Would it like to eat ______?
3. Philip enjoyed reading because he learned ______.
4. The hard-working farmer had very strong, ______ hands.

Review of Words with Sounds of ✎ o

You may remember that the vowel **o** makes several sounds? Here are three of them:
ô as in dôg, ŏ as in tŏp, and ō as in sōap.

✔ As you read these words, mark the **o** to show the correct sound that it makes. Use the underlined words to complete the following sentences.

côst	moss	cross	clock	frog
cōat	both	toe	toss	bow
shŏp	log	off	comb	hop
most	soft	gloss	long	hope
moth	home	wrong	flock	opened

1. Mrs. Hill went to the store to ________ for a ________ for Joan.
2. She bought a ________, red coat that had a ________ on it.
3. Mr. and Mrs. Hill came to Joan's ________ at six o'________.
4. After Joan ________ her gift, she hugged ________ of her grandparents as she thanked them.
5. She did not take ________ her coat until it was time for bed.

✔ Think before adding the suffix **-ed** to these words. When do you first have to change the **y** to **i**?

pray	prayed	study	________	stay	________
try	tried	hurry	________	carry	________
play	________	worry	________	enjoy	________
dry	________	cry	________	copy	________

✎ Review of the Apostrophe

The little mark called the **apostrophe** (') is used in two ways.
Rule 1: To show that someone or something ***owns or possesses*** something, an **apostrophe** and an **s** (**'s**) is added to the end of the word as in **the cat's dish**.

✔ Add **'s** to show possession or ownership.

ball of Dale Dale's ball dog of Connel

doll of Tara suit of Eric

truck of Calvin bed of baby

dress of Jane quilt of Mary

book of Jim rug of Kelsey

A **contraction** is a short way of writing two words. As they are written together, ***one or more*** letters are left out. Here is the second way in which the little mark called the **apostrophe** (') is used.
Rule 2: An **apostrophe** is put in the place of the missing letters. Usually the first word is not changed.

do not ⇒ don't **they will ⇒ they'll** **he is ⇒ he's** **you are ⇒ you're** **we have ⇒ we've**

✔ Take out the underlined letters. Add an **apostrophe** (') where the letters are removed: **let us ⇒ let's.**

we have we've they are has not

would not let us he is

we are have not they will

it will you have it is

she will here is we will

they have could not are not

should not she is he will

✔ Print the words that are in these **contractions**.

they've = here's = haven't =

✎ Synonyms, Antonyms, and Homonyms

Synonyms are words that have the ***same or similar*** meaning as in **small ⇒ little.**
Antonyms are words that have the ***opposite or almost opposite*** meanings as in **in ⇒ out**.
Homonyms are words that ***sound alike***, but have ***different*** meanings and spellings as in **be ⇒ bee.**

✔ In the blanks between the words, print an **S** if the words are **synonyms**, words that have the ***same*** meaning, print an **A** if the words are **antonyms**, words that have the ***opposite*** meanings, or print **H** if the words are **homonyms**, words that ***sound alike*** but have ***different*** meanings and spellings.

soft	A	rough	foolish	______	wise			
protect	S	guard	big	______	large			
weight	H	wait	tight	______	loose	repair	______	fix
careful	______	careless	blue	______	blew	present	______	absent
under	______	below	lost	______	found	through	______	threw
light	______	dark	sick	______	ill	strong	______	weak
rode	______	road	thought	______	idea	shut	______	open
go	______	leave	see	______	sea	quick	______	slow

✔ Complete these sentences with these **synonyms** and **antonyms**.

quickly Woods noisy building glistened journey

1. The boys enjoyed hiking in the forest called Butler ______________.
2. At times it was quiet, but sometimes it was quite ______________.
3. They went on a trip or ______________ through the forest.
4. A rabbit hopping slowly, suddenly went ______________ away.
5. They watched as a bird was making or ______________ its nest.
6. A little brook sparkled or ______________ as they hiked past it.

Words with Short Vowel Sound of ✎ u

The vowel **o** has the <u>short vowel</u> sound of **u** as in **mother**, **shovel**, and **dove**.

✔ Print these short vowel **o** words under the correct pictures.

glove	shovel	oven	money	dove

✔ Use these words to complete the following sentences.

month	done	come	mother	some
brother	other	son	loving	nothing

1. Victor and his younger ____________ have just ________ inside.
2. They have ________ their homework. What should they do now?
3. It is the ____________ of April so the weather is warm.
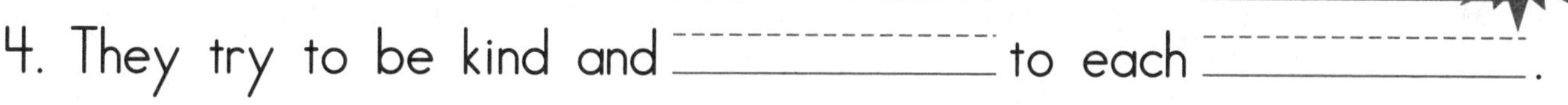
4. They try to be kind and ____________ to each ____________.
5. Their father and ________________ are so thankful for them.
6. Did you ever have a day when you had ____________ to do?
7. The older ________ has ____________ paper they will color.

The vowel **a** has the ***schwa*** sound or <u>short vowel</u> sound of **u** as in **ago** and **away**.

✔ Divide these words. How quickly can you read them? Put the accent mark after the last syllable.

a–rose′	asleep	abide	ashore	adorn
a–like′	anoint	aloud	agree	anew
a–wait′	about	again	awhile	ahead

✎ Words in Alphabetical Order

Do you know what the word ***raiment*** means? How would you use a ***tambourine***?
A good place to look for answers is in a **dictionary**. The words are arranged in alphabetical order, so they are easily found. You can learn about many words as you study a **dictionary**.

a b c d e f g h i j k l m n o p q r s t u v w x y z

These words are written in **alphabetical order**. The word beginning with **a** is written first.

apple basket cross deer envelope fish gift

If you do not have words that begin with each letter, just skip the letter and go to the next word.

boat desk elephant flake heart seal tools

✔ Number these papers in **alphabetical order**. REMEMBER: Skip letters that are not used.

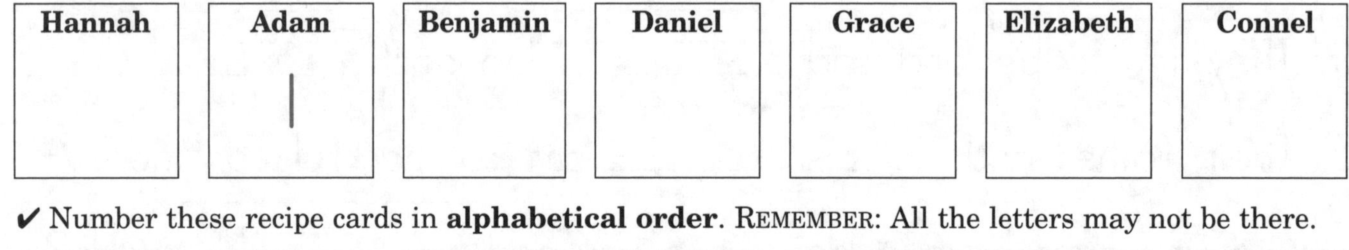

Hannah	Adam	Benjamin	Daniel	Grace	Elizabeth	Connel
	1					

✔ Number these recipe cards in **alphabetical order**. REMEMBER: All the letters may not be there.

breads	vegetables	desserts	cookies	appetizers	meats	salads
				1		

✔ Put these words in **alphabetical order**. Think about the alphabet. You may look up at the top.

wagon ______
swing ______
bicycle ______
helmet ______

chicken ______
salad ______
apples ______
carrots ______

Let's have a picnic!

✎ Words in Alphabetical Order

A Christian man named **Noah Webster** was the first American to produce a good **dictionary**. It was printed in 1828. He worked very hard and spent a great deal of time to organize this important book. It is such a helpful book for us, so we need to learn how to use it properly.

a b c d e f g h i j k l m n o p q r s t u v w x y z

✔ Think of the alphabet; look at the first letter of each word. Put the words in **alphabetical order**.

jet		rabbit	
boat		kangaroo	
helicopter		panda	
cab		squirrel	
train		giraffe	

Some words begin with the same letter, such as **Connel** and **Calvin**. We then need to look at the ***second*** letter to see which word should come ***first*** in the dictionary: **Connel** or **Calvin**? The letter **a** comes before **o**. The name **Calvin** would come before **Connel** in a dictionary.

✔ Think about the ***second*** letter as you alphabetize these names that begin with the same letter.

Doris	2	Samuel		Bobby		Timmy		Anna	
Danny	1	Susan		Billy		Tommy		Alex	

✔ Carefully alphabetize all the words in both lists. NOTE: Some of them begin with the same letter.

feet		head	
hands		soul	
legs		eyes	
arms		mouth	
heart		ears	

I will praise Thee; for I am fearfully and wonderfully made.... Psalms 139:14

The Short Vowel Rule

Short Vowel Rule: When there is ***one*** vowel in a word, either at the beginning or between two consonants, it usually has the short vowel sound.

1. Short vowel a words

ax	pan	tag	tap	cat	bad
tax	ran	wag	am	bat	dad
wax	tan	cap	ham	hat	had
can	van	lap	jam	pat	lad
fan	gas	map	as	rat	mad
man	bag	nap	has	sat	pad

2. Short vowel a words with consonant blends

glass	and	brand	snap	stamp	drag
grass	band	grand	trap	tramp	glad
class	hand	stand	camp	lamb	ant
bass	land	clap	damp	brag	pant
pass	sand	slap	lamp	flag	plant

3. Short vowel e words

egg	hell	pet	tent	hen	smell
leg	well	set	went	men	tell
bed	web	wet	bent	pen	nest
red	jet	bless	rent	ten	rest
bell	met	dress	spent	step	test
fell	net	press	stem	spell	vest

The Short Vowel Rule

Short Vowel Rule: When there is ***one*** vowel in a word, either at the beginning or between two consonants, it usually has the short vowel sound.

4. Short vowel i words

big	dip	tin	fib	sit	hill
dig	hip	win	rib	bit	pill
fig	lip	did	crib	fit	milk
jig	tip	hid	fist	hit	dim
pig	pin	lid	list	pit	him
wig	sin	bib	mitt	dill	swim

5. Short vowel o words

God	hop	stop	pot	fox	bond
nod	mop	cot	rot	mom	pond
pod	pop	dot	spot	cob	clock
rod	top	hot	ox	rob	lock
sod	drop	not	box	sob	sock

6. Short vowel u words

fun	but	cuff	bug	tug	bus
gun	cut	muff	dug	cub	bump
run	hut	puff	hug	tub	dump
sun	nut	yum	jug	cup	hump
bud	fuzz	gum	mug	pup	jump
mud	buzz	gull	rug	us	pump

Words Ending with ck and Consonant Digraphs

If short vowel words end with the sound of ***k***, it is usually spelled with **ck**.
A consonant digraph has ***two*** consonants that make ***one*** sound.

7. Short vowel words that end in ck

back	lock	knock	pluck	quack	brick
jack	rock	stock	cluck	snack	quick
pack	sock	smock	lick	track	stick
sack	block	buck	pick	neck	trick
tack	clock	duck	sick	wreck	tuck
dock	flock	puck	black	speck	truck

8. Words with consonant digraphs (sh and ch)

shack	shop	hash	brush	chick	such
shed	shot	rash	rush	chin	bench
shell	shut	crash	chap	chip	inch
shelf	ash	flash	check	chop	pinch
ship	cash	smash	chess	rich	lunch
shock	dash	mesh	ranch	much	bunch

9. More words with consonant digraphs (th and wh)

that	they	bath	thumb	when	whiskers
than	mother	thank	thump	which	whale
them	father	think	math	whim	wheel
then	brother	thick	path	whip	white
the	gather	thin	with	whisper	wheat

The Long Vowel Rule (1)

Long Vowel Rule (1): When a word has ***two*** vowels, usually the ***first*** vowel says its name and the ***second*** vowel is silent.

10. Long vowel a words

rail	came	wave	rake	paint	way
sail	game	save	take	day	gray
tail	name	bake	wake	may	tray
mail	same	cake	flake	pay	play
nail	mane	lake	quake	pray	stay
pail	vane	make	shake	say	stray

11. More long vowel a words

gain	brain	tape	rate	grade	wait
main	grain	ate	date	pale	bait
pain	train	hate	gate	sale	hay
rain	ape	late	made	tale	lay
vain	cape	mate	fade	whale	clay

12. Long vowel e words

sea	weak	sheep	ear	bee	feel
tea	deep	steep	dear	fee	heel
flea	peep	sweep	fear	wee	peel
plea	weep	heap	hear	tree	beef
key	creep	leap	near	free	meek
beak	sleep	reap	deer	three	seek

The Long Vowel Rule (1)

Long Vowel Rule (1): When a word has ***two*** vowels, usually the ***first*** vowel says its name and the ***second*** vowel is silent.

13. More long vowel e words

beet	reach	feed	steam	wheat	seal
feet	teach	need	beam	treat	veal
meet	green	weed	meat	deal	zeal
greet	screen	seem	heat	heal	steal
beach	bean	seam	beat	meal	seen
peach	mean	team	seat	real	teen

14. Long vowel i words

bite	prize	fine	wine	pie	tide
kite	wipe	line	shine	tie	wide
quite	pipe	mine	thine	hide	bride
white	ripe	pine	twine	ride	pride
size	dine	vine	die	side	wire

15. More long vowel i words

dime	hive	mile	my	bike	why
lime	nice	pile	cry	like	fire
time	price	tile	dry	hike	hire
chime	rice	smile	fly	shy	tire
dive	slice	while	fry	sky	rise
five	file	by	try	spy	wise

The Long Vowel Rule (1) and Exceptions

Long Vowel Rule (1): When a word has ***two*** vowels, usually the ***first*** vowel says its name and the ***second*** vowel is silent.

16. Long vowel o words

note	goat	hope	load	home	low
vote	bone	rope	toad	joke	mow
quote	cone	rode	hole	poke	row
wrote	lone	foam	pole	woke	tow
boat	tone	roam	stole	yoke	oak
coat	zone	road	dome	bow	soak

17. More long vowel o words

boast	spoke	glow	snow	rose	hoe
roast	smoke	grow	throw	close	toe
toast	blow	know	hose	chose	globe
dove	crow	show	nose	soap	scone
stove	flow	slow	pose	groan	stone

18. Exceptions: o words that make the sound of the short vowel u

done	shove	honey	hovel	wonder	flood
none	oven	money	shovel	month	govern
dove	does	other	cover	Monday	son
love	color	mother	hover	nothing	ton
glove	come	brother	from	tongue	won
above	some	another	front	blood	of

The Long Vowel Rules (1-3)

Long Vowel Rule (1): When a word has ***two*** vowels, usually the ***first*** vowel says its name and the ***second*** vowel is silent.

19. Long vowel u words

suit	June	true	new	chew	flew
fruit	tune	use	pew	drew	slew
juice	prune	fuse	crew	grew	stew
cute	blue	dew	knew	screw	mew
flute	clue	few	mule	threw	cube
dune	glue	hew	rule	blew	tube

Long Vowel Rule (2): If a word has ***one*** vowel and it comes at the end of the word, that word usually has a long vowel sound.

20. Long vowel words that follow Rule 2

he	we	why	lo	yo-yo	**Exceptions:**
me	by	go	no	be	do
she	my	so	so	hi	to

Long Vowel Rule (3): The vowels **i** and **o** usually have the long vowel sound when followed by two or more consonants.

21. Long vowel i words that follow Rule 3

child	find	blind	high	light	bright
mild	kind	grind	nigh	might	blight
wild	mind	remind	sigh	night	flight
bind	rind	behind	sign	right	fright
hind	wind	delight	fight	sight	slight

The Long Vowel Rule (3) and Diphthongs

Long Vowel Rule (3): The vowels **i** and **o** usually have the long vowel sound when followed by two or more consonants. A diphthong is ***two*** vowel sounds in ***one*** syllable.

22. Long vowel o words that follow Rule 3

old	hold	host	toll	colt	folk
bold	mold	most	knoll	dolt	both
cold	sold	post	scroll	jolt	scold
fold	told	poll	stroll	molt	polka
gold	wold	roll	bolt	volt	stollen

23. Words with diphthongs ow and ou

cow	owl	our	out	scout	plow
bow	fowl	hour	pout	shout	allow
how	growl	sour	route	snout	ouch
now	howl	flour	about	sprout	couch
pow	towel	loud	clout	mouth	pouch
sow	vowel	proud	doubt	south	crowd

24. More words with diphthongs ow and ou

cower	grouse	mound	count	crown	county
tower	house	pound	ounce	frown	flounder
power	mouse	round	bounce	down	powder
flower	bound	sound	pounce	gown	fountain
shower	found	ground	brown	town	mountain
blouse	hound	amount	clown	noun	thousand

Diphthongs and **Vowel Digraphs**

A diphthong is ***two*** vowel sounds in ***one*** syllable. The diphthongs **oi** and **oy** make the **oi** sound **as** in **oil**. A vowel digraph has ***two*** vowels that make ***one*** sound. The digraph **oo** makes the sound of **oo** as in **zoo**.

25. Words with diphthongs oi and oy

oil	broil	voice	poise	coin	loyal
boil	spoil	choice	poison	join	loyalty
coil	joint	foist	boy	ploy	royal
foil	point	hoist	coy	employ	royalty
soil	void	moist	joy	enjoy	recoil
toil	avoid	noise	toy	destroy	rejoin

26. Words with the vowel digraph oo as in zoo

loom	room	scoop	goose	boot	toot
boom	coop	scoot	loose	root	doodle
bloom	goop	stoop	moose	hoot	noodle
broom	hoop	snoop	noose	loot	poodle
groom	loop	caboose	choose	shoot	pooch

27. More words with the vowel digraph oo as in zoo

boo	loon	roost	spool	zoo	smooth
goo	moon	rooster	stool	roof	food
too	noon	tool	school	hoof	mood
boon	soon	fool	goober	proof	baboon
coon	spoon	cool	goofy	booth	balloon
goon	boost	pool	moo	tooth	buffoon

Vowel Digraphs and Modified Vowels: är Words

A vowel digraph has ***two*** vowels that make ***one*** sound. The digraph **oo** makes the sound of **oo** as in **look**.

28. Words with digraph oo as in book; o, u, and ou also can say oo

book	brook	stood	foot	wolf	bull
cook	crook	wood	soot	wolves	full
hook	shook	wooden	booklet	put	pull
look	cookie	woody	brooklet	bush	could
nook	good	wool	unhook	push	would
took	hood	woolen	lookout	cushion	should

When the consonant **r** comes after the vowel **a**, it changes the sound of the vowel as in **ark**.
The **ar** sound may be marked with two dots over the **a** like this: **ärk**.

29. Modified vowel är words

bar	par	bark	park	farmer	harp
car	tar	dark	shark	harm	sharp
far	spar	hark	spark	charm	large
jar	star	lark	arm	alarm	barge
mar	ark	mark	farm	carp	charge

30. More modified vowel är words

barb	guard	art	tart	march	harness
barber	hard	cart	chart	market	harvest
barley	yard	dart	start	garden	pardon
bard	barn	mart	arch	hardly	regard
card	yarn	part	parch	harbor	sparkle

Modified Vowels: ôr and er Words

When the consonant **r** comes after the vowel **o** or **e**, it changes the sound of the vowel as in **for** and **herd**. The **or** sound is marked like this: **côrn**. The **er** sound is a combination of the ***schwa*** (ə) and **r** sounds.

31. Modified vowel ôr words

Lord	corn	port	cork	torch	order
cord	horn	sort	fork	core	score
ford	torn	short	pork	more	snore
door	worn	sport	horse	sore	store
floor	thorn	storm	force	tore	shore
born	fort	north	porch	wore	stork

32. Modified vowel er words (er and ir)

herd	sister	germ	sir	bird	skirt
fern	verse	term	fir	dirt	circle
father	serve	derby	stir	third	circus
mother	person	cracker	girl	firm	thirsty
brother	eternal	pitcher	first	shirt	birthday

33. More modified vowel er words (ur, ear, and wor)

church	curb	injure	earn	worship	worst
fur	curl	turtle	learn	word	worth
nurse	hurt	hurry	earth	world	worthy
purse	burst	sure	early	worldly	work
burn	curtain	furniture	heard	worm	worker
turn	purple	turkey	pearl	worse	worry

Modified Vowels: âre Words and ô Words

You have learned the sound of **är** as in **arm**. These letters also make the sound of **are** as in **squâre**. The vowel **o** makes different sounds and one of them is the sound of **ô** as in **dôg**.

34. Modified âre words (are, arr, air, ear, eir, ere, err, and wor)

bare	aware	air	berry	tear	parrot
care	blare	fair	ferry	wear	barrel
dare	flare	hair	merry	their	dairy
hare	share	pair	cherry	where	square
rare	carry	stair	bear	there	errand
ware	marry	chair	pear	carrot	error

35. Words with the sound of ô as in dog (o, al, and au)

off	log	moss	ball	wall	faucet
bog	frog	cross	call	small	auto
dog	smog	cloth	fall	walk	because
fog	boss	wrong	hall	stalk	laundry
hog	toss	strong	tall	salt	autumn

36. More words with the sound of ô as in dog (aw, augh, and ough)

draw	saw	lawn	brawl	awesome	ought
flaw	straw	pawn	crawl	caught	bought
gnaw	thaw	yawn	shawl	taught	fought
law	dawn	drawn	sprawl	daughter	brought
paw	brawn	awning	awful	naughty	thought
raw	fawn	hawk	awkward	haughty	cough (f)

The Soft Sounds of c and g and Vowel Digraphs

The letter **c** usually has the sound of **s** when it is followed by the vowels **e**, **i**, or **y**. This is called the soft sound of **c**. Likewise, the soft sound of the letter **g** makes the **j** sound when it is followed by **e**, **i**, or **y**.

37. The soft sound of the letter c

ice	vice	juice	place	cymbals	prince
dice	price	face	space	ounce	lettuce
lice	slice	lace	trace	bounce	celery
mice	spice	pace	chance	pounce	necklace
nice	splice	race	glance	fence	circle
rice	twice	brace	city	pencil	circus

38. The soft sound of the letter g

age	sage	charge	gypsy	pledge	giant
cage	stage	gem	Egypt	engine	orange
gage	wage	ridge	badge	giraffe	range
page	large	bridge	wedge	hinge	change
rage	barge	gym	hedge	danger	manger

39. Words with the vowel digraph ea which has the short vowel e sound

dead	dread	thread	meant	threat	sweater
head	spread	deaf	weapons	breath	weather
lead	stead	breakfast	peasant	death	headache
read	steady	health	pleasant	feather	treasure
ready	instead	wealth	pleasure	heather	measure
bread	tread	cleanser	sweat	leather	meadow

Vowel Digraphs

The vowel digraphs **ea**, **ei**, and **ey** can have the sound of the long vowel **a** as in **break**, **eight**, and **they**.

40. Words with the vowel digraphs ea, ei, and ey

break	eight	weigh	freight	sleigh	obey
steak	eighty	weight	veil	neigh	survey
great	reign	neighbor	vein	they	prey

41. Words with consonant digraphs (ng and nk)

king	sling	gang	thong	bank	sink
sing	sting	hang	wrong	rank	wink
ring	swing	rang	hung	link	think
wing	thing	sang	sung	blink	bunk
bring	bang	long	stung	drink	dunk
fling	clang	song	wrung	mink	trunk

42. Words with consonant digraphs (kn, wr, and gn)

knead	knife	knock	knuckles	wrench	gnash
knee	knight	knoll	wrap	write	gnat
kneel	knit	knot	wreath	wrong	gnaw
knew	knob	know	wren	gnarl	gnu

43. Words with consonant digraphs (gh and ph) that make the f sound

alphabet	phase	photo	digraph	telephone	cough
phonics	phrase	phony	dolphin	trophy	rough
pheasant	phone	graph	elephant	laugh	tough

The Alphabet

Here is a chart to help you study how to properly write the letters and numbers.

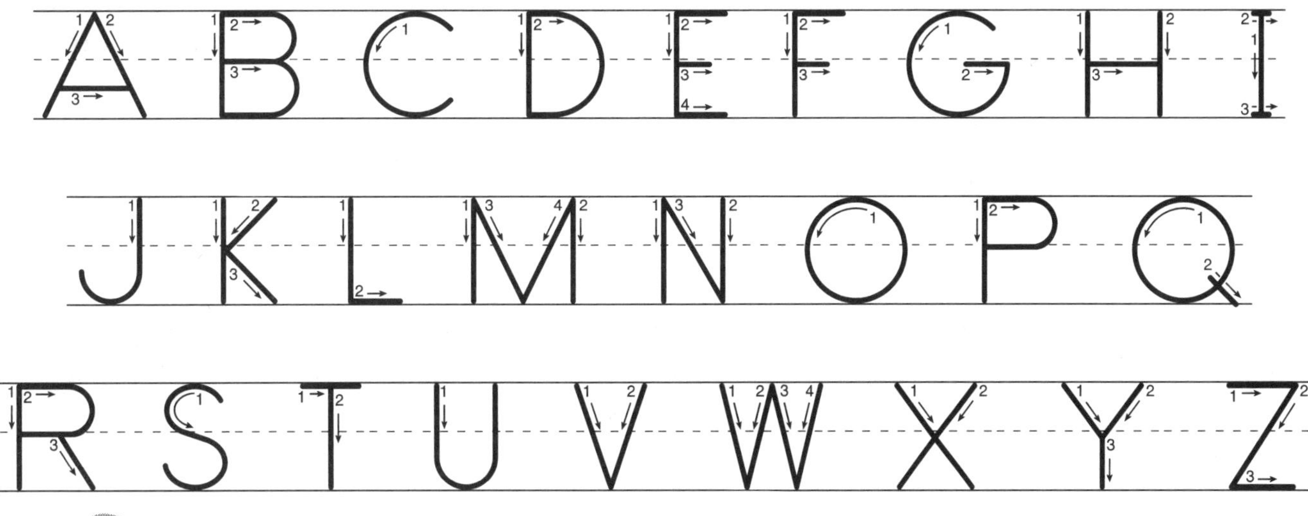

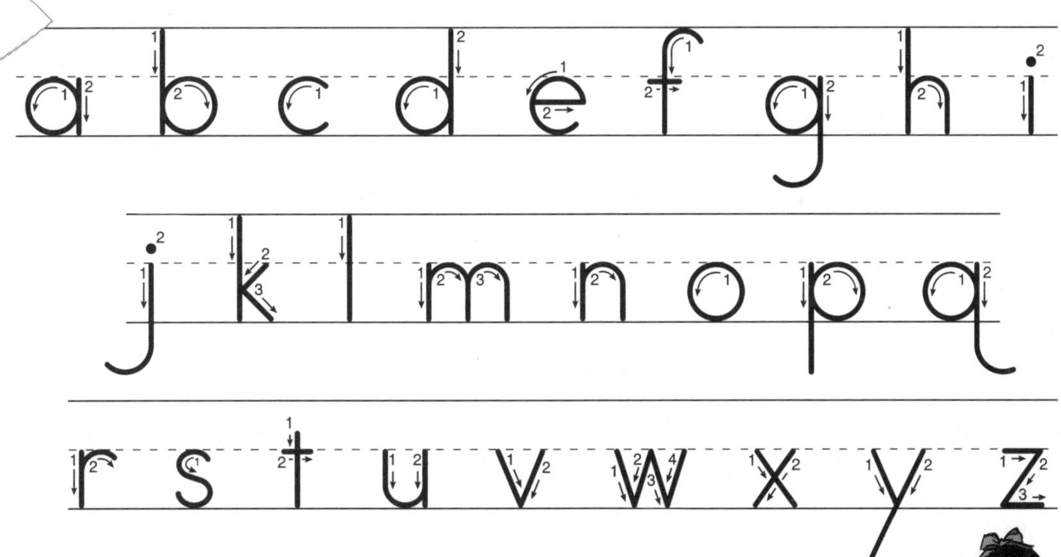

0 1 2 3 4 5 6 7 8 9

Upper and Lower Case Letters

This chart will help you learn the differences between the upper and lower case letters.

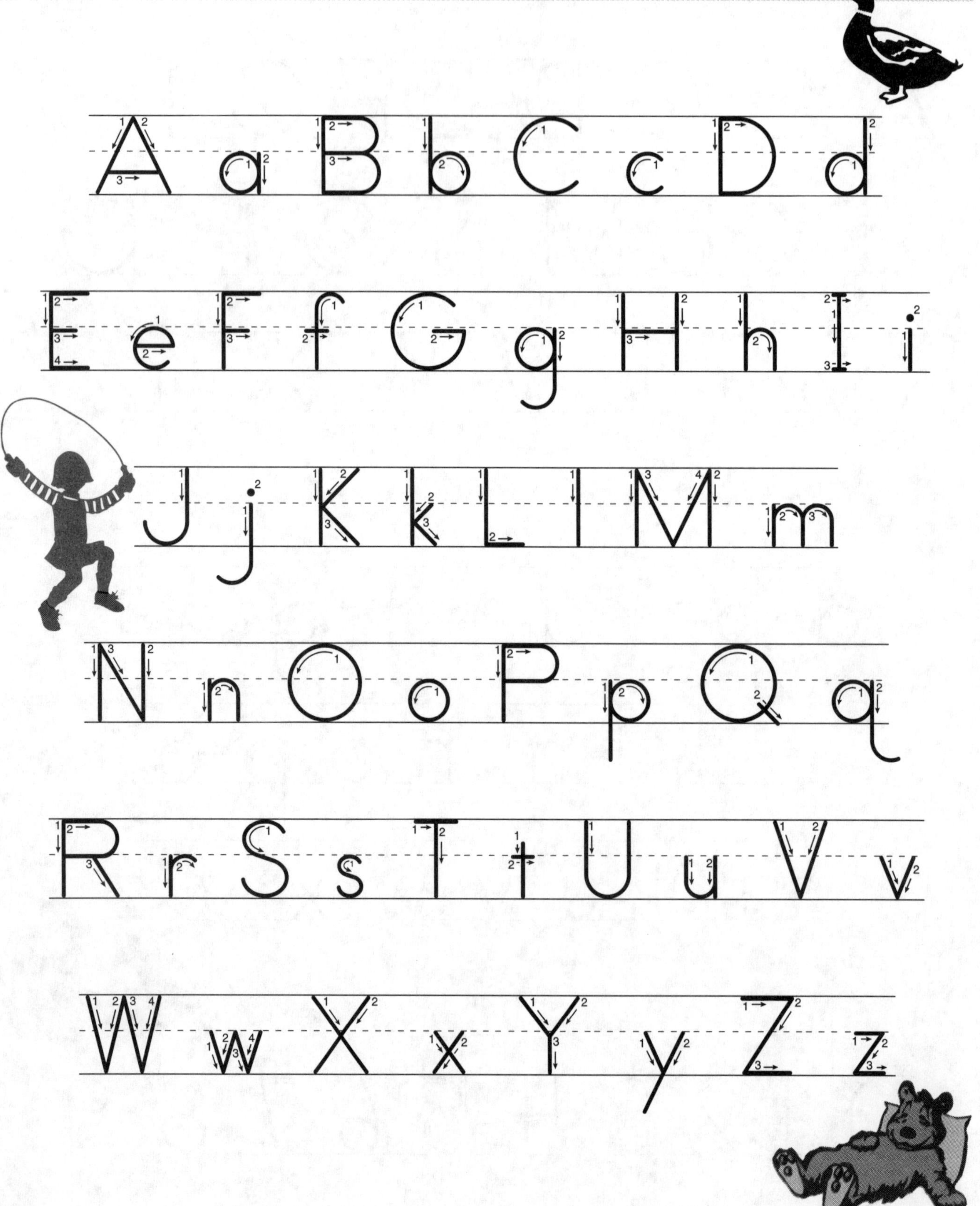